Cross-Cultural Teaching and Learning for Home and International Students

Cross-cultural teaching and learning for home and international students maps and discusses the increasing internationalisation of teaching and learning at universities around the world. This new phenomenon brings both opportunities and challenges, as it introduces what can be radically different teaching, learning and assessment contexts for both students and staff. This book moves beyond the rhetoric of internationalisation to examine some of the more complex issues for practitioners, researchers, students and those working in transnational or non-Anglophone contexts. It recognises that although universities around the world enthusiastically espouse internationalisation as part of their mission, there is currently little information available about carrying out this vision in terms of pedagogy and curriculum at a practical level. This book fills that gap comprehensively, organising its information around four main themes:

- **New ways of teaching, learning and assessing**: challenges and opportunities for teaching practice, student engagement and participation, assessment and supervision of learning.
- **New ways of designing and delivering curriculum**: internationalising the curriculum for all students within 'home' and 'abroad' contexts.
- **New ways of thinking and acting**: developing the global citizen, intercultural learning and respectful dialogue, responding to student diversity and equity, enhancing graduate employability and future life trajectories.
- **New ways of listening**: discovering and responding to new or unfamiliar voices among students and staff, embracing 'other' academic and intellectual traditions.

Illustrated by a wide range of examples from around the world, this book brings together contemporary work and thinking in the areas of cross-cultural teaching and internationalisation of the curriculum.

Dr Janette Ryan is Director of the UK Higher Education Academy *Teaching International Students* Project and Research Associate of the China Centre at the University of Oxford.

Cross-Cultural Teaching and Learning for Home and International Students

Internationalisation of pedagogy and curriculum in higher education

Edited by Janette Ryan

Routledge
Taylor & Francis Group

LONDON AND NEW YORK

First published 2013
by Routledge
2 Park Square, Milton Park, Abingdon, Oxon OX14 4RN

Simultaneously published in the USA and Canada
by Routledge
711 Third Avenue, New York, NY 10017

Routledge is an imprint of the Taylor & Francis Group, an informa business

© 2013 selection and editorial material, The Higher Education Academy;
individual chapters, the contributors.

The right of The Higher Education Academy to be identified as the author
of the editorial material, and of the authors for their individual chapters, has
been asserted in accordance with sections 77 and 78 of the Copyright,
Designs and Patents Act 1988.

All rights reserved. No part of this book may be reprinted or reproduced
or utilised in any form or by any electronic, mechanical, or other means,
now known or hereafter invented, including photocopying and recording,
or in any information storage or retrieval system, without permission
in writing from the publishers.

Trademark notice: Product or corporate names may be trademarks or
registered trademarks, and are used only for identification and
explanation without intent to infringe.

British Library Cataloguing in Publication Data
A catalogue record for this book is available from the British Library

Library of Congress Cataloging in Publication Data
Ryan, Janette, 1956-
Cross cultural teaching and learning for home and international
students : internationalisation, pedagogy and curriculum in
higher education/Janette Ryan.
  pages cm
ISBN 978-0-415-63012-2 (hardback)—ISBN 978-0-415-63013-9 (pbk.)—
ISBN 978-0-203-09803-5 (e-book) (print) 1. Students, Foreign—Case
studies. 2. Multicultural education—Case studies.
3. College teaching—Case studies. I. Title.
LB2375.R93 2012
378'.0162—dc23   2012008709

ISBN: 978-0-415-63012-2 (hbk)
ISBN: 978-0-415-63013-9 (pbk)
ISBN: 978-0-203-09803-5 (ebk)

Typeset in Galliard
by Cenveo Publisher Services

MIX
Paper from
responsible sources
FSC
www.fsc.org   FSC® C004839

Printed and bound in Great Britain by the MPG Books Group

Contents

Contributors

Jos Beelen is researcher and consultant on internationalisation of the curriculum at the Centre for Applied Research on Economics and Management (CAREM) at Hogeschool van Amsterdam, University of Applied Sciences. He chairs the Special Interest Group Internationalisation at Home of European Association for International Education and is a Visiting Fellow at Leeds Metropolitan University.

Associate Professor Valerie Clifford recently joined the Teacher Development Unit at Victoria University. Previously, she was Deputy Head of the Oxford Centre for Staff and Learning Development at Oxford Brookes University and inaugural Director of the Centre for International Curriculum Inquiry and Networking (CICIN). She has published widely on curriculum and pedagogy from a feminist and cultural perspective.

Dr Jeannie Daniels lectures in Academic Language and Learning at La Trobe University, Australia. She previously taught in England and South Australia. Her current research explores the non-traditional student experience in the contexts of the internationalisation of education and increasing participation of mature age students.

Hans de Wit is Professor of Internationalisation of Higher Education at the Hogeschool van Amsterdam University of Applied Sciences, Academic Director of the Centre for Internationalisation of Higher Education at the l'Università Cattolica del Sacro Cuore in Milan, Italy and visiting professor at CAPRI, Leeds Metropolitan University. He is co-editor of *Journal of Studies in International Education* and has (co)written books and articles on international education.

Dr Christine Edmead is a Senior Teaching Fellow in the Department of Pharmacy and Pharmacology at the University of Bath. Her role as an Educational Projects Officer within the Learning and Teaching Enhancement Office involves supporting staff across the institution in developing activities to enhance student integration and group work experiences.

Dr Monika Foster is Senior Lecturer and Senior Teaching Fellow at Edinburgh Napier University. She has extensive experience of staff development in the UK and overseas. Her current research interests lie in effective and culturally appropriate support to assist international students in transitions to higher education.

Fenella Galpin is a Senior Lecturer at the Open University Business School in the UK. She has worked with leading business schools in the development and delivery of global MBA and other programmes. She has a particular interest in online learning, online communities and effective online tutoring skills.

Martin Haigh is Professor of Geography at Oxford Brookes University and, formerly, editor of the *Journal of Geography in Higher Education*. He is a National Teaching Fellow, a Senior Fellow of the Higher Education Academy and the 2010 recipient of the *Taylor and Francis Award for Excellence in Geography Teaching (Higher Education)* of the Royal Geographical Society, London.

Juliet Henderson is Senior Lecturer in English Language and Communication at Oxford Brookes University. Her research interests include language, identity and globalisation. She is an executive member of CICIN (the Centre for International Curriculum Inquiry and Networking). She has published in *Language and Intercultural Communication* and the *Journal of Studies in International Education*.

Professor Helen E. Higson is currently Senior Pro Vice Chancellor at Aston University and Professor of Higher Education Learning and Management at Aston Business School. She has degrees from Newnham College Cambridge, the Open University and Birkbeck College London and has developed innovative practice in teaching intercultural communications over many years.

Dr David Killick is Head of Academic Staff Development and leads the Post Graduate Certificate in Higher Education at Leeds Metropolitan University. He has published widely on internationalisation in higher education. He works on curriculum development around cross-cultural capability and global perspectives and his current research is on links between internationalisation and equality and diversity.

David Leat is Professor of Curriculum Innovation and Director of the Research Centre for Learning and Teaching at Newcastle University. His research focuses on pedagogy and curriculum, teacher research, teacher coaching and professional resilience.

Dr Kai Liu is Lecturer in International Business at Northampton Business School, University of Northampton. His research interests include economic sociology, entrepreneurship and innovation in regional and community contexts, intercultural communication and creative and cultural industries in China and the UK.

Rachel Lofthouse is Head of Teacher Learning and Development (Education Section) at Newcastle University and a member of the Research Centre for Learning and Teaching. Her research interests focus on professional learning, coaching models to support professional learning and the use of blogs and ePortfolios in learning.

Dr Susan McGrath-Champ is Associate Professor in Work and Organisational Studies at the University of Sydney Business School. She teaches international and strategic human resource management and has been a recipient of an Award for Teaching Innovation. Her research includes the geographical aspects of employment, equity and diversity, international assignments and the construction industry.

Sabine McKinnon is Lecturer in Employability and Manager of the Real WoRLD project at Glasgow Caledonian University. She has had a long career teaching modern languages and intercultural communication at different UK universities. Her research focuses on the role and impact of cultural values in learning and teaching.

Dr Patricie Mertova is a Research Fellow in the Department of Education, University of Oxford. She has previously worked at the University of Queensland and Monash University. She recently completed her PhD on the academic voice in higher education quality and her background is in linguistics, cross-cultural communication and foreign languages.

Dr Catherine Montgomery is Associate Director for Research in the Centre for Excellence in Teaching and Learning at Northumbria University. She has taught in higher education for 20 years, most recently in the field of sociolinguistics. Her research interests centre on the social and cultural context of student learning.

Dr Paul Prinsloo is an Education Consultant at the University of South Africa (Unisa). His academic qualifications and research interests include religious studies, art history, learning theories, business education, online learning, curriculum development, corporate citizenship, student success and throughput and the use of social technologies in open distance learning.

Dr Stuart Reid is Associate Fellow at the University of Warwick and Senior Associate at The Partnering Initiative. He contributes to postgraduate and executive education programmes in Cambridge and Warwick and is co-founder of Warwick's Global People Resource Bank (www.globalpeople.org.uk). He has managed or contributed to international projects in planning, development and evaluation of cross-sector partnership and intercultural management.

Sue Robson is Head of the School of Education, Communication and Language Sciences and a member of the Research Centre for Learning and Teaching at Newcastle University. Her research interests include the internalisation of higher education exploring academic perceptions of internationalisation on professional lives, the student experience and on learning and teaching.

Dr Janette Ryan is Director of the UK Higher Education Academy *Teaching International Students* Project and Research Associate of the China Centre at the University of Oxford. Her publications include *China's higher education reform and internationalisation* (Routledge, 2011), *Education reform in China* (Routledge, 2011) and *International education and the Chinese learner* (Hong Kong Press, 2010).

Dr Tony Shannon-Little is Principal Lecturer at the University of Wolverhampton Teaching English as a Foreign Language and TESOL. His research interests include the tensions between the agendas of employability and global citizenship, particularly as manifested in group work experiences in higher education.

Dr Sharon Slade is Senior Lecturer at the Open University Business School in the UK. She has focused on the support and development of tutors and students on online-only international management programmes since 2000, and has an interest in student profiling and tracking study behaviours to improve retention.

Gordon Slethaug has most recently been at the University of Southern Denmark and is Adjunct Professor at the University of Waterloo, where he focused on communications, globalisation and internationalisation. He was also Lingnan Professor at the University of Hong Kong and Sun Yat-sen University in China. His research centres on cultural studies, cross-cultural pedagogy and film and literature.

Helen Spencer-Oatey is Professor and Director of the Centre for Applied Linguistics at the University of Warwick. She has published extensively in the field of intercultural communication (e.g. *Intercultural/Interaction*, Palgrave, 2009) and currently leads the Global People project (www.global-people.org.uk).

Lucy Taylor evaluates student and staff experiences of learning and teaching at the University of Sydney. Her research interests include learning technologies and interactive pedagogies. She regularly reviews for the *British Journal of Educational Technology* (BJET) and the *Australasian Journal of Educational Technology* (AJET).

Dr Yvonne Turner lectures in Management at Aberdeen Business School at the Robert Gordon University. Her interests focus on cross-cultural learning, the globalisation of knowledge and cultural pedagogy. She is currently working in the area of higher education internationalisation and transnational graduate work and employment.

Associate Professor Jane Vinther is Head of English Studies at the University of Southern Denmark Kolding Campus. Her teaching and research interests include applied linguistics, international teaching and learning, motivation and philosophies of education. She has presented papers at conferences in the UK, Hong Kong and China on these themes.

Dr Kate Wall is Senior Lecturer and Divisional Director Postgraduate Taught Programmes in the HYPERLINK "http://www.dur.ac.uk/education/" School of Education at Durham University. Kate's research interests revolve around the enquiry question, how do participatory methods support authentic conversations about metacognition between teachers and students and what do they tell us about the learning process?

Rachel Wicaksono is Head of Subject for Languages and Linguistics at York St John University, UK. She is a co-author of *Mapping applied linguistics: A guide for students and practitioners*, published by Routledge in 2011, and a founder member of www.mappling.com, an online community of applied linguists.

Mimi Zou is a Commonwealth Scholar reading for a doctorate in Law at St John's College, University of Oxford. Her research focuses on a comparison of labour migration policies in Europe and Australasia. She has taught international law, employment law and industrial relations at Sydney, Utrecht, Tsinghua and Rhodes universities.

Acknowledgements

This book was made possible through funding provided by the Higher Education Academy. This book arises from the conference on *Internationalisation of Pedagogy and Curriculum in Higher Education: Exploring New Frontiers* held at the University of Warwick from 16 to 17 June 2011. The conference was hosted by the Higher Education Academy/UKCISA Teaching International Students (TIS) project in partnership with the Centre for Academic Practice and Research in Internationalisation (CAPRI) and the Centre for Internationalised Curriculum and Networking (CICIN).

Introduction

Janette Ryan

Challenges and opportunities of internationalisation

The internationalisation of universities around the world provides both opportunities and challenges, in sometimes radically different teaching and learning contexts for home and international students and for the staff who teach and support them. This book seeks to move beyond the rhetoric of internationalisation to examine the more complex issues for staff and students in these contexts (whether Anglophone or non-Anglophone) and to explore possible solutions to some of these questions in order to enact the rhetoric of internationalisation.

The past decade has seen a rapid acceleration and expansion of international education and a change in the nature of debates surrounding the broader issue of internationalisation in higher education. It is clear that the presence of international students on university campuses does not automatically bring about internationalisation of curriculum and pedagogy and that broader initiatives are required. Internationalisation now features as a goal in the mission statements of universities around the world, and internationalisation debates no longer occupy the periphery; they have firmly moved into the mainstream. Added to earlier debates about the challenges of teaching and learning for international students are discussions about the nature of the curriculum and pedagogy for all students in these changing contexts. These discussions are beginning to extend to ideas about knowledge and intellectual traditions in the wake of an unprecedented global movement of people (both students and scholars) and ideas (through collaborative research and joint programmes).

Teaching and learning for international students is becoming more important as their numbers increase and they are no longer a 'minority group' within the classroom. International education increasingly encompasses joint programmes, branch campuses and transnational or multimodal education. These developments call for a reconsideration of contemporary realities and practices and a re-examination of systems of knowledge and intellectual traditions. These global flows mean not only the exchange of people but also the exchange of ideas and academic traditions.

The growing numbers of international students as well as their diverse pathways means that the label 'international' is becoming less helpful in determining their needs or separating them out from the needs of other students. Some argue that such labelling marginalises these sojourners and instead call for new ways of working and thinking. In virtual learning environments, ethnicity or nationality becomes less 'visible' and in transnational learning environments, the teacher can be the cultural 'outsider'. Educators everywhere and perhaps most importantly in Anglophone countries, need to 'reverse the lens' (and practise what they preach to their students about internationalisation) by examining their own thinking and practice and viewing international learning as an enterprise that occurs not within a single system of cultural academic practice but as an endeavour between civilisations and intellectual traditions.

Internationalisation remains a fuzzy concept, however, and despite good intentions, can be hard to conceptualise and even harder to operationalise. It is appropriated for all kinds of agendas, which is perhaps ironically limiting its development and progress. On the other hand, this fuzziness means that debates can be broad with many rich veins for exploration. In this book, we focus on internationalisation of curriculum and pedagogy (the 'what' and the 'how') and its corollaries such as global citizenship, transcultural learning and intercultural competencies. This book is aimed at those working to internationalise teaching and learning policy and practice and who are seeking ideas and evidence to support this endeavour.

Given the rapid expansion in this area, it is timely to reflect on what has been achieved and what is still to be done. Some commentators argue that debates about international students and internationalisation have not moved on significantly in the past decade and that staff report the same difficulties that they have always reported (Singh, 2009; Turner & Robson, 2008). This raises questions about whether the field lacks a coherent definition and whether a lack of cohesion is inhibiting progress. That these debates exist is encouraging and evidence of a field finding its feet and establishing its presence; they need to be encouraged and conducted in a candid and open way. As the numbers of students and countries involved rises, so do moral and ethical questions about issues such as academic imperialism, the dominance of the Anglo-American model or the implications of English as a *lingua franca*. The purpose and impacts of internationalisation and international education need to be interrogated: Is international education an altruistic endeavour, an enterprise of mutuality of regard and respect, a foreign policy initiative, an economic imperative or merely an arm of fiscal policy? And what does it mean for nations, individuals and its many stakeholders?

What is clear is that international student mobility – meaning those who study academic programmes of another country either in that country or their own – continues to accelerate and is expanding its reach. The direction of flow has been from 'developing' to 'developed' (primarily Anglophone) countries but this is beginning to change. In 2008, 3.3 million students were studying outside their country of citizenship, almost double the number in 2000, and this figure is predicted to increase to 7 million by 2020 (OECD, 2010). As the Institute of International Education (IIE, 2011, p. 1) states, the nature of the 'flow' and the 'overall context of global mobility, both in terms of who is going where, and the mix of host and sending countries' is changing. There is increasing competition for the international education market as universities around the world pursue internationalisation agendas and invest in international student recruitment, academic exchanges, research collaborations and joint academic programmes. These moves are not just based on economic imperatives but are claimed to be 'critical components for sharing knowledge, building intellectual capital and remaining competitive in a globalizing world [in order to] foster mutual understanding and cooperation, especially in a climate of increased diplomacy and security' (IIE, 2011, p. 2).

Many countries in Europe, Scandinavia, Asia, South Africa and the Middle East are vigorously entering the international education market and offering programmes in English. China now accepts more international students than it sends abroad and aims to attract half a million foreign students by 2020 (IIE, 2011). The core–periphery model of international education (Jiang, 2005; Pan, 2011) is thus beginning to break down, changing from 'a unidirectional "brain drain" type of mobility of students moving from "developing" to "developed" nations to one of dynamic, mutual exchange' (IIE, 2011, p. 7) and 'brain circulation'. These developments call for new relationships and stances towards knowledge and other intellectual traditions and universities are responding by seeking to internationalise their curriculum not just for their students from abroad but also for 'home' students who will be living and working in a more globalised world.

This global drive towards international student recruitment and internationalisation of the curriculum for both international and home students represents a 'new frontier'. It not only alters the demographic within student cohorts, in disciplines, across campuses and in the local communities in which universities operate, but also provides opportunities for universities to better prepare their graduates for the global era. This trend opens up debates about epistemologies and paradigms and the development of the intercultural skills and knowledge of all students as well as staff in contemporary higher education systems.

These changes have brought to the fore the implications of the rapid increases of international students especially in Western learning contexts, and the challenges for those working with them. But these shifts also provide opportunities for new ways of working for all stakeholders: opportunities to explore what it means now and into the future to be a citizen of the world in changing political and economic times. They also position higher education at the forefront of these changes in ways that can benefit not only nations and regions but also individuals within them.

Much internationalisation work is already being done within universities in many countries by practitioners and researchers but often these initiatives occur in isolation or through the enthusiasm of committed individuals. The aim of this book is to bring together some of this work and share it with others who are experiencing similar challenges, and to prompt and inform debate amongst those wishing to internationalise their teaching and learning policies, practices and programmes.

Origins of this book

The chapters in this book illustrate how practitioners and researchers are responding to the challenges outlined above within their own contexts. They originate from an international conference at the University of Warwick in the UK in June 2011 which brought together researchers, practitioners, policy makers and students interested in the internationalisation of curriculum and pedagogy in higher education. The purpose of the conference, *Internationalisation of Pedagogy and Curriculum in Higher Education: Exploring New Frontiers*, was to explore new and emerging thinking, practice and research and was a joint initiative of the UK Higher Education Academy's Teaching International Student (TIS) Project, the Centre for Academic Practice and Research in Internationalisation (CAPRI) and the Centre for Internationalised Curriculum and Networking (CICIN). The Call for Papers invited those working in internationalised higher education contexts around the world to share their work and to explore and debate the following issues:

- What are the challenges and opportunities for universities, teachers and students of increased student mobility (both inbound and outbound)?
- How can the diversity of student and staff perspectives and experiences be used for more internationalised learning for all?
- How can these shifts shape imaginative and creative approaches to teaching, learning and assessment; curriculum and programme design and delivery; research paradigms and epistemologies and interactions and transnational partnerships?
- How can these inform more complex issues such as global citizenship and intercultural learning, and foster respectful dialogue between and among diverse cultures and knowledge traditions on university campuses and across the communities in which they exist?
- Whether 'internationalisation' is an exclusively Western (or 'Westernising') notion or are there other cultural academic paradigms or perspectives that can inform a wider debate?

As the conference focus was on emerging and innovative research, much of the research described in this book is in its early or embryonic stages as researchers explore alternative paradigms, methods and practices. The chapter authors question underlying cultural assumptions about pedagogy and curriculum and investigate innovative approaches to knowledge, behaviour and interactions in increasingly internationalised contexts and for more global learning. They examine new ways of knowing, being and acting and their personal, intellectual, professional and institutional journeys are illustrated as they explore these 'new frontiers'. Many are taking tentative but courageous steps, like their international students, to move out of their comfort zones and experiment with new approaches and ideas in practice or policy.

Although there is much goodwill amongst university policy makers and practitioners, this is harder to translate into policies and programmes that address these ideals, are suited to diverse contexts and offer sustainable solutions. The real challenge is to find ways that individuals can work more effectively with their own students in their own contexts in ways that are sustainable for them and that can benefit all of their students and chapter authors provide diverse ideas and models of how they are doing this.

Whether internationalisation is conceptualised at the 'micro' level of the classroom or at more 'macro' policy level, its nature and impacts are complex and diverse. The sections of this book follow the original conference themes that address these various levels and are organised around the following domains:

Part 1: **New ways of teaching, learning and assessing**: this section addresses challenges and opportunities for teaching practice, student engagement and participation, and assessment and supervision of learning.

Part 2: **New ways of designing and delivering curriculum**: this section covers internationalising the curriculum within 'at home' and 'abroad' contexts, adaptive and flexible models of programme delivery and transcultural and transnational programmes and partnerships.

Part 3: **New ways of thinking and acting**: this section includes developing the global citizen, intercultural learning, responding to student diversity and equity and enhancing graduate employability and future career trajectories.

Part 4: **New ways of listening**: this section delves into deeper issues of personal and cultural academic values such as responding to new or unfamiliar voices among students and staff, and embracing 'other' intellectual traditions.

Together the chapters provide an overview of contemporary policy and teaching and learning contexts in universities engaged in international education. Authors discuss the challenges in this work but also point to the opportunities that these changes can bring such as more internationalised learning for all; imaginative and creative approaches to teaching, learning and assessment and programme design; the development of new research paradigms and epistemologies and the enhancement of international education interactions and transnational partnerships.

The authors point to broader debates, such as whether 'internationalisation' is an exclusively Western (or 'Westernising') notion, or whether other cultural academic paradigms and perspectives can inform wider debate and foster dialogue between and among diverse cultures and knowledge traditions. They describe how culture influences the ways that people both within and across cultures operate and how an awareness of this can lead to more reflective relationships and dialogue and the generation of new knowledge and understanding. This calls for institutions and individuals to re-examine their core cultural beliefs and adopt more ethnorelative rather than ethnocentric (or even Eurocentric) approaches. Much of the research reported shows how it is through contact with cultural 'others' that both staff and students come to understand the impacts of culture on their own expectations and values. Themes also emerge about concerns to work in more democratic and respectful ways even in the midst of the sometimes considerable difficulties facing staff and students working in changed conditions. These chapters show that the focus has shifted away from earlier practices where international students were expected to adjust and adapt, to one where universities recognise the need for institutional, curriculum and pedagogical change for all students as internationalisation has become a core mission for universities across the world.

The chapters are written by new and more experienced practitioners and researchers in both Anglophone and non-Anglophone contexts. Authors come from the UK, the Netherlands, Denmark, South Africa, Canada and Australia and all have first-hand experience of studying or working in cross-cultural contexts. They discuss not just the diversity of student cohorts but also diverse responses; chapters are underpinned by different theoretical or conceptual positions which provide a smorgasbord of choices and approaches. This demonstrates that there is no one 'correct' way to address the challenges of internationalisation. Authors do not aim to tell people how to teach or design curriculum but rather share their successes and failures and provide ideas for exploration and experimentation. They give practical guidance and often step-by-step descriptions of initiatives they have introduced so that others can adopt or adapt these.

A theme running through all of these chapters is the benefit for all students, not just those who are called 'international', when attention is given to students' needs, and practitioners actively work to address them: this moves beyond an approach where only students are expected to adapt and change – to 'sink or swim'. As the various chapter authors point out, they have discovered that the initiatives they have introduced are beneficial for all students and help to create more responsive and respectful learning environments where international students become part of the group. As the authors show, these 'new frontiers' open up exciting and challenging pathways to new destinations.

Part I

This book begins by identifying the challenges that international students can face in teaching, learning and assessment. Part 1 moves from the 'classroom' – induction, group work, postgraduate writing groups and feedback – to change at programme and Faculty level. The possible negative effects of internationalisation in countries outside the Anglophone world are also discussed due to pressures on academics in non-Anglophone universities to teach in English.

In Chapter 1, Christine Edmead focuses on the difficulties that international students can face in group work but argues that all students benefit from the intercultural learning that can arise from multicultural group work when it is well organised. Edmead describes attempts to improve group work at a university in the southwest of England following reports of 'disenchantment' amongst both home and international students in their group work experiences. Feedback from participants in the research studies she reports, shows that all students benefit when training is provided to the whole cohort, leading to better learning outcomes and experiences for all those involved.

In Chapter 2, Susan McGrath-Champ, Mimi Zou and Lucy Taylor argue that the future needs of a global workforce will require workers who can work in multicultural and diverse settings. This provided the impetus for a programme at an Australian university that aims to increase the intercultural competencies of Business students to prepare them for their future working lives. The programme uses a combination of team-based learning with critical reflective journals so that students of all backgrounds learn how to work together to not only learn more about the diverse cultural knowledge and perspectives of their peers but also to become more aware of their own. These approaches are embedded within the whole course and thus have a deep and enduring impact.

In Chapter 3, Jeannie Daniels addresses the challenges of writing at doctoral level for students whose first language is not English, and where cultural considerations add another layer of complexity. Daniels draws on the notion of 'capability' to interrogate competing notions of the purpose of doctoral work and argues that educators need new ways of working that address their students' complex and diverse learning needs. She describes the use of writing groups for doctoral students increasingly being implemented in Australian universities and shows how they provide supportive learning environments and help students to develop higher-order academic skills.

In Chapter 4, Sue Robson, David Leat, Kate Wall and Rachel Lofthouse examine the role of feedback for postgraduate international students. In a study of the views of students and staff at a university in the north of England, international students reported that their previous experiences of feedback had been limited. They saw assessment as a summative judgement of their performance rather than an opportunity for learning through formative or 'feed forward' assessment. The authors recognise that there are tensions about time and resources needed to provide effective formative feedback for students and argue that there is much work to be done to achieve students' full learning potential through forms of feedback better suited to their previous experiences and diverse learning needs.

In Chapter 5, Patricie Mertova compares the perspectives of senior British, Australian and Czech academics towards internationalisation. Mertova looks at 'critical events' in academics' experiences as a catalyst for improved teaching and learning practice and programmatic responses to internationalisation. Her research shows that although these academics are generally positive about internationalisation, some have concerns about loss of national or ethnic identity as well as English language dominance. Mertova's comparison of Anglophone, Danish and Czech academics reminds us that internationalisation is not a 'neutral' concept and can raise different issues or ethical concerns in differing contexts.

In Chapter 6, Gordon Slethaug and Jane Vinther explore one of the major challenges that international students face, which is learning in English as a foreign language, not just in Anglophone but also in non-Anglophone universities. With the expansion of international education in non-Anglophone countries, this presents a challenge for lecturers expected to teach in English. Slethaug and Vinther describe the situation in Denmark where domestic and international students are increasingly expecting a high standard of English. This chapter explores the challenges for both students and teaching staff and the difficulties for students learning in English as a foreign language as well as dealing with the additional language of the country in which they are studying.

Part 2

This section addresses curriculum design and development and includes initiatives that have been specifically designed to address academic preparation for international students as well as the development of intercultural competencies for all students.

In Chapter 7, Monika Foster focuses on induction programmes. She argues that traditional university induction may not be best suited to the needs of diverse student groups. She explores initiatives that aim to enhance the engagement of international students in their learning transitions and provide effective support. She describes two projects at a university in Scotland involving an online study skills resource called SPICE and an e-mentoring scheme. Foster describes the rationale for the projects, how they work and how to adapt them in different contexts.

In Chapter 8, Helen E. Higson and Kai Liu describe a training programme in a Business School in England that is designed to increase students' intercultural competencies and which uses an arts-based approach to facilitate student interactions and understanding. It thus 'levels the playing field' amongst students of different cultural backgrounds while simultaneously making (all) students aware of their own cultures. A pre- and post-intervention survey showed that the UK and EU students reported the most significant increases in their 'cultural intelligence', with all students welcoming such teaching methods and calling for sessions to be delivered earlier and more frequently.

In Chapter 9, Stuart Reid and Helen Spencer-Oatey argue that approaches to internationalising the curriculum for home students such as study abroad or exchange programmes often do not result in the intended outcomes and can even have negative outcomes. They argue that programmes aiming to develop students' intercultural skills need to be grounded in a theoretical and professional competencies framework. They describe the *Global People* competency framework that supports effective intercultural behaviour and is embedded into the learning process for undergraduate students.

In Chapter 10, Sharon Slade, Fenella Galpin and Paul Prinsloo report on a survey of MBA students and other stakeholders undertaking study in the UK, EU and internationally about their perceptions of the purposes of MBA study. The research showed that staff and students differ about the need for the programme to be 'international'. The authors discuss options for catering for the different needs of students, depending on their contexts, and call for further research to more precisely pinpoint students' needs to inform the development of these types of programmes.

In Chapter 11, Hans de Wit and Jos Beelen question the instrumentalist nature of internationalisation and internationalisation of the curriculum initiatives, which they argue don't adequately consider the purposes and outcomes of the learning process. They describe an initiative at a university in the Netherlands where 'coaches' assist teaching staff to internationalise their curriculum. This has proven more effective than a 'top-down' approach to staff development and in this chapter they examine some of the complex questions that have arisen from such initiatives and provide a step-by-step description of how this process works.

Part 3

This section moves beyond the 'classroom' to deeper issues of personal transformation through international learning. The authors explore the changes that occur to students' identities through intercultural contact, whether this learning takes place at 'home' or 'abroad'. They point to the need for new 'mindsets', new 'literacies' and new 'lifeworlds' to equip students in changed and changing world conditions and realities. They critique what they claim is a lack of theoretical or conceptual clarity in the international education field and explore alternative theories of interculturalism and the possibilities of transformative change, not only for international students but also for 'home' students.

In Chapter 12, Catherine Montgomery draws on the New London Group's theories of 'multiliteracies' that future graduates will need in a radically changing and interconnected world. She draws parallels between the imperatives of internationalisation and the work of the New London Group, arguing that this conceptualisation of curriculum as developing 'multiliteracies' has major benefits in the internationalisation of the curriculum arena, which, she argues, is beset by contested and disparate language and terms and lacks a clear theoretical underpinning.

In Chapter 13, David Killick uses theories of learning to investigate how experiences such as study abroad influence students' 'lifeworlds'. Killick argues that such experiences move beyond simple development of intercultural 'competencies' and have a profound impact on students' views of the world and their role within it. Killick reports on a study of Study Abroad students at one university in the UK showing their breadth and depth of learning not just about 'others' but also them 'selves'. Killick argues that these kinds of experiences are also possible 'at home' by creating communities of social practice where students become 'global learners' through learning about the lifeworlds of others.

In Chapter 14, Martin Haigh explores how intercultural learners not only change their identities but also 'awaken' to their own culture and identity. Haigh explores the transformative effect of international study and intercultural learning by examining the life history of Mahatma Gandhi. He analyses Gandhi's memoir of his time as a law student in London from 1888, showing its influence on his subsequent political career. Gandhi's story provides a sober reminder of the lasting impacts of identity change, which for international students can mean they feel they no longer belong in either culture. Few studies of international students take a longitudinal view; this case provides an excellent example not just of the longer-term impacts of international study but also of its potential for profound influence on the world.

In Chapter 15, Sabine McKinnon examines different cultural values and expectations of teaching and learning: in this case, of employability skills. The focus groups with international students at a university in Scotland reported in this chapter showed that different expectations about contact hours, students' progress and lack of personal recommendations for students when seeking employment post-study were a source of disappointment for many international students. This illustrates the need for not only very clear explanations of teaching and learning requirements and practices but also for sensitivity to potential sources of misunderstandings and disappointment and the need to explain why different approaches are adopted and their benefits.

Part 4

This section explores issues of cultural differences in academic values and attitudes. These may be unexamined or unrecognised, but lie at the core of the interactions between teachers and learners and influence the ways that students are treated, judged and assessed. Chapter authors consider issues of marginalisation and the agency of international students, rejecting 'deficit' notions of international students and instead looking at the benefits for all when international students can exercise agency in the classroom and become members of a truly internationalised community of learners.

In Chapter 16, Yvonne Turner examines approaches to talk in the classroom, contrasting different cultural approaches and questioning the characterisations in the Anglophone literature of international students as passive, dependent learners rather than recognising their intellectual traditions as more reflective than Western argumentative styles. Turner argues that lack of understanding about different cultural approaches in teaching and learning can marginalise and exclude international students in Western higher education contexts.

In Chapter 17, Rachel Wicaksono considers how English as the medium of mixed nationality and language classrooms in the UK results in both opportunities and threats for both the UK and bi- or multilingual international students.

For the UK students at her university, their ideas about their 'ownership' of English can mean that responsibility for intelligibility rests wholly on the international students. For international students, ideas about the UK students' ownership of English can mean that their (international) communication skills are not widely recognised. Wicaksono explores how this thinking plays out in students' classroom talk and discusses how new ways of listening, acting or talking can benefit the UK students who will be using English in international situations.

In Chapter 18, Valerie Clifford, Juliette Henderson and Catherine Montgomery describe an online course designed for academic and other staff in the UK, Australia and South Africa to explore conceptions of internationalisation of the curriculum in their own contexts. The authors describe how over several iterations of the course, changes in responses by institutions to internationalisation have been reflected in the responses and concerns of course participants. This suggests a deeper and more nuanced understanding of the need for reform of teaching and learning practices to be transformative for all students (and staff) to become 'global citizens' and 'internationalised, intercultural beings'.

In Chapter 19, Tony Shannon-Little describes how long-stay international students are able to negotiate membership of a 'community of practice'. The students in his study move beyond merely adapting to local British cultures and instead view themselves as active agents choosing strategies to engage with those around them and to build support networks. Shannon-Little describes the need for progressive strategies and structured interventions from the point of induction to establish collaborative learning so that all students see the benefits of a multicultural student body.

In the final chapter, I interrogate the dichotomisation of 'international' and 'Western' students using the Chinese learner as a case study. This chapter attempts to fill the vacuum about knowledge of other intellectual traditions by examining differences and commonalities of Western and Chinese higher education systems through the views and practices of senior academics within them. It addresses criticism of the 'Westernisation' of internationalisation and explores alternative conceptions of internationalisation that position cultural academic systems not in hegemonic relations of power but as partners in a mutual intellectual enterprise.

References

Institute of International Education (2011). *Student mobility and the internationalization of higher education: National policies and strategies from six world regions.* New York: Institute of International Education.

Jiang, K. (2005). The centre–periphery model and cross-national educational transfer: The influence of the US on teaching reform in China's universities. *Asia Pacific Journal of Education, 25*(2), 227–239.

OECD (Organisation for Economic Cooperation and Development) (2010). *Education at a glance 2010.* OECD Indicators. Available at: http://www.oecd.org/dataoecd/42/45/45941837.pdf (accessed 14 December 2010).

Pan, S. Y. (2011). Education abroad, human capital development, and national competitiveness: China's Brain Gain strategies. *Frontiers of Education in China*, 6(1), 106–138.

Singh, M. (2009). Using Chinese knowledge in internationalising research education: Jacques Rancière, an ignorant supervisor and doctoral students from China. *Globalisation, Societies and Education*, 7(2), 185–201.

Turner, Y. & Robson, S. (2008). *Internationalizing the university*. London: Continuum Press.

Part 1

New ways of teaching, learning and assessing

Chapter 1

Capitalising on a multicultural learning environment

Using group work as a mechanism for student integration

Christine Edmead

Introduction

The increase in student numbers and diversity is creating both challenges and opportunities for universities in terms of the effective delivery of an internationalised, inclusive curriculum (see Caruana & Ploner, 2010 and further relevant literature reviewed by Caruana and Spurling, 2007). In 2006, a three-year Teaching Quality Enhancement Fund (TQEF) project was undertaken at the University of Bath to identify learning and teaching strategies that make, or could make, our courses more inclusive to our increasingly diverse student population (Diversity in Academic Practice Project). Initial findings from this study identified the main barrier to inclusive learning to be a lack of student integration, particularly but not exclusively, between home and international students. Although not unexpected, these findings clarified the need to identify new approaches to meet the University's Learning and Teaching Strategy statement of 'capitalising on the benefits of the multicultural learning environment'.

Simultaneously, support was being requested by departments looking to implement effective group work activities within their academic programmes. Irrespective of discipline, the use of group work as an effective strategy to support learning has long been recognised in pedagogical literature (Race, 2003; UTDC, 2004) whilst being able to work effectively as a member of a multicultural team is a generic skill that is highly valued by employers. For these reasons, as well as being a mechanism for coping with increasing student numbers, elements of group work are included in the majority of degree programmes at the UK higher education institutions (Learnhigher, 2011).

Group work in its simplest form enables students to interact, share knowledge and experiences and build confidence to express their views. Therefore, using group work as a platform on which to build intercultural relationships and to help students recognise the value of diversity seems a logical progression (Montgomery, 2009; Osmond & Roed, 2010; Teaching International Students Project, 2011; and explored in more detail by McGrath-Champ and her colleagues in Chapter 2 of this volume). Since students engage better with tasks in which they can see the relevance, it makes sense to focus the group work task around subject specific learning. However, this creates the challenge of increasing pressure on the students to succeed and often resentment of the extra challenges of 'mindful' interactions – thinking carefully before they speak or act to ensure that their words or actions will not cause offence or misunderstanding whilst also paying more attention to interpreting the information imparted to them – and 'taboo' topics faced when working in a multicultural group (Harrison & Peacock, 2010). The learning outcomes of the task must therefore be structured such that students are encouraged to develop intercultural competency alongside the generic employability skills of teamwork and communication (Carroll & Ryan, 2005).

This was obviously not a novel idea and many departments were already utilising group work to encourage intercultural learning. However, the requests for guidance on how to enhance the effectiveness of the group work, coupled with student feedback which revealed a low level of satisfaction in their academic group work (see below; personal observation from student interviews), indicated that, as often reported in other studies, the approaches being used were not meeting the needs of the tutor or the student (De Vita, 2001). A review of the group work assessments commonly revealed the focus to be on a single product, the marks from which usually contributed to the final degree. Such output-based activities, however, are usually counterproductive in terms of development of group work skills as the pressure to succeed overrides the student's desire to engage with the process (Gibbs, 1995). If the activities take place within a multicultural environment the pressures faced by students are multiplied, resulting in resentment between group members and a tendency for some high achievers to 'take over' and 'do it all themselves'.

As part of the University's Innovations Week, an independent survey was carried out across campus to ascertain students' views of the effectiveness of different learning and teaching environments. Although overall the comments were positive, much of the student dissatisfaction recorded about group work seemed to arise from a perceived lack of training in preparation for group work; a lack of perception about the benefits of multicultural working or a lack of clarity of the learning outcomes of the exercise, as these student quotes illustrate:

> *You don't get taught how to work with each other. We're just expected to get together and learn.*
>
> *In most cases group work is a particular disaster – people usually follow their own goals rather than the team in general.*

These views are not unique and have been reported in other studies of group work (Mutch, 1998).

To address these perceptions and improve student satisfaction with group work, the project team set out to identify effective strategies for supporting staff in the design, implementation and assessment of multicultural group work tasks. Departments were asked to hold discussions during staff and student meetings to identify and record examples of good practice connected with group work activities for institution-wide dissemination. From the reports, the project team identified four departments, spanning three different disciplines, which were undertaking specific studies and activities designed to investigate and potentially improve the group work experiences of their students. This chapter outlines the approaches undertaken by the different departments and highlights some initial findings, although much of the work is still in the early stages of the research.

Use of a skills development approach to enhance group work participation

In September 2009, the Department of Electronic and Electrical Engineering requested support for their newly initiated 2 + 2 integrated programme of study. Twenty-two students who had studied Engineering for two years in China were joining the second year of the three-year Bachelor of Engineering (BEng) degree programme at the University of Bath. Whereas the Chinese students could demonstrate comparable levels of subject-specific knowledge with the existing second-year cohort, support was required to facilitate their integration into the academic and social culture of the University. A two-week induction programme was implemented to aid the students in this transition process. Owing to little prior experience of group work and the fact that the students would have to undertake a semester-long group student project, it was felt that the induction programme should address group work. A workshop was designed to encourage the students to explore the concept of group work, including the skills required and the benefits in terms of social integration and sharing of prior knowledge and experiences with home students (Huxham & Land, 2000). During the work-shop, the students were asked to describe any previous experiences of group working; interestingly, this revealed that most of their prior experience had been gained during extracurricular activities such as participation in clubs and volun-tary work and revolved mainly around leadership. The workshop therefore pro-vided an opportunity for the students to explore and discuss the different skills and roles required in effective group work, with a focus on contribution to a common goal and negotiation skills. To practise these skills, the students then engaged in a 'Dragons' Den' style activity (a television programme where new entrepreneurs pitch for investment from experienced business people).

All the students engaged very well with the activity, practising their communi-cation and negotiating skills. Their 'products' were extremely creative, with sev-eral relating to Chinese culture. This highlighted the importance of providing open topics for group work which enable students to draw upon their own prior knowledge, culture and experiences. At the end of the session, the students were asked to vote for their favourite product and the winning group received a small prize.

Although the students gained a deeper understanding of the skills, strategies and benefits of group working, which better prepared them for the upcoming group project, this approach did not result in significantly more multicultural project groups or appear to enhance student integration. This finding showed that simply redressing the issue of a lack of group work skills was insufficient to provide the confidence or incentive for students to opt to work in multicultural groups. Discussions with the remainder of the second-year cohort revealed that despite prior experience of group work, they felt they would also have benefitted from similar support. This follows the principles underpinned by the Universal Design for Learning, which endeavours to encourage consideration of curriculum design 'to give all individuals equal opportunities to learn using flexible approaches that can be customized and adjusted for individual needs' (Centre for Applied Special Technology, 2009).

Use of a skills development approach to enhance integration and intercultural competency

The Master of Pharmacy programme attracts a diverse cohort of students, around 25 per cent of whom are international, although many have studied previously in the UK schools and colleges. However, despite departmental initiatives such as integrated tutorial groups, peer mentoring schemes and social group-based induction activities, there was still a clear lack of integration of home and international students. This was particularly evident in workshops and laboratories when students self-selected their work partner(s). This meant the opportunities for students to engage in intercultural peer learning and sharing of prior experience was not being maximised. Based on the lessons learnt from Engineering, it was decided to develop a core, skills-based approach in order to facilitate integration and intercultural competency. To inform the development of effective approaches, discussions were held with both home and international students, and, as with the Engineering students, these discussions highlighted considerable variation in prior academic experience of group work. The pharmacy degree programme is accredited by the General Pharmaceutical Council (GPhC), which broadly dictates the knowledge and skills expected of a pharmacy graduate, including working as a member of a multicultural team and effectively communicating both with peers and patients in a variety of vocational settings. A learning outcome of the first-year programme therefore became to engage students in a range of subject-related group tasks focusing on skills needs analysis and opportunities for development. The rationale for the approach was that by focusing on skills development rather than integration per se, students could be encouraged to identify similarities in their learning needs rather than focusing on cultural differences and so develop both their intercultural communication and subject-specific knowledge to form a more integrated cohort.

In the first semester, all pharmacy students take a Study Skills module, which is designed to facilitate the development of key academic and employability skills. Although group work was an existing element of this unit, there was no explicit instruction in the group work process or more specifically in the skills and benefits of intercultural working (De Vita, 2001; Fiechtner & Davies, 1985; Volet &

Ang, 1998), it being wrongly assumed that they had acquired such skills and appreciation of the benefits of group work during their prior academic experiences. Using the Engineering model we therefore designed a two-hour workshop, delivered to students in groups of 30. This provided an opportunity to discuss the group work process and theory, member roles, personal and group goals and the necessary skills required to be an effective group member, including intercultural competencies such as communication, respect for others' beliefs and strategies for supporting peers for whom English is not their first language. Students were encouraged to discuss these skills and then rate themselves in terms of their perceived current competency. This focus on levels of skills competency was used as a mechanism to establish common territory within diverse student cohorts, which they could then use to support each other's development (this concept of utilising groups to facilitate skills development through peer support and feedback is further explored by Daniels in Chapter 3 of this volume).

Building on the workshop discussions and using guidance in the literature about group selection (De Vita, 2001), students were then randomly assigned to groups of five or six, given a short activity and asked to take on a role in the group which either enabled them to practise their strengths or preferably to address their weaknesses. As exemplified by the quotes below, feedback on these workshops was very positive, indicating that students found it a useful and enjoyable exercise. Although many expressed initial concern when they were assigned to groups with students they had not previously met, the structure of the activity enabled them to get to know each other; this was reported as one of the main benefits. Randomly assigning students to groups had the benefit of encouraging students to talk to others they may not normally have associated with due to differences in language, culture or interests.

It was a wonderful and fantastic experience to work together with my group mates as a team especially it is my first time to work with local students in U.K. They are really patient and helpful to guide us as international students on different issues and try to lead us to develop the group discussion as much as possible.

This is my first time to have a group work with people who come from different countries, so the feeling was quite fresh and I could learn some new things from my group mates and this project.

The principal dilemma encountered was communication due to language barriers, as each student in the group was from a different country. However, this was overcome by conscientious listening, patience and showing tolerance when verifying points. The group was effective because everyone was treated with dignity and respect.

The main negative feedback was that many students felt that the short task was insufficient for them to practice the skills. In response to this, subsequently, workshops were embedded within the Study Skills module and extended to include an assessed assignment. Students were either randomly assigned or were allowed to self-select groups, to enable an evaluation of how group composition influenced engagement with the task (see the following section). The assignment was to produce a magazine article about an aspect of community pharmacy and was specifically structured to encourage input from all members of the group (De Vita, 2001). In order to capitalise on the diversity of student perspectives and experiences, students were encouraged to draw on their own knowledge and experiences of community pharmacy, resulting in some groups comparing practice in different countries, discussing different legal and ethical practices or describing the historical role of different cultures in the development of medicines and pharmacy as a profession. This facilitated internationalised learning and also ensured that students who had little actual experience of the UK pharmacies could contribute effectively to the discussion. Often in group work, some members find it more difficult to participate due to lack of familiarity or knowledge of the topic, language barriers or shyness. One focus of the activity was to support students in developing strategies for encouraging all members to participate in the discussions either by commenting on the contributions of others, taking on key roles in the group such as organiser or note taker and being given time to think and formulate comments rather than being put under pressure to contribute creative ideas. This focus on the skills aspect benefitted both the international students, but also the quieter home students who gained confidence in expressing their ideas. The activity encouraged the students to discuss their prior knowledge and experience of the pharmacy profession and so facilitated a deeper understanding of different cultures, which would be important in their future career.

The article itself, however, only contributed 40 per cent to the assessment mark. The key learning outcome of this exercise was that '*students should be able to demonstrate knowledge of the group work process*' and '*critically evaluate their engagement with this process*'. To assess whether they had met this learning outcome, students were asked to write a 300-word reflective account of their group work experience, identifying how they resolved challenges, developed a skill and/or helped other group members to develop theirs. As explored further by McGrath-Champ and her colleagues in Chapter 2 of this volume, the process of reflection, based on Kolb's (1984) model of experiential learning, underpins much of the student learning from group work activities, providing them with an opportunity to consider what they have achieved and how this could be improved upon.

The final part of the assessment required the students to anonymously assess their peers on their group work skills such as attendance, organisation and contribution to meetings and to the workload. Encouraging peer marking in group work tasks has been proposed as an example of good practice as it helps students to engage better with the group work process (Keppell et al., 2006; Walvoord, 1986) and also helps to address the 'fairness' of the assessment by rewarding contribution. These latter parts of the assessment were deemed to be the more important as they assessed the development of intercultural group work skills rather than the final product and were therefore a more accurate measurement of the success of the integration aspect of the exercise.

Staff evaluation and student feedback were very positive. Students' reflective commentaries indicated they felt the task had given them the opportunity to develop their own skills and support the skills development of their peers. They encountered few challenges, which were mainly time management and differences in work ethics. Many students felt that they had gained confidence in speaking out in groups, whereas others reflected that the group work made them more aware of the needs and viewpoints of their peers:

> *At the beginning, I had trouble giving criticism and expressing my opinions for fear of being rejected. This improved as the weeks went by. As I got to know my group members, I realised that they were very understanding and willing to listen.*
>
> *After the team assignment I feel that my faith in my own opinions and communication skills has increased, offering me the confidence I lacked. Also, I learned that sometimes compromises are needed and that the true challenge lies in your flexibility rather than the way you convince others to accept your views.*

The main limitation was pressure on the students to rush the discussion/ negotiation phase in order to devote more time to researching the article. This has since been addressed by basing the article on a previous period of work experience. As they already had their research findings, more time could be spent on discussing the focus and negotiating how to structure the article. The second limitation was a tendency for the students to write descriptively about their experience. This we have addressed by structuring the article with reflective-style questions to encourage students to consider the impact on their social and intercultural skills.

Analysis of factors which may impact on students' approaches to group work

The pharmacy workshops conveniently coincided with the commencement of an independent study by colleagues in the Department of Education. The focus of their study was to identify good practice in multicultural group working through exploring how group composition, prior knowledge and experience of the group work process impacted on students' strategies and approach to group work. The study aimed to assess student expectations of the group work process and its outcome; their engagement with the group task; their perceptions of their own learning and the development of group (and individual) strategies to meet the challenges of working together to meet the assessment demands of the task.

A short presentation by the project leaders about the aims of the study was given to all pharmacy students and their participation was requested on a voluntary basis, either as individuals or as a group. To enable evaluation of group composition, students were either randomly assigned to multicultural groups or were allowed to self-select group members. We were mindful to ensure that participation in the study should not positively or negatively impact upon their assignment in any way – in terms of bias due to interview comments, guidance in thinking reflectively about their experience or through undue imposition on their time – and so strategies were put in place to address these issues. The students were interviewed individually at the start of the group work exercise to ascertain their prior experience and expectations of the group work activity. They were encouraged to keep a log of their experience during the group work and were then re-interviewed on completion of the task. Unfortunately, only 18 students elected to participate in the study, probably because (despite assurances of minimal demands on their time) they perceived it as increased workload. Despite the small numbers, it is hoped that a comparison of the responses of students who were randomly assigned to groups with people they didn't previously know with those of students who worked with their friends will give an insight into the effectiveness of the approach in enhancing social integration and intercultural skills. One quote from a student in her reflective commentary indicated that, despite electing to work with friends, on reflection, she felt she may have missed a learning opportunity:

> *Although it was lovely to work with friends I now feel it may have been a better learning experience for me if I had worked with people I didn't know. I find it much easier to communicate in groups if I know the people but can find it nerve racking voicing my opinions in front of virtual strangers. This task would have helped me overcome this while also enabling me to get to know others on the course.*

It is hoped that the responses of the participating students will help to inform best practice in group work structuring. It seems that if improving intercultural communication is an intended learning outcome of the group work task, then allocation of students to multicultural groups is essential. In such cases, it is necessary to be explicit in the reasoning behind this approach and the benefits the students may expect to gain both academically and socially from the opportunity. Furthermore, this must be supported by the task design such that intercultural communication is an essential activity for the effective completion of the task.

The study is continuing with input from other student groups undertaking group work activities and, as this was an independent study, the findings will be reported separately by colleagues from the Department of Education at a future point.

Facilitating improved group dynamics to enhance student integration and satisfaction with group work

Although the focus on skills development to enhance intercultural competency and student integration in a first-year cohort was successful, continued support and opportunities for intercultural working must be provided for students throughout their academic studies. Unless the longer-term benefits of intercultural competency skills are emphasised, then, given the extra challenges students face while working in multicultural groups, it is unlikely these relationships will be maintained.

Funding was obtained from the Higher Education Academy Engineering Subject Centre for a pilot study to assess the impact of prior experience on student engagement and satisfaction with group work. The study initially focused on the perceptions of students undertaking a third-year group business design project. This provided the opportunity to assess the extent of integration amongst diverse student groups comprising students who were more than halfway through their study programme.

The majority of the students had engaged in group work tasks previously either during their university academic studies or school/college curricula and many had also completed a period of work-based study. However, in previous years there had been considerable diversity in their reported satisfaction with their third-year group work projects. For the design project, students select the broad topic area for their project and are then assigned to groups by the Director of Studies and thus are often grouped with students they do not know. Prior to the start of the group work, the students were surveyed to capture their perceptions of the enjoyment and learning opportunities offered by their previous experiences of group work. They were also asked to rate the importance to them of various factors when undertaking group work, such as prior training in group work skills and the opportunity to work with new people. The aim of this part of the study was to identify factors that encourage or discourage students from actively engaging with the task and each other.

Although preliminary analysis of their responses showed considerable diversity in their attitudes to group work, the opportunity to work with new people was rated highly by many of the students. Qualitative comments suggested that this approach enabled them to develop their communication and team working skills better than when they worked with their friends:

> *Due to a friendly, hardworking and supportive team I was able to produce some of my best work.*
> *I learnt about adjusting to others.*

Interestingly, compared with the previous campus survey responses, which indicated disillusionment in group work was due in part to a perceived lack of training, very few of this cohort of students reported that they felt they needed further support in developing group work skills, most being confident that they had achieved knowledge of and competency in these skills during previous group work and placement opportunities.

A follow-up focus group discussion near the end of the project revealed that most groups had integrated extremely successfully and reported satisfaction with their group work experience. This was attributed to a number of factors, including a focus on and enthusiasm for the task due to its direct relevance to industry and their future careers. Many students, however, attributed the success of their integration to the undertaking of a short group task prior to the start of the project. This competitive, but non-assessed task, enabled the students to get to know the other members of their group, to learn the skills they each brought to the group and how to organise themselves to make most effective use of these skills. Thus, by the time they began the project, they had built up a level of understanding and respect for each member and so were able to work more effectively as an integrated group with a common goal. Whereas this establishment of group dynamics is important for the success of any group, it may be even more critical in supporting the integration of multicultural groups where the increased challenges of language and cultural differences put extra tension upon the group members.

These initial observations, in agreement with the findings of Fiechtner and Davis (1985), indicate that providing students with an opportunity to participate in social integration in a structured but more relaxed setting prior to undertaking subject-specific tasks enhances the effectiveness of the group. Unfortunately, due to restricted time and resources such activities are often dispensed with in favour of students 'getting on with the task'. However, if one of the desired outcomes of group work is to facilitate student integration and the development of intercultural competency then dispensing with such pre-task activities could be detrimental to student learning.

Conclusion

The findings from each of these approaches have already helped to inform our understanding of the factors that impact most on student integration within a multicultural group work learning environment and which strategies are most effective in preparing and supporting students in undertaking such work. Initial findings from these studies have indicated that assumptions about prior experience equating to competency in group work skills and process may not hold true and that for students to work effectively in groups, time should be set aside to educate them in these strategies. If one purpose of undertaking group work is for students to develop intercultural competency then this should be more explicitly outlined in the learning outcomes of the exercise and marks awarded for demonstration of awareness of and/or reflection on these skills. Additionally, careful thought needs to be given by staff as to the inclusive nature of the task to ensure that all students have an equal opportunity to contribute and are not unfairly discriminated against due to lack of cultural knowledge or experience.

Finally, careful consideration should be given to the provision of opportunities for students to establish group dynamics prior to undertaking assessed group work tasks. This is even more critical for students working in multicultural groups where opportunities to develop intercultural competency and explore the similarities and differences of diverse cultures can prove invaluable to the learning experience and the task ahead.

In their responses to paper questionnaires, and in interviews, students often indicate a desire to work in a multicultural environment; however, the challenges which occur in practice can often override these good intentions. By using group activities to support integration and personal skills development, including intercultural competency as a key learning outcome within a subject-related task, it is hoped that we can encourage students to see past the barriers of diversity and capitalise on the benefits of a multicultural learning environment.

References

Carroll, J. & Ryan, J. (eds.) (2005). *Teaching international students: Improving learning for all*. London: Routledge.

Caruana, V. & Ploner, J. (2010). *Internationalisation and equality and diversity in higher education: Merging identities*. Equality Challenge Unit. Available at: http://www.ecu.ac.uk/publications/internationalisation-and-equality-and-diversity-in-he-merging-identities (accessed 10 June 2011).

Caruana, V. & Spurling, N. (2007). *The internationalisation of UK higher education: A review of selected material*. The Higher Education Academy. Available at: http://www.leedsmet.ac.uk/world-widehorizons/index_resource_bank.htm (accessed 10 June 2011).

Centre for Applied Special Technology (2009). Transforming Education through Universal Design for Learning website. Available at: http://www.cast.org (accessed March 2011).

De Vita, G. (2001). The use of group work in large and diverse business management classes: Some critical issues. *The International Journal of Management Education*, *1*(3), 27–35.

Fiechtner, S. B. & Davis, E. A. (1985). Why groups fail: A survey of student experiences with learning groups. *The Organisational Behaviour Teaching Review*, *9*, 58–73.

Gibbs, G. (1995). *Assessing student centred courses*. Oxford: OCSLD.

Harrison, N. & Peacock, N. (2010). Cultural distance, mindfulness and passive xenophobia: Using Integrated Threat Theory to explore home higher education students' perspectives on 'internationalisation at home'. *British Educational Research Journal*, *36*(6), 877–902.

Huxham, M. & Land, R. (2000). Assigning students in group work projects. Can we do better than random? *Innovations in Education and Training International*, *37*(1), 17–22.

Keppell, M., Au, E., Ma, A. & Chan, C. (2006). Peer learning and learning oriented assessment in technology enhanced environments. *Assessment & Evaluation in Higher Education, 31*(4), 453–464.

Kolb, D. A. (1984). *Experiential learning: Experience as the source of learning and development.* Englewood Cliffs, NJ: Prentice Hall.

Learnhigher (2011). *Group work website.* Available at: http://www.learnhigher. ac.uk/Staff/Group-work.html (accessed March 2011).

Montgomery, C. (2009). A decade of internationalisation: Has it influenced students' views of cross-cultural group work at university? *Journal of Studies in International Education, 13*(2), 256–270.

Mutch, A. (1998). Employability or learning? Groupwork in higher education. *Education + Training, 40*(2), 50–56.

Osmond, J. & Roed, J. (2010). Sometimes it means more work: Student perceptions of group work in a mixed cultural setting. In E. Jones (ed.), *Internationalisation and the student voice.* New York: Routledge.

Race, P. (2003). *Learning in small groups.* The Higher Education Academy. Available at: http://www.heacademy.ac.uk/assets/York/documents/resources/resource-database/id475_learning_in_small_groups.pdf (accessed 8 June 2011).

Teaching International Students Project (2011). International Student Lifecycle Resource Bank – Group Work. Available at: http://www.heacademy.ac.uk/resources/detail/internationalisation/ISL_Group_work (accessed 11 June 2011).

UTDC (2004). *Improving teaching and learning: Group work and group assessment, UTDC guidelines.* University of Wellington, Victoria: University Teaching Development Centre. Available at: http://www.cad.vuw.ac.nz/resources/guidelines/GroupWork.pdf (accessed 16 July 2012).

Volet, S. E. & Ang, G. (1998). Culturally mixed groups on international campuses: An opportunity for inter-cultural learning. *Higher Education Research and Development, 17*(1), 5–23.

Walvoord, B. F. (1986). *Helping students write well: A guide for teachers in all disciplines.* New York: Modern Language Association.

Chapter 2

Exploring new frontiers in an internationalised classroom

Team-based learning and reflective journals as innovative learning strategies

Susan McGrath-Champ, Mimi Zou and Lucy Taylor

Introduction

Education has become a global endeavour with 'more people than ever before choosing to undertake an international education' (Arkoudis, 2006, p. 5). This global drive towards the internationalisation of higher education represents a 'new frontier' that is changing the demographic of classrooms, campuses and local communities within which universities operate. Workplaces have also become highly globalised and multicultural. Countries like Australia have seen changes in demographic structure, labour shortages and the deployment of immigration as a key source of skilled labour. Accordingly, the need for greater intercultural competence of employees is increasingly crucial to business success. Higher education institutions represent a particular organisational context for the development of intercultural competence, and are 'especially relevant because they provide students with the opportunity to pre-empt these issues prior to entering the workforce' (Freeman et al., 2009, p. 9). The sheer number and presence of students from diverse cultural backgrounds within today's higher education classrooms, along with the necessity of intercultural competence within professions and the workforce generally, 'creates a pressing need for academics to consider the (associated) learning and teaching implications' (Arkoudis, 2006, p. 5).

The aim of this chapter is to outline and evaluate two mechanisms that potentially contribute to internationalising the curriculum and classroom. One involves application of a specific form of team-based learning (TBL) developed by Larry Michaelsen (see Michaelsen Bauman Knight & Fink, 2004) that constitutes an overall approach to course design and curriculum delivery, entailing a student-centred, active-learning philosophy of teaching. The other mechanism, a critical reflective journal, is a major piece of assessment that has been used in conjunction with TBL. Under both mechanisms, international and local students work together and draw upon their lived and learned knowledge, which models much of the course subject material. This study reports a quantitative and qualitative evaluation of the use of TBL and reflective journals in six semesters across three different courses or 'Units of Study' (UOS).

The study includes six postgraduate and undergraduate UOS taught at the University of Sydney Business School from 2007 to 2010. The subject content of the units covered strategic, international and geographical aspects of human resource management (HRM): that is, the world of people at work. In these UOS, there is a mix of local and international students (see Table 2.1). Typically, a unit is composed of students with 15 to 25 different nationalities. The subject content of these UOS is often complemented by acquisition of generic or 'soft' skills via the learning process. The UOS were taught by an academic coordinator from the discipline of Work and Organisational Studies, supported by a Tutor/s and Faculty Learning Technologies Officer who assured the quality and sustainability of the TBL process.

The purpose of this chapter is to explore the contribution of these two mechanisms to enhancing students' academic learning and intercultural capabilities. The next two sections briefly consider literature on aspects of internationalising the classroom, followed by an overview of the teaching approach, research methods and evaluation findings. The chapter concludes that TBL and the critical reflective journal contribute to harnessing the resource embodied in a diverse, multicultural student body, a genuine internationalising of the courses, classroom and curricula, and developing students' intercultural competences for global workplaces.

Engaging cultural diversity in the classroom

The student demographic in Australian universities is already highly internationalised. However, this is not always reflected in actual internationalisation of the classroom in a manner that allows learning processes to unlock and utilise the 'resource' of a culturally diverse body of international and local students. It is thus appropriate to distinguish between the existence of an internationalised classroom – the national origins and affinities that students have – and 'internationalisation' of the classroom that entails active processes which utilise the asset that such diversity offers to enhance learning processes and outcomes.

Table 2.1 Participating UOS in the discipline of Work and Organisational Studies

Year	Semester	Level*	Students enrolled	Unit code	Unit name
2007	2	PG	67	WORK1	Human Resource Strategies
2008	1	PG	150	WORK2	International Dimensions of HRM
2009	1	UG	38	WORK3	Work and Globalisation
2009	2	PG	142	WORK4	International Dimensions of HRM
2010	1	PG	125	WORK5	International Dimensions of HRM
2010	2	PG	81	WORK6	Human Resource Strategies

*PG, postgraduate; UG: undergraduate; UOS: Units of Study.

Sulkowski and Deakin (2009) warn educators to beware of adopting unjusti-fied cultural stereotypes. An example is the perception that deep learning is attained through educational processes that emphasise abstraction and evaluation common in Western settings, but generally not through rote learning. By con-trast, research highlighting the 'Confucian Paradox' (Sulkowski & Deakin, 2009) contrasts the Western use of rote learning with rote learning in Chinese settings which, it holds, serves the purpose of memorisation but can also deepen understanding.

Freeman et al. (2009) report that '[r]esearch has shown that academic staff and domestic students tend to perceive student difference as a barrier to learning' and argue that '[t]he development of intercultural competence in staff and students is practically and strategically important' (Freeman et al., 2009, p. 9). Citing Volet (2004), they argue that internationalisation creates opportunities for improving the quality of higher education through two specific channels: enhanc-ing intercultural competence, and fostering skills for critical reflection (Freeman et al., 2009, p. 10), both of which are evaluated in this study. Ryan and Carroll (2005), along with others, identify that many educators associate learning differ-ences with cultural differences and, when faced with internationalisation issues, take a 'deficit' perspective. Biggs (1997, cited in Freeman et al., 2009, p. 11) discerns that this 'deficit perspective' focuses on 'what students are' and 'what teachers do'. But since the cognitive processes that students use in learning are universal, the best focus for educators is on 'what students do': that is, students' learning activities. Taking up Biggs' (2003) point, Freeman et al. (2009, p. 11) propose that '[s]uch cognitive processes can be stimulated by active teaching strategies such as problem-based learning', and further, that *all* students (not only international and culturally diverse local students) benefit from such inclu-sive teaching and learning environments (see also Ryan & Carroll, 2005). Corresponding with this, TBL is an active, problem-solving-based approach to learning that aims to engage all students.

An enduring assumption – that 'proximity' automatically results in intercul-tural contact which leads to intercultural learning – has been refuted by research (Robertson et al., 2000; Ryan & Carroll, 2005; Volet & Ang, 1998). Our class-room experience supports Freeman et al.'s (2009, p. 12) view that '[a]t the very least, active engagement is a necessary ingredient'. We demonstrate below that TBL establishes the broad architecture for a course that is founded in active learning which is reinforced and complemented by the reflective journal. Heyward (2002) proposes that *self-reflection* is central to the development of intercultural capabilities. As outlined below, the 'critical reflective journal assignment' (CRJA) is a key mechanism that facilitates students' subject-relevant, reflective activity.

Eisenchlas and Trevaskes (2007) argue that the development of intercultural skills is most effective 'within the very context of their own curriculum content and assessment practices' and propose that the immediate 'micro-level of every-day experience' with, and in, culture is most effective (Eisenchlas & Trevaskes, 2007, p. 416). In the UOS examined below, students were required to interface their experiential ('everyday') knowledge with formally acquired knowledge in assessed work. Furthermore, our teaching practice corroborates Eisenchlas and Trevaskes' (2007) insight that international and local students need to be partners in this process.

Teaching approach and tools

Team-based learning

Group work is common nowadays in higher education and various forms of team learning exist. Michaelson-style TBL is a particular type of team learning, used in widely ranging subject areas (Michaelsen et al., 2004; Team-based learning, n.d.; Thompson et al., 2007). It provides a broad architecture for the courses (see below) and deploys enduring student teams, which are established through a transparent, instructor-led process and formed according to specified criteria (in this application: work and professional experience, nationality, gender, local or international student status and prior TBL experience). TBL entails a modularised, topic-based sequence of learning activities extending usually over a two- to three-week cycle.

The sequence commences with independent (individual) study by students of instructor-specified learning materials (readings, backgrounding documents, a video or other materials) containing essential knowledge for the topic. This is followed by a brief in-class, multiple-choice test of foundational knowledge, conducted first individually (to ascertain the level of individual knowledge and create learning accountability), then repeated in student teams, the latter creating opportunity for peer teaching, collaboration and negotiation between students to achieve the best answer to the questions. Through question design that includes interpretive, causal and key concepts, these multiple-choice questions facilitate deep learning, averting a rote-learning approach for which multiple-choice tests are sometimes criticised (Freeman et al., 2006; Michaelsen et al., 2004). Results of the individual tests are scanned in class by the instructor using a portable scanner while the team test is underway. The team test is completed using 'Immediate Feedback Assessment Test' ('scratchie') forms, which immediately reveal whether or not teams have achieved the correct answer, and allow them to progress successively towards correct knowledge (see Dihoff Brosvic & Epstein, 2003). From the scanned individual test results, the instructor identifies the class's knowledge deficiencies and provides guided corrective input. The individual test and group retest is known as a 'Readiness Assurance Process', assuring students' knowledge of, and readiness to use, foundational knowledge. The next stage is an applied exercise in which students deploy the conceptual knowledge established through the above steps to solve a real-world problem (a case-based exercise). This again involves individual preparation, team-based collaboration and negotiation to reach a shared solution, followed by class-wide debate and argumentation by teams to present and defend their choices.

It has been found that TBL significantly enhances learning outcomes. For example, Freeman et al. (2006) found that students who scored lowest in the individual multiple-choice tests improved their outcomes by 56 per cent when repeated as a team test, average-scoring students' marks improved by 20 per cent, while the top-scoring students gained a team-based mark-up of 2 per cent. Separate comparison of overall results for courses taught (over a 14-year period by the first co-author, Susan McGrath-Champ) in TBL with the same content taught using traditional mode (lecture-based, exam and essay-assessment method) showed a higher average student result in TBL by 10 percentage points.

Furthermore, TBL fosters participative, collaborative learning in which the notion of 'arguing to learn' (Andriessen, 2006) and peer teaching (Falchikov, 2001) are central, and establish a student-centred 'learning community'. It has been observed repeatedly in these courses that students in a team become a trusted resource such that an individual student will commonly seek assistance, advice and help with learning challenges from other team members, supplementing the role of the designated instructor/s. Supportive components are used to enable students to develop necessary team-working skills and to initiate the internationalising process. These include transparent, instructor-directed team formation (outlined above), a workshop in which students negotiate and agree a 'team contract', including agreed expectations regarding grade outcomes, an exercise in 'Exploring and Valuing Diversity' and a guest workshop on cross-cultural work and negotiation skills in practice. All teamwork is undertaken within the classroom, creating transparency. Whereas the TBL process itself operates to substantially preclude 'free-loading' and 'social loafing' in teamwork, formative and summative self and peer assessments are also deployed to create transparency of individual contribution to teamwork and avert or resolve adverse popular perceptions of learning in group settings.

TBL establishes, within quite large classes, small working groups of five to six students so that the classroom experience is primarily one of 'smallness', even though the whole class group may be substantial in size. TBL entails a wholly different philosophy of learning and teaching which shifts the instructor's role from 'sage on a stage' to 'guide on the side' and 'delivers' learning and teaching by establishing a student-centred learning community.

Critical reflective journal assignment

Within the teams established for TBL, students were further matched to establish cross-national pairs or trios. Throughout the semester, students worked individually and in partnered arrangement on a reflective journal assignment, their main written assessment. This requires them to each write at least one weekly journal entry relating to the themes of the course, which may include aspects of relevant lived experience which they combine with formally acquired knowledge from the course. Weekly in-class time to discuss their journal entries with their partner/s follows during which students listen, challenge and present their partner/s with alternative views, interpretations and perspectives. Workshops assist students with the requisite (critical) style of writing and to ensure they can identify quality of work and understand the marking criteria. Students 'revisit' earlier journal entries later during the semester to add or extend early insights as their subject knowledge grows. The individually compiled, submitted assignment focuses on two or three of a student's strongest journal themes, presenting how their values, beliefs and assumptions have been challenged or changed through their learning in the UOS. The experience is that reflective writing is usually unfamiliar to students; however, instructor guidance, dedicated in-class time to undertake partnered work, along with other learning supports outlined above enable students to take up these new learning tools.

Instead of the message being that students should leave their personal lives 'at the classroom door', this assignment invites them to blend their lived and learned knowledge. For example, cross-cultural adjustment, with which international students have direct personal experience, is a key issue for multinational organisations in managing international assignees and a topic in the UOS 'International Dimensions of HRM'. As one of many themes relevant to the course content, this aspect enables students to interface their lived experience with formal knowledge, augments the knowledge of local students (who commonly did not have extensive cross-cultural adjustment experience) and validates the experiential knowledge of non-local students who often had less professional or work experience to draw upon than their local student peers. This opening up and mixing of cross-cultural knowledge helps to extend the intercultural competency of both local and international students. The opportunities for intercultural exchange and insight can be applied to a range of subject areas where contrasting human and cultural knowledge is relevant.

Research scope and methodology

The scope of the study reported here addresses the following questions relating to students' perceptions of TBL and the reflective learning journal:

Do students perceive that:

1   TBL assists them to develop critical thinking skills?
2   TBL helps them to collaborate with people from diverse backgrounds?
3   TBL helps them enhance their communication skills?
4   the CRJA assists them to develop critical thinking skills?
5   the CRJA helps them to collaborate with people from diverse backgrounds?
6   the CRJA helps them enhance their communication skills?
7   the CRJA facilitates blending of relevant lived (personal) knowledge and formally learned knowledge?
8   being partnered with another student of different national background for the CRJA assists their learning?

In making this exploratory study robust, a mixed-method approach was taken using three research instruments – a customised survey,[1] two focus groups and qualitative feedback from university-wide Unit of Study Evaluation (USE) surveys. Paper-based surveys were held during the last fortnight of the courses. The USE was conducted immediately after the customised evaluation, deploying standardised University of Sydney protocols. Focus groups consisting of student volunteers were additionally used for evaluating units WORK1 and WORK2. The focus group questions sought depth on the questions asked by the customised survey. Each focus group was recorded and transcribed. Of the 594 students enrolled in the UOS, there is an 86 per cent (average) customised survey return rate (510 students). A total of 20 students participated in the focus groups.

The survey asked for some initial demographic information (Table 2.2) and included questions about the students' perceptions of whether TBL in-class exercises supported their learning. Additionally, in the survey for WORK4, 5 and 6, students were asked whether the critical reflective journal process enhanced their learning. Specifically, nine key questions in the survey asked students about the role of TBL and the critical reflective journal in encouraging critical thinking about:

- the UOS subject content
- promoting cross-cultural learning and collaboration
- enhancing their communication skills.

The focus group used a series of semi-structured questions to extract details about students' thoughts of TBL.

A grounded approach was taken with the analysis of focus group data so that any findings could be directly linked to the student comments. Transcripts were open coded (Glaser, 1992) using NVivo, with general categories identified such as 'working in teams', 'working with students from diverse background' and 'negotiating ideas'. The survey results were descriptively analysed using Excel. USE written feedback was manually collated.

Table 2.2 Student demographics (% of total)

Unit (WORK)	1	2	3	4	5	6
Female	69	74	59	70	76	84
Male	31	26	41	30	24	16
Local	47	18	74	26	18	59
International	53	82	26	74	82	41

Table 2.3 TBL and the CRJA process: Contribution to learning and associated skills (% agreement/disagreement)

UOS – WORK 1, 2, 3, 4, 5, 6	Strongly/Agree							Neutral							Strongly/Disagree						
	1	2	3	4	5	6	Av	1	2	3	4	5	6	Av	1	2	3	4	5	6	Av
1. Helped me take responsibility for my learning	90	76	63	77	88	73	78	4	20	31	17	8	24	11	6	4	6	6	6	3	5
2. Helped me actively engage with the learning material/course*	81	85	72	83	89	72	80	13	11	22	8	7	24	14	6	5	6	9	3	4	5
3. Encouraged me to think critically about the different topics/theories/contents/experiences	79	72	56	65	80	68	70	13	22	25	25	16	22	20	8	6	19	10	5	10	10
4. Encouraged me to collaborate with people from diverse backgrounds	85	86	81	82	90	81	84	11	13	13	15	7	14	12	4	1	6	3	3	4	3
5. Enhanced my communication skills	79	67	56	75	87	49	69	13	24	25	17	11	39	22	8	9	19	7	2	12	v9
The critical reflective journal assignment process...																					
6. Helped me integrate learned (formal) and lived (informal) knowledge	na			68	85	63	72	na			23	9	25	19	na			9	7	12	9
7. Helped me actively engage with learning in this course	na			58	77	55	63	na			31	16	33	26	na			11	7	12	10
8. Helped me to think critically about the different topics/ theories/contents/experiences	na			63	82	64	70	na			27	14	23	21	na			10	4	13	9
9. Encouraged me to collaborate with people from diverse backgrounds	na			69	87	64	73	na			26	9	26	20	na			5	3	10	6
10. Enhanced my communication skills	na			61	79	53	64	na			22	19	34	25	na			17	3	13	5
11. Having a student partner to work with on the CRJA assisted my learning.	na			52	80	63	65	na			34	15	24	24	na			15	4	13	10

* The differing nature of TBL and CRJA necessitated slightly different wording of evaluation questions on learning engagement. For TBL: 'TBL helped me actively engage with the learning material'; for the assignment: 'The critical reflective journal assignment process helped me actively engage with the learning in this course'.
CRJA: critical reflective journal assignment; na: not available; TBL: team-based learning; UOS: units of study.

Findings

Overall, there was strong support among surveyed participants for the use of TBL and critical reflective journal as learning strategies to promote critical thinking, cross-cultural learning and communication skills (see Table 2.3).

Team-based learning

A very substantial proportion of students reported that they experience TBL as helping them to take responsibility for their learning (average 78 per cent: Table 2.3, item 1) and enabling engaged learning (average 80 per cent; Table 2.3, item 2). Arguably these are fundamental to success in internationalising learning processes. A significant majority of respondents across all UOS believed that TBL encouraged them to think critically about diverse topics, issues and experiences relating to the course (average 70 per cent; Table 2.3, item 3).

Team-based learning enhanced students' learning by drawing on the diversity and richness of their cultural backgrounds and experiences. Focus group participants appreciated the value of TBL in this regard:

> we were able to have... a mix of thoughts and patterns in which we were able to interact and appreciate each other's perspectives

TBL utilised the 'resource' of an internationalised classroom to enhance students' learning. As an international student commented, TBL enables:

> [l]earning other cultures. I've come from the [United] States and then meet someone from Australia and some from... (another) culture. So you... get like a different perspective which is great for the business world because we're so global now... we don't all work in one country.

Importantly, this learning of other cultures is largely experiential, learning arising from students' active engagement with one another, not solely from their formal intellectual learning activity.

Focus group participants identified the peer-to-peer feedback aspect of TBL as a catalyst in encouraging their critical thinking about learned and lived experiences in a cross-cultural setting. One participant noted:

> The role of the instructor definitely is very important and it does set the stage for it but I think the more you do peer-to-peer it sort of engages people with each other... . Peer-to-peer feedback was very valuable in this course (International HRM); the appreciation of how you can relate to different contexts.

Another participant also highlighted the relevance of peer-to-peer learning to their future professional experiences:

> *If you're going to be gaining a position where you have to deal with expatriates you almost start getting just a bit of initial feedback from those people living in these countries on how things are. So it's almost like gaining some bit of insight from this peer-to-peer thing.*

The strongest support for TBL facilitating internationalisation is indicated by students' evaluations concerning the capacity to promote cross-cultural collaboration. For all six semesters, over 80 per cent of respondents agreed that TBL exercises encouraged them to collaborate with people from diverse backgrounds (average 84 per cent; Table 2.3, item 4).

The value of team-based learning in encouraging students to collaborate and forge partnerships across cultures is best summed up by a local student with professional human resource management experience:

> *[M]aybe 80 percent of the knowledge (from this course) I already know.... What I'm gaining is the ability to sit down with some people I do not know, understand their perspectives, appreciate what they have to contribute, give them the opportunity to speak up and you know become team members, understand how different cultures interact, because for the first time I was linking with some people who were from some countries I've never interacted with.*

The focus group participants highlighted TBL's particular value in advancing their cross-cultural communication skills. The students espoused the value of this process in overcoming the challenge of cultural barriers in communication:

> *In the beginning... people were a bit hesitant to give feedback because they found it might be criticism and that sort of a cultural hurdle had to be overcome within our team as we moved along, and gradually people were more open.*
>
> *For us it was a challenge to deal as a group with different cultural backgrounds coming across with people who might not be too comfortable in presenting their ideas.... What we did in our group was actually encouraged them to speak and give them more leadership or opinion leading opportunities.*

As the teams worked together on weekly TBL exercises throughout the semester, students' ability to successfully consult and collaborate as a team strengthened over time. As one student stated:

> *it was actually team dynamics that evolved for us....*

By requiring that all teamwork is carried out in class and through mechanisms that establish individual accountability for knowledge contribution via individual readiness assurance tests, TBL largely designs out the 'free-rider' problem.

However, one or two focus group participants believed that free-loading was still a problem in some cases where particular team members opted to do most of the writing for team-based application exercises. However, other students recognised that the issue of free-loading is:

> *how you manage it, how you actually put in some strategies that you can sort of tackle it, and how you inculcate the level of confidence in different team members that you have, that you're able to do it.*

Mechanisms for managing inequitable effort have been successively enhanced and in Semester 2, 2009 onwards, 100 per cent of students chose to take shared, not individualised marks, from team assessments, reflecting a very high level of perceived equity in contribution and learning outcomes. Students noted that TBL strategies:

> *benefited us in terms of assessing how we are able to view each other and how everybody can bring positive aspects to the table.*

Critical reflective journal

The critical reflective journal was intended to enhance the benefits gained from TBL. To glean whether students agreed on its learning value, those students in WORK4, 5 and 6 were asked specific questions in the survey (Table 2.3, items 6–11).

A considerable majority of students supported the use of the critical reflective journal as a learning strategy. There was strongest agreement on its value in encouraging collaboration with people from diverse backgrounds (average 73 per cent; Table 2.3, item 9). There was also strong agreement on how the critical reflective journal helped students integrate lived and learned knowledge (average 72 per cent; Table 2.3, item 6).

USE comments reflect the benefits students derive in exploring cross-cultural and related aspects of their learning through the critical reflective journal:

> *The opportunity to understand the experiences of an international student who I would not have otherwise had the opportunity to understand or appreciate was a great benefit – this led to me challenging my values, beliefs and assumptions.*

Variable and slightly weaker support was indicated in regard to the reflective journal assignment enabling active engagement with the learning material (average 63 per cent; Table 2.3, item 7), enhancement of communication skills (average 64 per cent; Table 2.3, item 10) and assistance which student partnering provided in undertaking the assignment (average 65 per cent; Table 2.3, item 11). These outcomes may appear inconsistent with students' broad support for its cross-cultural collaboration value. This inconsistency can be explained by some students' tendency to opt for group discussions during allocated journal partnering sessions (communication skills item), the perception that 'lived', experiential knowledge is less directly related to course content (active engagement item) and that in some semesters, the late-in-the evening seminar is most popularly chosen by local students, which reduces the proportion of students working in cross-cultural pairs (student partner item).

Comparing TBL and critical reflective journal

To provide a comparison of how TBL and the critical reflective journal impacted on students' learning in internationalising the classroom, four corresponding questions were asked in the survey in relation to critical thinking, cross-cultural collaboration and communication skills (Table 2.3, items 2 & 7; 3 & 8; 4 & 9; 5 & 10).

The results show slightly higher student support for TBL than the reflective journal exercise across all these areas, suggesting a preference for learning in a group environment with greater diversity of experiences and perspectives than a paired/partnered arrangement. Nevertheless, the significant support for the critical reflective journal demonstrates its potential in complementing TBL in supporting students' learning, particularly in enhancing cross-cultural collaboration and helping students to integrate learned knowledge and the diverse lived experiences of the internationalised classroom.

Conclusion

It is evident that in the courses evaluated in this study, TBL and the reflective journal assignment contribute significantly to unlocking the resources represented by a diverse, multicultural student body, and to a genuine internationalising of the courses, classroom and curricula. These 'resources' include such dimensions as students' knowledge and experience of different cultures, insights from cross-cultural adjustment experiences, potentially contrasting values, beliefs, assumptions and the perspectives and views that arise from these. In particular, by encouraging collaboration between people of diverse backgrounds and enhancing communication skills, the evidence confirms that these learning tools can contribute to enhanced learning for international and local students, and staff, for whom ongoing acquisition of cross-cultural knowledge and enhanced teaching techniques are integral to the process. This teaching approach is effective in deploying student diversity in the classroom as a microcosm of the world in which students will eventually work – where cross-cultural engagement and management are necessary skills.

The research corroborates a program evaluation at the University of Michigan (Miller & Fernandez, 2007) which identified that the aspects having greatest success in facilitating internationalisation of teaching and learning were the use of reflective journals and working as part of a culturally diverse team. A third 'impact' mechanism – close interactions with faculty – was also a possible factor (though not evaluated) via relatively small seminar classes, in WORK1 and WORK3. In the other units the seminar classes, with approximately 45 and 70 students, respectively, were substantial in size. However, TBL provides a structure that enables economy and efficiency – an instructor can interface with each team closely enough so that this overcomes the larger actual size of these classes. Peer-to-peer learning augments teacher-focused input so that students learn from multiple people-sources, not just the instructor. Thus, in WORK2, 4, 5 and 6, and consistent with experience elsewhere (Michaelsen et al., 2004), substantial class sizes were experienced by staff as beneficial, not adverse, to the learning process because the diversity of experience and views that exist within the student group can be harnessed and shared by a larger class.

The study indicates that active learning in effective student teams initiates cross-cultural partnerships and relationships. Anecdotal evidence from students who have reported that they keep in contact with former team members from TBL-taught UOS, and the experience that some students have deliberately sought out and enrolled in TBL UOS suggests that such cross-cultural classroom relationships are valued and can be enduring.

Although this research took gender and local/international background of students into account to create a complete profile of the sample, the data analysis did not unpack the evaluation questions using these variables. Further research could be done to determine how these (or other) variables affect aspects of internationalising the classroom. Furthermore, Freeman et al. (2009, p. 16) note that '[i]f students are to focus on the development of their intercultural competence it must be clearly identified as a learning goal which is assessed'. The evidence from this study shows that the assessment tools achieve this goal and while internationalisation of the learning process is presented to students in introductory sessions, it was not formally articulated as an explicit learning goal in course documents until WORK6 (in 2010). Other limitations are: the data are self-reported and would be strengthened by validation data (for example, ratings by other people to whom the students are known), the need to pre- and post-test to deeply understand the effect of TBL and related interventions, and the need to extend to other universities and faculties to be able to generalise the findings. Longitudinal study that follows up participating students six months and one year later could reveal the durability of changes arising from TBL and journaling techniques.

Notes

1 Customised online evaluation surveys of TBL were conducted in prior semesters and used to develop and enhance the learning tools and processes.

References

Andriessen, J. (2006). Arguing to learn. In R. K. Sawyer (ed.), *The Cambridge hand-book of the learning sciences*. New York: Cambridge University Press.
Arkoudis, S. (2006). *Teaching international students: Strategies to enhance learning*. Melbourne: Centre for the Study of Higher Education, University of Melbourne.

Biggs, J. (1997). Teaching across and within cultures: The issue of international students. In R. Murray-Harvey & H. Silins (eds), Learning and Teaching in Higher Education: Advancing International Perspectives. Proceedings of the Higher Education Research & Development Society of Australasia Conference, Adelaide: Flinders Press.

Biggs, J. (2003). *Teaching for quality learning at university*. Buckingham: Open University Press.

Dihoff, R. E., Brosvic, G. M. & Epstein, M. L. (2003). The role of feedback during academic testing: The delay retention effect. *The Psychological Record*, *53*(4), 533–548.

Eisenchlas, S. & Trevaskes, S. (2007). Developing intercultural communication skills through intergroup interaction. *Intercultural Education*, *18*(5), 413–425.

Falchikov, N. (ed.) (2001). *Learning together: Peer tutoring in higher education*. London: RoutledgeFalmer.

Freeman, M., McGrath-Champ, S., Clark, S. & Taylor, L. (2006). The case for in-class team-based assessment. In *Symposium Proceedings: Assessment in Science Teaching and Learning*, 28 September. University of Sydney.

Freeman, M., Treleven, L., Ramburuth, P., et al. (2009). *Embedding the development of intercultural competence in business education*. Strawberry Hills: Australian Learning and Teaching Council.

Glaser, B.G. (1992). *Basics of grounded theory analysis*. Mill Valley, CA: Sociology Press.

Heyward, M. (2002). From international to intercultural: Redefining the international school for a globalised world. *Journal of Research in International Education*, *1*(1), 9–32.

Michaelsen, L. K., Bauman Knight, A. & Fink, L. D. (eds.) (2004). *Team-based learning: A transformative use of small groups in college teaching*. Sterling, VA: Stylus Publishing.

Miller, A. T. & Fernandez, E. (2007). New learning and teaching from where you've been: The global intercultural experience for undergraduates. *New Directions for Teaching and Learning*, *111*, 55–62.

Robertson, M., Lane, M., Jones, S. & Thomas, S. (2000). International students, learning environments and perceptions: A case study using the Delphi technique. *Higher Education Research and Development*, *19*(1), 89–102.

Ryan, J. & Carroll, J. (2005). *Teaching international students: Improving learning for all*. Oxford: Routledge.

Sulkowski, N. B. & Deakin, M. K. (2009). Does understanding culture help enhance students' learning experience? *International Journal of Contemporary Hospitality Management*, *21*(2), 154–166.

Team-based learning (n.d.) *Team-based learning collaborative*. Available at: http://www.teambasedlearning.org/starting (accessed 5 December 2011).

Thompson, B., Schneider, V., Haidet, P., et al. (2007). Team-based learning at ten medical schools: Two years later. *Medical Education*, *41*(3), 250–257.

Volet, S. (2004). Challenges of internationalisation: Enhancing intercultural competence and skills for critical reflection on the situated and non-neutral nature of knowledge. In P. Zeegers & K. Dellar-Evans (eds). *Language & Academic Skills in Higher Education, Volume 6*, 1–10. Adelaide: Flinders University.

Volet, S. & Ang, G. (1998). Culturally mixed groups on international campuses: An opportunity for intercultural learning. *Higher Education Research & Development*, *17*(1), 5–23.

Chapter 3

Developing capability

International students in doctoral writing groups

Jeannie Daniels

Introduction

The internationalisation of higher education has seen increasing numbers of international students coming to Australia to undertake doctoral studies. For students whose first language is not English, writing at doctoral level poses particular challenges, with cultural considerations adding another layer of complexity to the doctoral experience. Educators are thus challenged to develop new and appropriate pedagogical tools that acknowledge these students' complex and diverse learning requirements. This chapter describes one project that aims to address these student needs, drawing on the notion of 'capability' to interrogate competing notions of the purpose of doctoral work. Capability is used as a lens through which to critique existing normalising constructions of doctoral study and to analyse the research data.

Writing groups for doctoral students are increasingly being implemented in Australian universities, as research shows these supportive, peer-learning environments offer students many additional benefits to the development of high-order academic skills. The formation of one such writing group has created a collegial learning environment in which students not only gain opportunities to further develop their academic English language skills but also engage in a comprehensive approach to building doctoral attributes that has the potential to extend beyond those of personal achievement and institutional requirements.

This chapter provides a contextual background before describing the implementation and progress of a writing group for international doctoral students in an Australian university. The conceptual framework applies an educational lens to Sen's (1999) Capability Approach to investigate learning through participation in a writing group. Discussion then focuses on preliminary findings from an accompanying research study that aims to investigate the potential of the writing group both as a pedagogical tool and a process of capability formation.

Capability and education

The notion of capability was developed by Sen as 'a critique of other approaches to thinking about human well-being' (Walker & Unterhalter, 2007, p. 1).

Central to capability theory is the idea that quality of life is dependent not just on access to, or acquisition of, commodities, but also the opportunities to benefit from those commodities through the ability to make choices based on individual circumstance and need. Sen refers to a range of 'freedoms', explaining that capabilities are 'substantive freedoms, rather than... just income or wealth' (1999, p. 24), and which must be individually evaluated since individuals are subject to different combinations of 'unfreedoms' – barriers or lack of opportunities – within their social contexts. Capability is not, however, a theory of individualism but is:

> *quintessentially a social product...[because] the specific uses that individuals make of their freedoms, depend on social associations – particularly on the interactive formation of public perceptions and on collaborative comprehension of problems and remedies.*

(Sen, 1999, p. 31)

Sen argues that it is these opportunities that must be accounted for when evaluating economic, social and educational policies.

Educational theorists have applied Sen's capability approach in a range of contexts (see Harreveld & Singh, 2008; Lessmann, 2009; Nussbaum, 2004; Unterhalter, 2003; Walker, 2005) as a way of evaluating the broader social agenda of education as well as of interrogating inequalities of opportunity within the system. An educational application addresses the ongoing productivity of individuals operating within and across society, exercising their capabilities through making informed choices and applying their knowledge. There is, however, little in the education literature that explores capability's application to doctoral studies or to international students, two areas that together form a significant part of the higher education landscape. The challenges to provide doctoral education for culturally and linguistically diverse student populations present openings to explore different ways of theorising the issues and developing more relevant doctoral pedagogies.

The notion of capability in an educational context focuses on conditions that enable students to make 'decisions based on what they have reason to value' (Walker & Unterhalter, 2007, p. 3). As such, it provides a balance for the current utilitarian approach that sees equality and social justice only in terms of resources and outcomes. The doctoral – and post-doctoral – identity, seen through the lens of Sen's notion of capability, therefore emerges from each student's ability to develop her/his decision-making capacity and exercise individual choice, through:

> *an integration of knowledge, skills, personal qualities and understanding used appropriately and effectively – not just in familiar and highly-focused specialist contexts but in response to new and changing circumstances.*

(Stephenson, 1998, p. 2)

Capability theory is a critical response to the particular ways in which the international doctoral student in Australia (and other Western cultural educational environments) is currently being constructed (Lee & Boud, 2009; Rizvi, 2010a). The demands on them, as for all doctoral students, are high and greater than simply producing research theses that demonstrate a good level of English academic writing and add to the knowledge base in their specialist field. As Rizvi (2007, p. 4) explains, '[t]he global age... requires students who are cognitively flexible, culturally sophisticated, and are able to work collaboratively in groups made up of people of diverse backgrounds and intelligences'. An investigation of such constructions through a lens of capability indicates the potential of the writing group process to produce such post-doctoral knowledge workers, well-prepared for the challenges of their internationalised social, economic and political environments – the transnational spaces (Rizvi, 2010a) within which these international students will operate beyond the doctorate.

International doctoral students: Issues and perspectives

Much has been written about the challenges faced by students from non-English-speaking countries undertaking doctoral studies in Australia (see Dawson, 1998; Novera, 2004; Rizvi, 2010a; Sawir, 2005). While exposure to Australia's Western education system can be perceived as advantageous by both students and their parents (Guruz, 2008; Rizvi, 2010a), with 'international qualifications [seen] as a marker of status and prestige' (Rizvi, 2010a, p. 162), students are faced with significant cultural differences in addition to the challenges of studying and writing in a second language.

Doctoral writing requires a high level of skills in any language. Many international students face the challenge of constructing complex ideas and arguments in a language they are still learning. Working between two languages, as Robinson-Pant (2005, p. 129) explains, is 'not only time-consuming but intellectually challenging'. These students may already be working more intensely than their Anglophone peers as they negotiate potentially unfamiliar academic concepts; in fact, international students experience the highest stress levels of all non-traditional students (Dawson & Conti-Bekkers, 2002).

Language is a social practice 'embedded in social, political and cultural contexts' (Robinson-Pant, 2005, p. 125). Unfamiliarity with a language can produce lack of confidence, misunderstandings and a reticence to engage in the interactive and sometimes abrasive activities of Western-style learning. Consequently, some international students have difficulty adjusting to social and educational expectations (Rizvi, 2010a). Cultural differences – both educational and social – create other difficulties and can lead to students becoming isolated. Compounding this isolation is the fact that doctoral work is, by its nature, a solitary undertaking. Geographic separation from familiar support networks adds to the risk of isolation and its resultant difficulties. Clearly these students must overcome significant hurdles to study successfully in Australia, and of these, acquiring skills in written academic English is perhaps the most immediate – although by no means the only – consideration.

While international students can find the educational environment in which they study culturally quite different from their own, it is also one where they are acknowledged, and understand what is expected of them. A high level of dependency on *the system* can easily eventuate for those whose own educational perceptions may be based on concepts of teacher-as-expert, and of knowledge as *given* (Robinson-Pant, 2005). This can be problematic, producing a supervisory relationship in which the students become dependent on the supervisors and so gain few of the skills required to negotiate the sometimes challenging, even conflicting, expectations of how they will eventually apply their doctoral expertise. Such an approach to doctoral work also concerns educators developing appropriate pedagogies for increasingly international postgraduate student cohorts.

Acknowledging the relations of power in which research training is embedded, Rizvi (2010a) talks of higher education's role in shaping professional identities, and the implications for international students: the tensions of identity formation they face when 'caught between the stress on individualistic skills and entrepreneurial competition, on the one hand, and on general humanistic concerns and national cultural values, on the other' (p. 163). Expectations about what these international students will do with their qualifications and skills are to some extent already forged in these 'transnational spaces', and further mediated both by the Western values embedded in their education and by their cultural values or even the expectations of the institution or government that has paid for their doctoral studies (see Rizvi, 2010a). Despite these tensions, within the doctoral process there is potential to produce both self and ethical awareness and so for international doctoral students to consider their current studies and future goals (Walker, 2010).

While a necessary part of doctoral work is undoubtedly 'the need to form a person who thinks and acts like a researcher and can draw on the devices – conceptual and practical – researchers need' (Lee & Boud, 2009, p. 21), capability extends these attributes, establishing a further level of awareness related to development of a socio-community consciousness informed by an understanding of differences. This includes the ability to reflect on and act in response to these differences. Students moving into or returning to professional environments different to those envisaged within Western doctoral frameworks are thus able to evaluate diverse situations and respond appropriately.

In the context of doctoral study, it is important to develop students' ability to use those resources, making individual choices about needs based on their own informed evaluation of *what matters to them*. One educational strategy that has the potential to do this, and that is increasingly being used in Australian postgraduate education, is the use of student writing groups.

Writing groups as pedagogical tools

Student writing groups are growing in popularity as supervisors and discipline lecturers recognise their value as effective pedagogical tools for improving academic writing skills (Aitchison, 2009; Aitchison & Lee, 2006; Li & Vandermensbrugghe, 2011; Maher et al., 2008). Such groups also provide, for some students, a learning environment that addresses additional needs.

Challenges already identified for doctoral students include working in comparative isolation, with little or no opportunity to share or receive peer support in their experience of doctoral work; minimal exposure to different ways of presenting ideas or crafting an argument; few opportunities to develop skills of critique or to receive critical feedback and little encouragement to engage reflectively with their work. While the doctoral process develops specialised academic skills and professional knowledge, the social community of the writing group, through engagement in 'critical peer learning' (Maher et al., 2008, p. 268), create collaborative spaces that can address many of these issues and have the potential to produce more confident and skilled writers (Aitchison & Lee, 2006; Maher et al., 2008). Growing interest in such collaborative writing processes, along with recognition of current students' writing needs, has led to the implementation of a doctoral writing group at La Trobe University in Australia.

Background to the project

The University's Faculty of Business, Economics & Law has approximately 220 postgraduate research students, mostly studying at doctoral level. Many are from countries other than Australia and are writing their theses in English as a second – or even third – language. Academic writing, a necessary part of doctoral work, is challenging for some of these students, who seek support from the Academic Language and Learning (ALL) staff. ALL staff are academics who work with discipline staff on curriculum design and the application of appropriate pedagogical tools to provide academic skills development opportunities for students. They also construct and deliver workshops and seminars on specific aspects of academic literacies. With such large numbers of international students in the faculty, writing and language support is a substantial part of the work of ALL staff; it has become apparent, however, that this strong focus on writing well in English is holding back the potential for students to develop other, equally important doctoral skills.

ALL staff identified that, in some disciplines, successful completion of the thesis is seen as the major purpose of doctoral study. As a consequence, many international students are simply encouraged to seek extensive language support and steered through the doctoral process. The experience of doctoral study itself is given scant attention. At times it seems students are being given little encouragement to build their intellectual curiosity, agency or ownership of their learning, or develop an awareness of how they might apply these attributes, and their knowledge and skills, postdoctorate. There is, in many cases, little evidence that doctoral identities are being encouraged and nurtured.

Whereas Australian doctoral students are also subject to these supervisory limitations, they may be better prepared, by virtue of their Western-style educational background, to shape their doctoral identity. As active participants within a (reasonably) familiar educational environment, they may already have the confidence to engage in debate with their supervisors and respond to challenges to their ideas. In doing so, they are more likely to gain opportunities to acquire the skills to negotiate their own learning needs.

It has been the experience of ALL staff that international students are more likely to accept the supervisory conditions set for them, without question. This situation often leads to an overemphasis on producing *correct* English grammar and punctuation to the neglect of developing the skills to become 'cognitively flexible, culturally sophisticated and able to work collaboratively in groups made up of people of diverse backgrounds and intelligence' (Rizvi, 2007, p. 4), a role that their increasingly global work environments will demand of them (Gardiner, 2004; Seddon, 2010; Rizvi, 2007, 2010a). A doctoral experience in which the student/learner is *given* knowledge by a supervisor/expert will not produce such an identity.

The globalised environments into which these students will move postdoctorate will require 'globally mobile researchers' who are agentic, self-directed and reflective and who are able to engage confidently in diverse situations and contribute to knowledge through 'self-reflexivity about location and effects in knowledge geopolitics' (Seddon, 2010, p. 223). Seddon's profile of relevant doctoral education 'acknowledges the diversity of disciplinary, workplace and professional knowledge communities and also the way these communities are framed by national cultures' (p. 224). And yet, she claims, tensions remain in what constitutes knowledge and knowledge-building; international students, applying their Western education skills post-doctorate, need to understand and be able to negotiate these tensions.

Although all doctoral students become learners within their candidature, these international students come into this learning environment already seasoned academics and/or professionals experienced in their fields (Rizvi, 2010a). It is reasonable to assume, therefore, that the intensive effort required to study in a different country and in a different language should add substantially to these students' already extensive body of knowledge and professional skills. This belief has led ALL staff to reflect on their capacity to enhance the learning experiences of these doctoral candidates, and to ask:

- How does doctoral study at this university benefit these students?
- What kind of professional identity is being built, or built upon?
- What role can the ALL staff take in facilitating the doctoral process as one of identity development, agency and facilitating students' ability to negotiate their roles, postdoctorate, as international knowledge workers?

Attendance at a workshop for higher education practitioners interested in developing postgraduate writing groups provided possible answers to these questions. Facilitators of existing writing groups explained how students achieve much more than the development of high-level English writing skills, which itself builds confidence in non-native speakers and writers (Dawson & Conti-Bekkers, 2002). As the literature affirms (Aitchison & Lee, 2006; Maher et al., 2008), writing groups offer students opportunities (or *freedoms*) to become reflexive, to consider multiple perspectives and to understand how ideas can be shaped and applied (and the implications of doing so). Viewed together with a growing self-confidence, Sen (1999) would call this a process of developing capability: that is, the agency and power to choose how to apply the functionings, or processes of their doctoral work, in future situations.

The research

At the same time as the writing group was formed, a small research project was implemented, guided by Walker's (2010, p. 31) suggestion that '[t]he opportunity exists for research into doctoral capabilities... to conceptualise opportunities and outcomes in doctoral scholarship and learning for diverse students'. The research aims to address the questions:

- Does the participation of international students in doctoral writing groups lead to capability through development of high-level academic and self-management skills?
- If so, how does this happen within the writing group?

While the eventual aim is to identify observable and demonstrable perceptions of capability development, it was decided that this first stage would investigate students' and researchers' perceptions of what happens in the writing group. Data were collected from interviews and journalling: students self-selected to be interviewed, and were asked to reflect on their own and others' actions and interactions during the sessions, as well as their perceptions of any changes in how the process is developing. The researcher's journal recorded the levels of discussion, types of responses and the methods used to address conflicting reviews of written work. These observations were recorded after each session. Data were categorised within a framework of capability elements, before attempts were made to apply a capability lens to the data analysis itself (subsequent categories and definitions for analysis of capability development are drawn from the analysed interview and journal data).

An analytic framework informed by narrative inquiry used, as data, students' own responses to participation in the writing group and facilitators' observations, while elements of Sen's capability approach informed the categories for analysis. Walker's (2010) educational perspective illustrates a number of features of capability development and these were used to categorise the interview data into personal (*confidence with self*) and communicative/social (*confidence with others*) attributes.

Confidence with self, that is, *personal attributes*, includes elements of:

- self-assessed improvement in thinking at doctoral level
- a sense of 'self'/purpose
- clarity of future goals
- self-assessment of personal and learner development.

Capability elements of *communicative attributes*, or confidence with others, are:

- increased confidence
- improved writing at doctoral level
- eagerness to give opinion
- demonstrated skills in giving critique, and receiving and acting on critique from peers.

Interviews with seven of the group's participants – Nirmali, Tuan, Ahn Dung, Mawar, Akmar, Adir and Rushani (not their real names) – were conducted with additional interviews planned in approximately 12 months. These subsequent interviews are expected to add substantially to the breadth of data, and to the depth of the findings.

Students were asked about the process and its effectiveness in developing their skills: Did they think it will change/has changed their way of thinking about themselves or their goals? In addition, the research sought to explore the dynamics of the group and the impact of the facilitator's approach, asking participants how they perceived the changes were happening: for example, was it the functioning of the group; the facilitation or perhaps each individual's attention to their own needs? Data were also collected from the researcher's journalling after each session, students' responses during the sessions and the feedback and comments received from the initial one-day workshop.

Early findings and future possibilities

From this first stage of the research some significant elements emerged. The interviews have given students opportunities to express their experiences of, and concerns about, writing in academic English (in itself a useful process in learner development). Some concerns point to different cultural understandings and expectations, while confidence, or the lack of, is a term frequently expressed. Students explain their initial reticence to share their writing – and, for some, even to engage in discussion – as a lack of confidence with their level of English language skills, a sentiment expressed by all except one participant.

The interview data together with the researcher's journal recording interaction and participation already indicate an increased level of confidence in students. This is demonstrated by greater willingness to offer their work to the group, to engage in discussion and to present their opinions and to engage with those of the other reviewers. Talk within the group has become not only more relaxed and frequent but also has taken on a more scholarly tone.

All participants claim that writing in English at academic level is their major concern, even though each had been able to choose their preferred institution and therefore had elected to study in an English-speaking university. Some had enrolled with confidence in their ability to address the high-level written requirements of their study, realising later their need for additional support; Nirmali from Sri Lanka, one of the newer doctoral candidates, identified concerns about her written language skills at her first writing group meeting, explaining, 'my English is not good, no'. Issues around the level of English are of course one of the core concerns within the group, and it is this shared experience that encourages self-identification of needs and the capacity to reflect on individual location within a community of shared – but not identical – experiences.

Students asked few questions in the first session, a reticence perhaps linked to cultural notions of the student as passive recipient of knowledge. Some did voice such an understanding of their doctoral role. Akmar, a Malaysian student, told the group her role was 'just being here to listen because I know little yet. I [have] just start[ed]'. She now participates at each session, and has reviewed others' writing, although is yet to offer her own work for review.

Most students, like Tuan from Vietnam, were also initially reluctant to produce written work to share. Tuan was convinced his writing was 'very, very bad', confiding that, 'at first I was very, very ashamed to show them [the other students] my work'. Rushani, from Bangladesh, expressed a similar opinion. By contrast, Mawar, a higher education lecturer in Indonesia, was one of the first to share her work. A confident student who 'love[s] to talk', she was happy to receive peer feedback – with reservations, only taking it on board when she thought the reviewer understood what she meant. After approximately seven meetings, however, members now claim to feel more confident in sharing their work and, importantly, in listening and responding to questions and critique.

When asked to consider the influence of the writing group participation on her writing, Mawar insisted that 'It isn't about the writing, no, no, it is *not* about the writing'. Participation in the group – at least for her – is about other perceived benefits, indicating the possibility of outcomes over and above those identified in the existing literature. She has her family with her in Australia, and is a confident and outgoing personality; Mawar appears less isolated than many international students and has a good support network; yet she insists that she gets from the writing group 'something more', although she has some hesitancy in articulating what that 'something' is.

Ahn Dung, like Tuan, is also from Vietnam. He works as a tutor in the faculty while studying and so is used to taking on the role of teacher. For him, there was a transition to be made from identifying and correcting mistakes to providing positive feedback. When asked to review, for the group, another student's work, he reflected on how difficult he found this, explaining, 'when she writes it like that, I want to tell her it's not [the] right way; I have to stop myself'.

Ahn Dung is still working through this transition, and seems impatient at times when other reviewers take a more reflective approach in their responses. It can be hard to offer constructive criticism without seeming judgemental, and yet this skill enables the giver to explore their own ideas in relation to those of others as only one amongst many ways of looking at the world (Aitchison, 2009). Embedded notions of *good* teaching and learning can be hard to leave behind, especially if, like Tuan, the student is also by profession a higher education teacher in their home country, or is tutoring in the traditional teaching environment that dominates this faculty, as Ahn Dung does.

Additionally, Mawar's claim that 'something' other than writing is the significant factor at work in her participation in the writing group will be explored further with her in a subsequent interview. Rizvi (2010b) considers the postdoctoral worker in current and future international contexts and imagines her/his potential to apply a highly polished critical lens to problems and situations encountered, and to be able to think about how *things might be otherwise*. Perhaps Mawar's perception that there is something being developed, something beyond expected outcomes, suggests there may be elements of capability formation in the processes of the international doctoral writing group.

The research has thus far confirmed some of the challenges faced when studying in an additional language, and that are recognised in the literature. Students have also identified that their participation in the writing group has led to an increase in their confidence, especially academically. Stephenson (1998) defines confidence as the 'distinction between the *possession* and *use* of skills' (p. 2 *italics in original*), a definition that is matched by the descriptions of participants such as Adir, from the United Arab Emirates (UAE), who talks of 'feeling confident now to apply what I think I know, but before wasn't sure to say'. The distinction drawn by Stephenson, and expressed by Adir, can similarly be identified in Sen's (1999) theoretical approach as the difference between *functionings* and (if those skills include the freedom to evaluate and to make choices) *capabilities*.

The preliminary work so far suggests the methodology is a relevant one for the research questions, with initial data used to further refine the focus of future interviews. With data collection not yet complete, some analysis remains to be done. Even in these early stages, however, interview data have produced some interesting results.

Conclusion

In this chapter, the notion of capability is used to explore the challenges facing international students undertaking doctoral studies in an Australian university. The collaborative approach to doctoral writing that develops within the writing group is suggested as a way to address some of these identified challenges, and to increase awareness and confidence amongst students in addition to giving opportunities to engage in high-level academic writing. As a pedagogical tool, the writing group has benefits for international doctoral students, having the potential to address many concerns expressed in the literature. The writing group described in this chapter, as well as the related research project, are attempts to investigate pedagogical strategies to address some of these concerns, and to begin to explore the potential of the writing group, suggesting possible outcomes linked to the formation of Sen's capabilities (1999).

Preliminary results of this ongoing research study suggest that while there are benefits to participation, further data collection and analysis is required. Similarly, more work is needed to understand if, and how, the writing group process has the potential to respond to the claims made about outcomes of capability formation. The current research will address only some aspects of the complexity of challenges that face international doctoral students, although participants are already reporting benefits of increased confidence in their academic skills and engagement in scholarly discussion. Other perceived benefits, acknowledged but not yet named and defined, illustrate the need for further research in this area. While the potential of educational applications of the capability approach are fully explored in this small project, it is planned to expand the research later to investigate capability's relevance to internationalisation in education more broadly.

As doctoral studies become more and more an international experience for many students, it is important that all aspects of that experience continue to be documented and interrogated. Research into international doctoral learning is therefore a necessary accompaniment to the increasing internationalisation in education, to ensure these students receive relevant and high-quality learning outcomes that enhance their personal and professional futures.

References

Aitchison, C. (2009). Writing groups for doctoral education. *Studies in Higher Education*, *34*, 905–916.

Aitchison, C. & Lee, A. (2006). Research writing: Problems and pedagogies. *Teaching in Higher Education*, *11*, 265–278.

Dawson, J. (1998). From accommodation to incorporation: Internationalising the classroom through structured dialogue. In *Proceedings of the HERDSA 21st Annual Conference*. Auckland, New Zealand: HERDSA.

Dawson, J. & Conti-Bekkers, G. (2002). Supporting international students' transitional adjustment strategies. In *Focusing on the Student. Proceedings of the 11th Annual Teaching Learning Forum*. Perth: Edith Cowan University.

Gardiner, H. (2004). How education changes: Considerations of history, science and values. In M. Suarez-Orozco & Quin-Hiliard (eds.), *Globalization: culture and education in the new millenium*. Berkeley, CA: University of California Press.

Guruz, K. (2008). *Higher education and international student mobility in the global knowledge economy*. Albany, NY: New York State University Press.

Harreveld, R. E. & Singh, M. J. (2008). Amartya Sen's Capability Approach and the brokering of learning provision for young adults. *Vocations and Learning*, *1*, 211–226.

Lee, A. & Boud, D. (2009). Framing doctoral education as practice. In D. Boud & A. Lee (eds.), *Changing practices of doctoral education*. Abingdon, Oxon, UK: Routledge.

Lessmann, O. (2009). Capability and learning to choose. *Studies in the Philosophy of Education*, 28, 449–460.

Li, L. & Vandermensbrugghe, J. (2011). Supporting the thesis writing process of international research students through an ongoing writing group. *Innovations in Education and Teaching International*, 48, 195–205.

Maher, D., Seaton, L., McMullen, C., et al. (2008). "Becoming and being writers": The experiences of doctoral students in writing groups. *Studies in Continuing Education*, 30, 263–275.

Novera, I. A. (2004). Indonesian postgraduate students studying in Australia: An examination of their academic, social and cultural experiences. *International Education Journal*, 5(4), 475–487.

Nussbaum, M. (2004). Women's education: A global challenge. *Signs*, 29, 325–355.

Rizvi, F. (2007). *Teaching global connectivity*. Curriculum.edu.au. Online at: http://www.curriculum.edu.au/verve/_resources/Rizvi_Teaching_Global_Interconnectivity_v.1.pdf (accessed 26 August 2011).

Rizvi, F. (2010a). International students and doctoral studies in transnational spaces. In M. Walker & P. Thomson (eds.), *The Routledge doctoral supervisor's companion: Supporting effective research in Education and the Social Sciences*. London: Routledge.

Rizvi, F. (2010b). Transforming lives, transforming learning. In *What does it take to transform a life through learning? The 3rd Annual Curriculum, Teaching and Learning Colloquium, La Trobe University*. Melbourne, Victoria: Curriculum, Teaching and Learning Centre, La Trobe University.

Robinson-Pant, A. (2005). *Cross-cultural perspectives on educational research*. Maidenhead, UK: Open University Press.

Sawir, E. (2005). Language difficulties of international students in Australia: The effects of prior learning experience. *International Education Journal*, 6(5), 567–580.

Seddon, T. (2010). Doctoral education in global times. In M. Walker & P. Thomson (eds.), *The Routledge doctoral supervisor's companion: Supporting effective research in Education and the Social Sciences*. London: Routledge.

Sen, A. (1999). *Development as freedom*. Oxford, UK: Oxford University Press.

Stephenson, J. (1998). The concept of capability and its importance in higher education. In J. Stephenson & M. Yorke (eds.), *Capability and quality in higher education*. London: Kogan Page.

Unterhalter, E. (2003). Crossing disciplinary boundaries: The potential of Sen's capability approach for sociologists of education. *British Journal of Sociology of Education*, 24(5), 665–669.

Walker, M. (2005). *Higher education pedagogies: A capabilities approach*. Maidenhead, UK: SRHE/Open University Press & McGraw-Hill.

Walker, M. (2010). Doctoral education as 'capability' formation. In M. Walker & P. Thomson (eds.), *The Routledge doctoral supervisor's companion: Supporting effective research in Education and the Social Sciences*. London: Routledge.

Walker, M. & Unterhalter, E. (2007). The capability approach: Its potential for work in education. In M. Walker & E. Unterhalter (eds.), *Amartya Sen's capability approach and social justice in education*. New York: Palgrave Macmillan.

Chapter 4

Feedback or feed forward? Supporting Master's students through effective assessment to enhance future learning

Sue Robson, David Leat, Kate Wall and Rachel Lofthouse

Introduction

This chapter reports on a small-scale research study at one institution that examined staff and Master's students' perceptions about assessment practices, and in particular about the role of feedback in students' learning. The study was funded by the University's Teaching and Learning Committee as part of a series of initiatives designed to enhance the student experience. The university in which this study took place takes pride in its diverse and cosmopolitan community, with almost 4,000 international students from over 110 countries studying at the institution. Its international strategy aims to address internationalisation at home, encompassing internationalisation of the curriculum, developing students as 'global citizens' with cross-cultural understanding and skills and internationalisation abroad, to encompass strategic partnerships and networks, transnational education and international recruitment.

The research study focused on students enrolled on Master's programmes in the Faculty of Humanities and Social Sciences, where one-year, full-time Master's programmes in Business and Education-related studies in particular attract increasing numbers of international students. The study used naturally occurring opportunities in a Graduate Skills Programme and a module on thinking skills for Master's students, and a staff development programme to invite students and staff to reflect upon and discuss their experiences of feedback, and what they regarded as the most useful and least useful forms of feedback. The research team aimed to create 'optimal contact situations' (Pettigrew & Tropp, 2000, p. 111) in which students could share their experiences and understandings about feedback and learn from each other, and staff could share their aims in providing feedback and explore the challenges associated with educating 'from, with, and for a multitude of cultural perspectives' (Nainby, Warren & Bollinger, 2003, p. 198).

The chapter explores the tensions between what students want from feedback, and the most common forms of feedback provided; and between academics' perceptions of the purposes and ideal forms of feedback, and what is achievable within their busy workloads. It considers the challenges associated with bridging the gap between the feedback that is made available to students and what is actually taken up by students to feed forward, and enhance their future work.

Literature review

Internationalisation has become an increasingly important goal for the higher education sector in many countries. Academic mobility is a key aspect of internationalisation, which Guruz (2011) relates to the global knowledge economy, the growing interdependence of international networks and communities and the requirement for 'a common language, a common base of skills, and the capacity to work in intercultural environments' (Guruz, 2011, p. 19). These factors promote academic mobility and motivate students 'to seek the best education they can afford anywhere in the world so that they can compete in the global labour market' (Guruz, 2011, p. 19). The number of students in tertiary education worldwide increased by 50 per cent between 2000 and 2009 (UNESCO, 2009) and demand for an international education is forecast to escalate from 2.1 million in 2003 to approximately 5.8 million by 2020 (Bohm et al., 2004). While the global economic crisis, the increase in university fees and more restrictive visa procedures may impact on international student recruitment in future, the rapid growth in numbers over the last decade has been attributed to student perceptions that they will receive a high-quality education in prestigious Western universities, enhancing their career prospects upon their return home (Edwards & Ran, 2009; Bohm et al., 2004). However, as McGrath-Champ, Zou and Taylor point out in Chapter 2 of this volume, how quality is achieved in practice is a very different thing and is challenging teachers within the sector.

Volet (2004) and Knight (2007) suggest that a crucial goal for internationalisation is to foster students' awareness of opportunities to develop intercultural competence as an integral part of studying in a multicultural higher education environment, an idea followed up by Mertova in Chapter 5 of this book. A review of assessment and feedback practices can determine the extent to which they reflect international perspectives, and promote intercultural learning, critical reflection and metacognitive awareness. Hattie and Timperley (2007) provide evidence that feedback is one of the most critical influences on student learning. Other studies illustrate the positive effects that feedback, mediated by the growth of self-concept and learner identity, can have (Black & Wiliam, 1998; Bloxham & Boyd, 2007; Gibbs & Simpson, 2004) to support learning as a 'social, socio-cultural and transformative process rather than... a purely cognitive and accumulative activity' (Kreber, 2010, p. 4).

Yorke (2003) notes that formative assessment is not a well-understood concept in higher education. This is perhaps due to the complexity of types of formative assessment, ranging from informal interactions in class to formal feedback that relates specifically to curricular assessment frameworks. Feedback often takes the form of descriptive comments accompanying coursework grades with the focus on what Edmead describes in Chapter 1 of this volume as an assessed product.

This combination has been found to provide more useful data on long-term learning of course content than exams (Gibbs & Simpson, 2004; Glover & Brown, 2006; Marzano, 2000). By contrast, other studies have found the practice of combining an assignment grade with qualitative information can have an adverse effect on student responses to feedback (Hattie & Timperley, 2007; Wiliam & Thompson, 2007). As Edmead notes, output-based activities and the pressure to succeed can override students' engagement with the process of learning with and from each other. Findings from a number of studies suggest that although students value feedback, not all feedback is perceived as useful (Hounsell et al., 2006; Gibbs & Simpson, 2004; Weaver, 2006). Concerns related to feedback were evident in the results of the first two years of the UK National Student Survey (Bloxham & Boyd, 2007).

What types of feedback are useful to students? Hounsell et al. (2006) suggest that students prefer personalised feedback which offers positive, clear links between the tasks, assessment frameworks and criteria. Feedback must be timely and provide constructive guidance on how to improve in the future (Nicol & Macfarlane-Dick, 2006; Hendry, Bromberger & Armstrong, 2011). Constructive alignment may be achieved when tutors interact with students through feedback as an integral part of the learning experience to correct misunderstandings, to acknowledge what was done well and to suggest ways to improve, thus enhancing engagement and motivation (Biggs, 2003; Nicol & Macfarlane-Dick, 2006). However, this can only be effective if students attend to it, understand it and act on it (Ferguson, 2011; Gibbs & Simpson, 2004). Black and Wiliam (2003) found that feedback is most likely to be useful to students if they are willing to be open about any problems that they are experiencing, or concepts that they have not understood. This helps tutors to gain insight into students' 'approaches to learning' and 'conceptions of learning' so that teaching and assessment can be adjusted to support future learning (Bloxham & Boyd, 2007, p. 19).

Admitting to failure to understand, however, may be a huge challenge for students from particular cultures. MacKinnon and Manathunga (2003, p. 131) suggest that students in Westernised universities are often required to become proficient in the dominant cultural literacy that pervades teaching and assessment and to subordinate their own cultural knowledge. As Mertova (Chapter 5 of this volume) recognises, a high level of tutor skill and commitment is required to create inclusive learning environments that 'enable all students to demonstrate to their full potential what they know, understand and can do' (Hockings, 2010, p. 2) and where assessment and feedback values different ways of knowing and learning in multicultural groups (Hockings, 2010; Leathwood, 2005; Butcher et al., 2010; Sadler, 2009). When judgements about academic work are negotiated feedback can be a powerful learning tool, helping students to become aware of their own and other cultural perspectives, and to recognise what counts as knowledge in different disciplines (Pryor & Crossouard, 2010; Montgomery & McDowell, 2010; Kreber, 2010). Involving students in collaborative learning in which they appraise their own and others' work can build understanding of the nature and functions of assessment criteria (Hockings, 2010).

Despite evidence of the positive benefits of formative feedback, the Quality Assurance Agency (QAA) in the UK have noted a continued emphasis on summative assessment in the higher education sector (QAA, 2007) with grades or numeric scores the most common type of feedback that students receive (Marzano, 2000). Modularisation has tended to shorten courses and reduce the timescale within which it is possible to set assignments and provide feedback, and tutors may provide feedback that simply relates to their own module outcomes rather than informing students' overall development. The crowding of assessments at the end of semesters can also reduce the benefits of feedback (Higgins, Hartley & Skelton, 2001; Yorke, 2003). Students may attend to feedback, but they may not act on it if it is module-focused and perceived to lack relevance to future assignments (Brown & Glover, 2005).

Method

This research project aimed to examine staff and student perceptions of effective feedback practices and to compare Master's students' preferred forms of feedback with those provided by tutors. The project also aimed to examine practices that support the development of graduate attributes such as metacognitive and intercultural awareness. The methodology provided opportunities for staff and students to discuss their experiences of giving and receiving feedback both personally and professionally.

Two student groups participated. All participants were studying on one-year, full-time Master's programmes. The first group (Table 4.1) involved 29 Master's students from five disciplines and nine countries who attended a Graduate Skills Enhancement Programme, and the second group (Table 4.2) involved 16 Master's students from five countries who attended a core Education module on thinking skills for successful learning.

Table 4.1 Student Group 1

Group 1, n = 29			
School	No. of students	Ethnicity	No. of students
Modern Foreign		Chinese	16
Language	1	African	3
Education	19	Middle East	3
Business	7	Thai	1
Architecture &		Japanese	1
Planning	1	English	1
Law	1	American	1
		EU	3

Table 4.2 Student Group 2

Group 2, n = 16			
School	No. of students	Ethnicity	No. of students
Education	16	Chinese	9
		African	1
		Middle East	4
		Thai	1
		UK	1

The project examined Master's students' perceptions about the purpose and role of feedback. In order to investigate *What types of feedback Master's students find most useful/least useful,* students were asked to submit a draft piece of written work reflecting on their experience of feedback (as school students, undergraduates or postgraduates). Following the initial data collection, the students were invited to join ethnically mixed focus groups (Table 4.3) to help with the analysis of the data and talk further about their perceptions of most useful/least useful types of feedback. The focus groups assisted with the analysis of the initial data using a diamond ranking technique (Figure 4.1) to rank feedback types in order of usefulness according to several priority levels.

To triangulate with the students' perspectives, a group of 18 academic staff from a range of disciplines also took part in the project. The tutors were all participants in a year-long research initiative delivered by the authors. During this initiative, participants researched aspects of their teaching practice and their students' experience. Over the course of the year participants came together for a number of days during which they shared their emerging research findings and engaged in discursive group tasks designed to elicit their views about aspects of student learning. Of particular relevance here were tasks designed to elicit their views about the role that feedback played in influencing students' learning. Tutors were asked about the most common forms of feedback they provided;

Table 4.3 Composition of focus groups

Focus Group 1: December 2010 n = 4	Focus Group 2: December 2010 n = 5	Focus Group 3: June 2011 n = 5
1 Chinese 2 European 1 African	3 East Asian 1 Middle East 1 African	4 Chinese 1 Middle East
All from education	2 Business 3 Education	2 Business 3 Education

Most useful

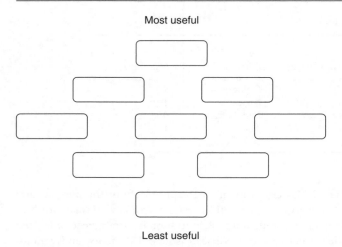

Least useful

Figure 4.1 Diamond ranking template

what they hoped to achieve when they provided feedback and what factors supported or inhibited feedback from feeding forward to enhance students' future learning.

Findings

Student perceptions

The initial data collection indicated that students' experiences of feedback prior to enrolling on Master's programmes were very diverse. Participants for whom this was the first period of study in the UK reported very limited earlier experience of receiving feedback:

> *As a student from China I didn't receive a lot of written feedback during my undergraduate life.*
>
> *I never received feedback from my university in Germany. We always got our grades and usually our assignments were exams instead of essays.*

Another student from the European Union (EU) commented:

> *In my previous studies I wasn't given proper feedback, it was just a grade and sometimes a few comments but never something that gave me a better understanding about how to improve in the weak areas.*

A mature student from the Middle East reflected:

> *When I was an undergraduate student ten years ago (Middle East) I did not use to be receive a feedback, because we just had a test at the end of term.*

However, students had clear ideas about what they would like from feedback. Data analysis in the focus groups led to the identification of the categories of most useful and least useful forms of feedback illustrated in Figures 4.2 and 4.3.

Discussion in the first two focus groups in month 3 of the Master's year revealed similar perceptions expressed by both international and European students. Feedback was strongly associated with the modular structure of their programmes. Participants did not appear to recognise dialogue with tutors or peers during the module as formative feedback, referring mainly to end-of-module grades and comments. Four students indicated that they valued prompt written feedback following the submission of assignments. As one participant noted:

> *What I do prefer in feedback is to receive it quickly as this will help me in the following assignments.*

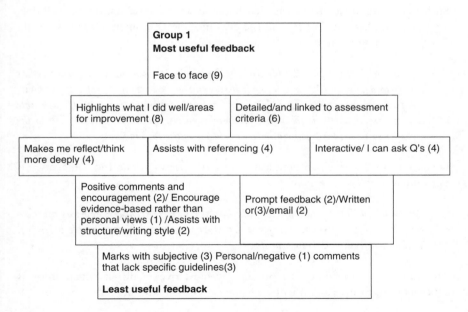

Figure 4.2 Group I most useful/least useful feedback

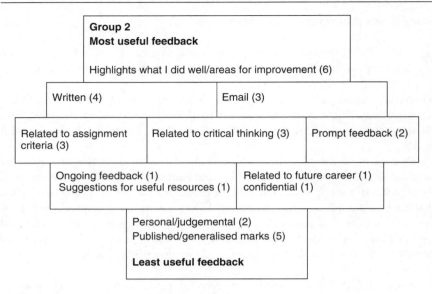

Figure 4.3 Group 2 most useful/least useful feedback

Students favoured face-to-face feedback as a means to understand how well they are going and how to do better in the next module assignment. A Focus Group 2 participant commented:

> *In general I really like the idea about feedback. It's a good way to know what was wrong and do I have to make it better in the next essays. I prefer to get written feedback because I am able to read this two or three times, and I am able to compare it with the following feedbacks. But it would be nice to talk to the lecturer so I could ask some questions related to the feedback*

Focus Group 2 participants indicated negative views about the value of self-assessment or peer assessment:

> *Personally, I don't really agree with peer assessment because it depends more on your luck of who you are doing the assessment with.... I believe people prefer an authorised feedback from a professor.*

The tutor was considered to provide authoritative feedback which informs approaches to future assignments. A Chinese student commented:

> *From the feedback I receive... I can get a brief idea about the grade of my assignments, the flaw and defects that exist in it, and... the comments tell*

me precisely about which part I should revise and which part can be deemed impressive.

These views of authoritative feedback can be interpreted through Bernstein's (2000) notion of 'framing' and the degree of control that tutors exert upon the assessment process. Whereas tutors views indicated weak 'framing' and wanted students to take control over their learning, student comments suggested strong 'framing' and a perceived power relationship with tutors. Tutors were expected to provide clear guidance, and feedback acts as a form of control that regulates and legitimises student behaviour. Feedback on both written work and group presentations was valued as a means to improve future learning:

> *The lecturers pointed out what our strengths and weaknesses were through our presentation. Hence this allowed us to continue working on our project and knowing where we should improve.*

Although the majority of participants wanted to know how they were going and how to do better, if they did not understand the feedback they were reluctant to seek help from the tutor unless they had failed the assignment. In the focus group 3 in month 9 of the Master's year a student from China commented: '*I will not meet this module in the future, so if the mark is pass, it is not necessary to understand feedback*'. '*Even you discussed with teachers...they wouldn't increase your marks, so no need to discuss with them*'.

The comments suggest that students had found it difficult to use feedback from one module to inform their learning in the next. Another Focus Group 3 student commented: '*I gradually adjust to learning and assessment here, and when I become more familiar with this educational form, I graduate*'. The student data, particularly from Focus Group 3, reveals a greater challenge related to student ambitions and motivation for completing their degree programme: '*some of the students think as long as they get good marks or results, its fine. Some of my friends who graduated last year said after a half year, they will forget what they have learnt in the UK*'.

Staff perceptions

Staff indicated that the most common forms of feedback provided were oral, such as answers to technical questions, comments in lectures or practicals or during seminar discussion groups. Responses by tutors indicated that they provided feedback to be constructive, to help students resolve issues and to encourage reflection. Five tutors agreed that they provided oral feedback with the intention to provide immediate clarification, to correct misunderstandings or to challenge students' assumptions. Three tutors also provided feedback to students in the form of annotated notes as both formative and summative records of progress. Their comments recognised the complexity of '*issues with defining the term formative assessment'*. They agreed that formative assessment approaches need to be adapted for different contexts to serve as '*mediating tools'*. One tutor explained this as a means to encourage '*social interaction in class'* as an important dimension of formative assessment that can '*give rise to more constructive teacher–learner relationships'*. Several tutors emphasised the importance of pedagogic relationships, which are created in the process of formative assessment. Tutors also recognised that:

> *formative assessment needs to be a conscious and deliberate effort to enable future learning with consistent approaches... and specific scaffolding.*

They regarded asking 'good' questions as an important mediating tool in feedback discussions with students to encourage critical reflection. Written feedback might be provided during the module with the intention to shape student's thinking or to encourage reflection, or at the end of modules to signal progress. Written feedback was also provided in electronic form and via email to both individuals and groups of students. Despite their efforts to provide multiple forms of feedback, several tutors expressed frustration that students had different demands with regard to feedback:

> *Students want different feedback, some want lots, some just want a grade.*

Tutors noted the resource constraints and imposed structures that they felt influenced the effectiveness of formative feedback. It was felt that there was a lack of a clear definition or common understanding within the university on the role of formative feedback. Ideally, tutors reported that they would like additional resources to get feedback to students more quickly, as workload, especially volume of marking, delayed the production of high-quality feedback, limited opportunities for continuous assessment and to help students act on feedback through individual action plans or 1:1 sessions. On the other hand, tutors were not confident that students used feedback appropriately. Concerns were voiced about the difficulty in modular programmes of knowing the long-term outcomes for individual students:

> *I'm not sure students pay attention to feedback. I'm keeping fingers crossed for longer term outcomes.... It's all I can do on modular programmes.*

Several tutors said that they would urge students to be proactive in seeking feedback ('*Don't wait, ask'*), to learn not only from written feedback but also from '*discussion with your teachers and peers'*, and to '*use the areas for development to set specific targets in a feed-forward process'*. In summary, tutors wanted students to take more responsibility to seek, understand and act upon feedback, to discuss with tutors any feedback that they don't understand, and to interact with feedback to set targets for their future learning, to '*use feedback to plan forward'*.

Discussion

In this small-scale research study, Master's students' and tutors' views of useful feedback were similarly focused on prompt feedback that leads to reflection, action and improvements in future work (Nicol & Macfarlane-Dick, 2006; Hendry et al., 2011; Hounsell et al., 2006). Positive impacts of feedback were strongly associated with the quality, type and timing of feedback. Face-to-face feedback in a constructive conversation was considered important. In addition, students appreciated written feedback that could be referred to more than once and compared with other module feedback. While tutors were keen to encourage collaborative learning and strongly encouraged students to peer assess and to learn from each other, students expressed little confidence in their peers as legitimate providers of feedback, and little interest in the role of peer assessment to enhance their understanding of different cultural values or ways of knowing.

Student participants' accounts illustrated a narrow view of feedback that related strongly to end-of-module assignments as products or artefacts that could be understood in terms of strengths, weaknesses and improvements. There was a strong emphasis on the marking scheme, and in line with Bernstein's (2000) notion of strong 'framing', a perception that tutors control the quality and future direction of students' work. By contrast, tutors wanted students to take control over their learning, but there was little sense that students sought to develop more independent thinking, creativity or self-regulation in learning. Many of the international students will have been exposed to a very different *pedagogic device* in their home country which Bernstein (1990) positions as the condition for the production, reproduction and transmission of culture. They have expectations of their relationships with their teachers which reflect a form of consciousness determined by power relationships in their home culture. These are being challenged, and adaptation might not be the most strategic move. Their tactical preoccupation with feedback as a means to achieve better grades implies that students' use of feedback has a limited role in helping them to reach their potential (Shalem & Slonimsky, 2010) but it may make sense in the short term. A critical issue raised by tutors was whether students in one-year, full-time Master's programmes 'get to the stage where they are able to identify their own achievements and gaps'. Tutors were both pressured by the expectation for prompt feedback on assessed work and frustrated by the lack of opportunity for dialogue and formative feedback over time to address students' assumptions about learning and to develop new and deeper knowledge and competences. Tutors recognised that this is a particular challenge for international students, and that new pedagogical approaches were required to facilitate this culture change towards an appreciation of autonomy and self-regulation in learning.

Although tutors were aware of evidence from the research literature about what works in feedback, the constraints of workload and volume of marking limited their opportunities to engage with students through feedback. One tutor commented that '*we have to be careful about making assumptions about the success of formative assessment and the critical reviews help us to stand back and evaluate'.*

Conclusion

The effectiveness of formative assessment is limited and shaped by the larger educational system within which it operates (Bennett, 2011) and by the perceptions of those who give and receive it. Yorke (2003) argues that formative assessment is essential to a key purpose of higher education, which is to facilitate the development of learner autonomy and produce lifelong learners. We concur with Bennett that '"formative assessment" is both conceptually and practically still a work-in-progress' (Bennett, 2011, p. 21) at our own institution, since our data suggest that we have some distance to travel to establish formative feedback that supports diverse cohorts of Master's students to move from their present to reach their potential (Shalem & Slonimsky, 2010). Feed forward to enhance future learning is particularly difficult to achieve in one-year modular programmes where tutors may not have ongoing contact with students beyond the modules on which they teach.

While tutors may strive to ensure a high-quality student assessment experience, resource constraints exacerbated by the economic recession are impacting on workloads, including volume of marking, so that feedback is provided less frequently, less immediately or may lack the necessary quality to have an effective formative function (Glover & Brown, 2006; Hounsell et al., 2006).

This research project created spaces for dialogue and reflection about assessment and feedback that were infrequently available to staff and students within the academic timetable. Tensions were revealed between what student participants want from feedback, and the most common forms of feedback provided; and between academics' and students' perceptions about the ideal functions and forms of feedback, and what is achievable within busy academic lives. While timing of feedback preoccupied staff and students, 'if feedback does not aid understanding, that is, enable the student to close the performance gap, and does not feed forward, it doesn't matter when it is returned. Such "feedback" serves only to justify the grade, and may as well not be given at all' (Glover & Brown, 2006). The data suggest that the disaggregation of grades and feedback would be beneficial with feedback that focuses on broader, rather than module-specific, achievement and learning outcomes (Bennett, 2011). This highlights the importance of providing more opportunities for Master's students to be involved in formative dialogue with their tutors and with each other (Black, 2009; Volet, 2004), so that assessment methods promote and value the international, intercultural and metacognitive competences necessary to life and work in the global economy (Knight, 2007). In this way, the cultural differences can be brought into the open and students can at least make more informed choices about how they approach formative assessment opportunities.

Further work is underway within a range of Master's programmes to trial electronic submission of assignments using Turnitin, encouraged by research findings from Denton, Roberts and Madden (2011) that e-technology can improve the quantity, quality and timeliness of feedback and that teacher reflection can be facilitated by the use of the allocation statistics to inform future teaching. The challenge to foster Masters' students' motivation to enhance their intercultural and metacognitive skills is being addressed by the explicit use of a framework for understanding thinking and learning (Moseley et al., 2004, adapted in Turner & Robson, 2008, p. 75) to provide guidance and a common language to describe the skills of inquiry, critical reflection and analysis valued within the institution and more widely (Volet, 2004), to underpin 'the capacity to work in intercultural environments' (Guruz, 2011, p.19).

Staff development initiatives might also explore with colleagues the 'sophisticated international perspectives' that Leask (2005) suggests are necessary to mediate students' interactions and encourage intercultural learning. Although our participants recognised both the value of feedback and the value of internationalisation, a high level of skill, commitment and time is required to develop adaptive pedagogies and appropriate feedback strategies when teaching multicultural groups (MacKinnon & Manathunga, 2003). This may be encouraged by the compelling evidence of the usefulness of feedback and by providing opportunities for colleagues to examine their teaching and learning practices through the lens of internationalisation. Strategic investment seems essential to support academic colleagues in their efforts to enhance the quality of the student experience and to maintain the reputation of universities in an increasingly competitive international student recruitment market.

References

Bennett, R. E. (2011). Formative assessment: A critical review. *Assessment in Education: Principles, Policy and Practice, 18*(1), 5–25.

Bernstein, B. (1990) *Class, Codes and Controls. Vol. IV: The Structuring of the Pedagogic Discourse.* London: Routledge.

Bernstein, B. (2000). *Pedagogy, symbolic control and identity* (2nd edn). London: Taylor & Francis.

Biggs, J. (2003). *Teaching for quality learning at university* (2nd edn). Buckingham: SRHE & Open University Press.

Black, P. & Wiliam, D. (1998). Assessment and classroom learning. *Assessment in Education, 5*(1), 7–74.

Black, P. & Wiliam, D. (2003). In praise of educational research: Formative assessment. *British Educational Research Journal, 29*(5), 623–637.

Black, P. (2009). Looking again at formative assessment. *Learning and Teaching Update, 30*.

Bloxham, S. & Boyd, P. (2007). *Developing effective assessment in higher education: A practical guide.* Maidenhead, UK: Open University Press.

Bohm, A., Follari, M., Hewett, A., et al. (2004). Vision 2020: *Forecasting international student mobility a UK perspective.* London: British Council & Universities UK.

Brown, E. & Glover, C. (2005). *Refocusing written feedback*. Paper presented at the 13th Improving Student Learning Symposium, Imperial College London.

Butcher, J., Sedgwick, P., Lazard, L. & Hey, J. (2010). How might inclusive approaches to assessment enhance student learning in HE? *Enhancing the Learner Experience in Higher Education, 2*(1), 25–40.

Denton, P., Roberts, M. & Madden, J. (2011). Returning formative feedback: Traditional versus electronic approaches. *Formative Assessment in Science Teaching*. Available at: http://www.open.ac.uk/fast/pdfs/Philip%20Denton.pdf (accessed 15 February 2011).

Edwards, V. & Ran, A. (2009). Building on experience: Meeting the needs of Chinese students in British higher education. In T. Coverdale-Jones & P. Rastall (eds.), *Internationalizing the university: The Chinese context*. Basingstoke, UK: Palgrave Macmillan, pp. 185–205.

Ferguson, P. (2011). Student perceptions of quality feedback in teacher education. *Assessment and Evaluation in Higher Education, 36*(1), 51–62.

Gibbs, G. & Simpson, C. (2004). Conditions under which assessment supports tudents' learning. *Learning and Teaching in Higher Education, 1*, 3–31. Available at: http://www2.glos.ac.uk/offload/tli/lets/lathe/issue1/articles/simpson.pdf (accessed 02 March 2012).

Glover, C. & Brown, E. (2006). Written feedback for students: Too much, too detailed or too incomprehensible to be effective? *Bioscience Education e-journal, 7*(3). Available at: http://www.bioscience.heacademy.ac.uk/journal/vol7/beej-7-3.pdf (accessed 02 March 2012).

Guruz, K. (2011). *Higher education and international student mobility in the global knowledge economy*. Albany, NY: State University of New York Press.

Hattie, J. & Timperley, H. (2007). The power of feedback. *Review of Educational Research, 77*, 81–113.

Hendry, G. D., Bromberger, N. & Armstrong, S. (2011). Constructive guidance and feedback for learning: The usefulness of exemplars, marking sheets and different types of feedback in a first year law subject. *Assessment and Evaluation in Higher Education, 36*(1), 1–11.

Higgins, R., Hartley, P. & Skelton, A. (2001). Getting the message across: The problem of communicating assessment feedback. *Teaching in Higher Education, 6*(2), 269–274.

Hockings, C. (2010). *Inclusive learning and teaching in higher education: A synthesis of research*. York: Higher Education Academy. Available at: http://www.heacademy.ac.uk/assets/documents/inclusion/wp/inclusive_teaching_and_learning_in_he.doc (accessed 02 March 2012).

Hounsell, D., McCune, V., Hounsell, J. & Litjens, J. (2006). *Investigating and enhancing the quality of guidance and feedback to undergraduate students*. Paper presented at the Third Biennial Northumbria/EARLI SIG Assessment Conference, Northumbria University, Newcastle.

Knight, P. (2007). Fostering and assessing 'wicked' competences. PBPL working paper. Available at: http://www.open.ac.uk/cetl-workspace/cetlcontent/documents/460d1d1481d0f.pdf (accessed 6 March 2011).

Kreber, C. (2010). Graduates for the 21st century. *TLA Interchange, 4*, 1–6. Available at: http://www.docs.hss.ed.ac.uk/iad/Learning_teaching/Academic_teaching/News/spring2010.pdf (accessed 6 March 2011).

Leask, B. (2005). *Internationalisation of the curriculum and intercultural engagement – a variety of perspectives and possibilities.* Paper presented at the Australian International Education Conference (AIEC), Queensland, Australia. Available at: http://www.aiec.idp.com/pdf/Leask,%20Betty.pdf (accessed 02 March 2012).

Leathwood, C. (2005). Assessment policy and practice in higher education: Purpose, standards and equity. *Assessment and Evaluation in Higher Education, 30*(3), 307–324.

MacKinnon, D. & Manathunga, C. (2003). Going global with assessment: What to do when the dominant culture's literacy drives assessment. *Higher Education Research and Development, 22*(2),131–144.

Marzano, R. (2000). *Transforming classroom grading.* Alexandria, VA: Association for Supervision and Curriculum and Development.

Montgomery, C. & McDowell, L. (2010). *Assessment for learning environments: Two case studies of the experience of international students. Occasional Papers 4.* Newcastle: Centre for Excellence in Teaching, Learning and Assessment for Learning CETL AfL, Northumbria University.

Moseley D, Baumfield V, Higgins S, Lin M , Miller J, Newton D, Robson S, Elliott J, Gregson M. (2004) *Thinking Skill Frameworks for Post-16 Learners: An Evaluation.* A research report for the learning and skills research centre. Trowbridge: Cromwell Press.

Nainby, K., Warren, J. & Bollinger, C. (2003). Articulating contact in the classroom: Towards a constitutive focus in critical pedagogy. *Language & Intercultural Communication, 3*(3), 198–212.

Nicol, D. & Macfarlane-Dick, D. (2006). Formative assessment and self-regulated learning: A model and seven principles of good feedback practice. *Studies in Higher Education, 31*(2), 199–218.

Pettigrew, T. F. & Tropp, L. R. (2000). Does intergroup contact reduce prejudice? Recent meta-analytic findings. In S. Oskamp (ed.), *Reducing prejudice and discrimination. The Claremont Symposium on Applied Social Psychology.* Mahwah, NJ: Laurence Erlbaum Associates.

Pryor, J. & Crossouard, B. (2010). Challenging formative assessment: Disciplinary spaces and identities. *Assessment & Evaluation in Higher Education, 35*(3), 265–276.

Quality Assurance Agency (QAA). (2007). *Enhancing practice. Integrative assessment: Managing assessment practices and procedures. Guide no 4.* Available at: http://www.enhancementthemes.ac.uk/documents/IntegrativeAssessment/IA%20Managing%20assessment.pdf (accessed 02 March 2012).

Sadler, D. (2009). Indeterminacy in the use of preset criteria for assessment and grading. *Assessment and Evaluation in Higher Education, 34*(2), 159–179.

Shalem, Y. & Slonimsky, L. (2010). Seeking epistemic order: Construction and transmission of evaluative criteria. *British Journal of Sociology of Education, 31*(6), 755–778.

Turner, Y. & Robson, S. (2008). *Internationalizing the university: An introduction for university teachers and managers.* London: Continuum Press.

UNESCO. (2009). *Communiqué: World conference on higher education: The new dynamics of higher education and research for societal change and development.* Paris: UNESCO.

Volet, S. 2004. Challenges of internationalisation: Enhancing intercultural competence and skills for critical reflection on the situated and non-neutral nature of knowledge. In P. Zeegers & K. Dellar-Evans (eds.), *Language and academic skills in higher education*, Vol. 6. Adelaide: Flinders University, pp. 1–10.

Weaver, M. L. (2006). So students value feedback? Student perceptions of tutor's written responses. *Assessment and Evaluation in Higher Education*, *31*(3), 379–394.

Wiliam, D. & Thompson, M. (2007). Integrating assessment with instruction: What will it take to make it work? In C. A. Dwyer (ed.), *The future of assessment: Shaping teaching and learning*. Mahwah, NJ: Laurence Erlbaum Associates.

Yorke, M. (2003). Formative assessment in higher education: Moves towards theory and the enhancement of pedagogic practice. *Higher Education*, *45*(4), 477–501.

Chapter 5

Internationalisation and quality in higher education

Perspectives of English, Australian and Czech senior academics

Patricie Mertova

Introduction

This chapter reports on two research projects: one project investigates senior academics' perspectives on quality in Czech and English higher education and the other project examines senior academics' perspectives on internationalisation and quality in English, Australian and Czech higher education. The research draws on previous research indicating that senior academics (such as heads of schools and associate deans academic) play significant roles in instigating and implementing change in higher education (Anderson & Johnson, 2006; Bell, 2004; Green & Mertova, 2010). There is also an expectation that senior academics have generally more experience in academic practice and may offer broader, better-informed opinions. The projects are brought together here because they focus on senior academics' perspectives and utilise the same methodology; and as the second project stems from the first. The second project was prompted by the attitudes of a number of Czech academics who viewed quality enhancement as intrinsically linked with internationalisation in their particular cultural context. As the second project is unfinished, this chapter does not outline substantial findings, but points to some issues and concerns voiced by academics with implications for academic practice.

Internationalisation in higher education

Internationalisation in higher education has become a widespread and strategically significant aspect of higher education (Van der Wende & Westerheijden, 2001) over the past three decades. However, it was only in the late 1990s that links to policy and practice began to be developed (Campbell & Van der Wende, 2000).

Internationalisation was pioneered particularly in Anglophone countries, such as the US, the UK and Australia. The initial focus of the research used Van Damme's (2001) outline of the forms of internationalisation:

- Student mobility – includes outgoing as well as incoming students.
- Teaching staff mobility.

- Internationalisation of curricula.
- Branch campuses – Van Damme indicated that this phenomenon is more widespread among Anglophone countries.
- Institutional cooperation agreements and networks – this includes collaboration between universities as not a particularly new phenomenon, as well as institutional cooperation in the field of teaching as a relatively recent one.

Knight (1999) described four different, complementary dimensions of internationalisation which are supplemented by Knight's (2004) later broadened understanding of internationalisation:

- *Activity* dimension – internationalisation as specific activities or programmes, this perception was associated with internationalisation in the 1970s and 1980s.
- *Competency* dimension – internationalisation in terms of the knowledge, skills, attitudes and values of students.
- *Ethos* dimension – relates to the culture and climate of the organisation to support particular principles and goals.
- *Process* dimension – relates to an integration of international, intercultural and global aspects into academic programmes as well as guiding policies and procedures within the institution.

Australian and English academics who participated in the research reported here referred to all these forms and dimensions of internationalisation. Czech academics did not discuss or gave only limited understandings of internationalisation of curricula and branch campuses; they referred to most dimensions outlined by Knight except for the *process*. The explanation for this may be less experience with internationalisation within Czech tertiary institutions and a cultural context to some degree, particularly regarding branch campuses.

Quality in higher education

Quality in higher education has gained increased attention in parallel with internationalisation (Van der Wende & Westerheijden, 2001). The focus on quality in higher education results from a range of competing factors, including:

- political control over higher education (particularly by national governments)
- growth in the number of students in higher education (including general changes in the student population and their expectations)
- financial control by national governments, frequently related to the previous two factors (Brown, 2004; Green, 1994; Harvey, 1998; Stoddart, 2004).

Quality monitoring has become a mechanism for governments worldwide to tackle these competing factors, and according to Harvey (2005), frequently also to disguise the dominant focus on accountability rather than enhancement. Among higher education institutions around the world, there have been various responses to this trend, ranging from implementing direct quality measurement scales to self-audit processes. Increasingly, the rationale for quality development has been driven by funding mechanisms, accreditation, keeping pace with international practice, national audits and other trends, such as massive growth in higher education and influences of information technology (Barnett, 1992; Harvey, 2004, 2005; Harvey & Green, 1993; Lomas, 2000; Morley, 2003). The rationale for internationalisation has in some ways coincided with that for quality in virtually all aspects, as outlined above.

There is a broad range of definitions of quality, but a summarised understanding is given here. Quality is a complex and multifaceted concept. According to Lomas (2004), there are two main understandings of quality: quality assurance and quality enhancement. Quality assurance is oriented mainly towards the product or service being of good standard. It is a 'preventative' measure (Lomas, 2004), which is 'regarded as a means of improving overall quality' (p. 158) and relates to the notion of 'fitness for purpose'. Quality enhancement, on the other hand, is 'directly concerned with adding value, improving quality... and implementing transformational change' (Lomas, 2004, p. 158).

Harvey and Green (1993) defined six notions of quality:

* *Traditional* concept – associated with exceptionally high standards.
* Concept associated with *consistency* and *'zero defects'* – associated with process and a set of specifications.
* *Fitness for purpose* – relates to a product or service meeting its purpose.
* *Value for money* – concerns accountability.
* *Transformative* process.
* *Pragmatic* approach – as a range of qualities (i.e. institution of a high standard in relation to one factor, may be low in relation to another).

The understanding of quality academics in this research mainly referred to was quality enhancement and a combination of the *traditional* and *transformative* concepts.

Internationalisation and its relations to quality in higher education

Over the last three decades, internationalisation and quality have developed in parallel; however, it was only in the 1990s that links to policy and practice started being perceived (Campbell & Van der Wende, 2000).

Throughout the 1990s, significant shifts in foreign policies, particularly in Anglophone countries, have occurred where education started being treated as an export commodity. Prior to that, education 'exported' overseas was primarily seen as a development activity or cultural programme. This change has led to a search for effective ways of improving the quality of provision, and thus maintaining a 'competitive edge' (Knight, 1999). This was also a point where links between internationalisation and quality started being more consciously developed. Internationalisation in Czech higher education started being forged more systematically, particularly in student and staff mobility, in the early 2000s (Ministry of Education, Youth and Sports of the Czech Republic, 2001a, b).

Internationalisation and quality have always existed in higher education, despite the renewed attention, with only perhaps more utilitarian and politicised meanings and values ascribed to them in recent times. Universities have always been influenced by social, cultural as well as physical movements (the 'wandering' scholar) and have not been confined within particular 'spatial boundaries' (Van Damme, 2001). There are notable exceptions, however, which relate to this research – for instance, the universities in non-democratic political systems, such as the former Communist regimes of Central and Eastern Europe, where these 'spatial boundaries' were firmly set for over 40 years (between the late 1940s and 1980s) and movement of thought and people was restricted.

The research reported in this chapter investigates academic perceptions of the trends of internationalisation and quality and relations between them in Czech, English and Australian higher education. The aim of the research is to establish:

- What senior academics understand by internationalisation and quality.
- What they perceive as the issues and impacts of the two phenomena on higher education and their students.
- Their perceptions of any links between internationalisation and quality.
- Lessons for improvement of future practices.

The research targets three contexts to find out the similarities and differences in two Anglophone systems with common historical and cultural roots compared with a system with quite different roots. The selection of senior academics was guided by previous research suggesting that they have a greater impact on change within the sector and greater experience in academic practice.

Methodology

Both projects used semi-structured, face-to-face interviews with academics in English, Australian and Czech higher education. Although the first one was mainly conducted in England and the Czech Republic, it was piloted in Australia. The first project consisted of 36 interviews (4 in Australia, 11 in the Czech Republic and 21 in England). The second one involved 75 interviews (13 in the Czech Republic, 35 in Australia and 27 in England). Both studies mainly targeted the Social Sciences and Humanities because of the researcher's own background and expertise within these fields. Academics were invited by email through recommendations of the researcher's colleagues and suggestions of interviewees. Interviews of 30 to 45 minutes were recorded and transcribed and analysed, extracting critical events in the professional practice of the interviewees. The interviewees were given pseudonyms to protect their identities.

Both projects utilised a *critical event* narrative inquiry method (Mertova, 2008; Webster & Mertova, 2007) which is well suited for investigation of issues of complexity and cultural and human centredness, such as internationalisation and quality as it identifies *critical events* in the professional practice of individuals (Mertova, 2008; Webster & Mertova, 2007). The identification of *critical events* was negotiated between the researcher, interviewees and at least two independent researchers.

A *critical event* is an event which significantly impacts on professional practice of, for instance, an academic, which might have entirely or considerably changed the academic's practice or even world view. A *critical event* can only be identified retrospectively, and it would have happened in an unplanned and unstructured manner. The causes of a *critical event* might be 'internal' or 'external' to professional practice of an individual, or entirely personal.

According to the degree of significance and unique characteristics, *critical events* were further distinguished as *critical*, *like* and *other* events. Stories that were collected through interviews were then analysed and identified as *critical*, *like* and *other* events.

A *critical* event is an event which has been selected because of its unique, illustrative and confirmatory nature in relation to the studied phenomenon. An event which has a similar level of significance as a *critical* event, and, is not as unique as the critical event, and which further illustrated, confirmed and/or repeated the experience of the critical event is referred to as a *like* event. A review of the *like* events is useful in confirming and/or broadening issues arising from the critical event (Webster, 1998). *Critical* and *like* events are distinguished according to the criteria outlined in Tables 5.1 and 5.2.

Furthermore, confirmatory event/s that may or may not have taken place at the same time as the *critical* and/or *like* events are referred to as *other* event/s.

Table 5.1 Features of a 'critical' event in professional practice

Feature	Presence/absence
(a) Has a major impact on people involved	√
(b) Is unplanned and unanticipated	√
(c) Is only identified after the event	√
(d) May have life-changing consequences	√ ×
(e) May reveal patterns of well-defined stages	√ ×
(f) May be intensely personal with strong emotional involvement	√ ×

Note: √ indicates presence; × indicates absence.

Table 5.2 Features of a 'like' event in professional practice

Feature	Presence/absence
(a) Has a major impact on people involved	x
(b) Is unplanned and unanticipated	√ x
(c) Is only identified after the event	√
(d) May have life-changing consequences	x
(e) May reveal patterns of well-defined stages	x
(f) May be intensely personal with strong emotional involvement	x
Additional features	Presence
(aa) Not as unique (as critical event)	√
(ab) Repeats and/or illustrates experience (of critical event)	√

Note: √ indicates presence; x indicates absence.

Typically, such events relate to other background information which may have revealed the same or related issues. The criteria which distinguish *other* events are described in Table 5.3. These *other* events are interwoven in the analysis of the *critical* and *like* events (Webster, 1998). *Critical, like* and *other* events may occur within the narrative of a single interview, but more often would occur across a number of different interviews.

There were limitations to these studies; the first did not focus on internationalisation but perceptions of quality where internationalisation was highlighted, and the second is in progress. Therefore, the findings reported here are at best partial and highlight some issues for practice; they do not enable extensive discussion or give any specific recommendations for policy and practice.

Table 5.3 Features of 'other' event in professional practice

Feature	Presence/absence
(a) Has a major impact on people involved	x
(b) Is unplanned and unanticipated	√ x
(c) Is only identified after the event	√ x
(d) May have life-changing consequences	x
(e) May reveal patterns of well-defined stages	x
(f) May be intensely personal with strong emotional involvement	x
Additional features	Presence
(aaa) Further background information	√

Note: √ indicates presence; x indicates absence.

Academic perspectives of internationalisation and quality

In the first study, few English and Australian academics highlighted internationalisation as a significant aspect of higher education quality enhancement. Two English academics (one previously worked in Australia and one participated in an institutional audit of an Australian university) and one Australian academic briefly touched upon the forms of internationalisation in Australian higher education through setting up overseas campuses and recruiting overseas students and related issues, such as feelings of isolation among overseas students, difficulties with academic writing and different cultural perspectives on plagiarism. These were not understood as quality enhancement aspects, but rather as measures that Australian tertiary institutions resorted to through external pressures on revenue raising; and thus, these academics felt, had negative impacts on quality. In comparison, some Czech academics viewed internationalisation as an emerging positive, quality enhancement trend in the Czech higher education context. This was despite the fact that internationalisation was not the topic of the interviews and academics were asked about their perception of quality.

In the second study, where internationalisation was an explicit focus, English and Australian academics generally portrayed the relation between internationalisation and quality as complex and by no means 'clear-cut'. A number gave examples of events where internationalisation has enhanced quality. On the other hand, they felt it is often unclear whether a particular aspect of internationalisation would enhance quality. Some gave examples of negative impacts or outcomes of internationalisation where specific contexts (frequently cultural contexts) or reasons for internationalisation were not carefully considered.

In comparison, many Czech academics drew a fairly positive link between internationalisation and quality enhancement. In some cases, this might have been because they had relatively little experience with various forms of internationalisation. A majority of these academics understand internationalisation as student and staff mobility, and some highlighted international research collaboration and publishing. Internationalisation of teaching and learning was hardly brought up; nevertheless, it might have been implicitly understood as a component of mobility or a form of personal development.

The perceived positive role of internationalisation in quality enhancement within Czech higher education was explained by one senior university leader who pointed out that the relation would work very differently in different cultural, political, historical and socio-economic contexts. He further underlined the dangers of 'implanting' particular frameworks which work in a certain cultural, political and socio-economic context into very different contexts.

Critical events in professional practice of senior academics

Both studies identified at least one type of *critical event* concerning internationalisation and/or quality in each interview. The individual events were distinguished according to their level of criticality, using the criteria outlined in Tables 5.1, 5.2 and 5.3. This chapter mainly draws on descriptions of *critical events* from the first project; thus, the proportion of events from Czech higher education dominate, which by no means indicates that similar events in Australian and English higher contexts are less important.

The first example of a *critical* event was related by Pavel, a Czech professor of Sociology. He described his trip to the US where he taught for one semester. This experience represented not only a cultural 'shock' for him, because it happened shortly after the end of communism (he experienced the difference between a post-communist and a liberal education system), but also helped him to enhance his own teaching practices.

This experience made him re-evaluate and significantly change his own teaching when he returned to the Czech Republic. This was one example where internationalisation led to a positive change in an individual's teaching practices, here through international mobility of the academic.

Krystof (a senior Czech academic and former dean of a faculty) told a story of another *critical* event – describing his sabbatical at a prestigious research institute in Holland after which he made a major shift in the faculty's style of teaching and learning based more on debate, reflection and thinking processes. Like the previous academic, this was enabled by academic mobility.

Richard (a senior Czech academic and former head of a central university unit) described a *critical* event involving a transformation of the pedagogy in the department he was heading in the early 1990s (shortly after the political change-over):

> *We shifted more towards courses focusing on certain area, theme or whatever, where people could explore and find connections...*

This was another example of a positive impact of an event involving a form of internationalisation in Czech higher education; in this case, it involved inward academic mobility.

Pedagogy was also a concern in the *critical* event described by Deborah (a senior Australian academic) involving teaching Film to a culturally diverse group of students.

> *The event made me realise that teaching a group of students of a wide range of cultural and ethnic backgrounds from an Anglo-centric perspective was extremely limiting and potentially intimidating for students.*

Encountering such a situation made Deborah dramatically transform her style of teaching to become more engaging and sensitive to a range of different perspectives based on culture, ethnicity and religion. Thus, the event (which involved inward student mobility) had a highly positive impact on Deborah's professional and personal development.

James (a senior English academic and previously head of several departments) described a *critical* event which involved setting up an educational programme in partnership with an overseas institution.

> *My English colleagues and I involved in setting up the programme were particularly concerned with the programme's sustainability to make sure that our overseas partner were eventually able to run the programme by themselves.*

James's approach was based on his previous experience in English higher education but also having experienced other cultural contexts in higher education, and understanding how cultural contexts are crucial to the success and sustainability of programmes set up by English institutions overseas. This event reflects the complexity of the relationship between internationalisation and quality.

Deborah told a story of a *like* event in her current institution. The event involved her teaching and working with a culturally diverse group of academics, some of whom had recently joined the university from overseas.

> *Last semester, I taught a group of new academics here. I could see that academics particularly from non-Anglophone environments frequently struggled to adapt to the very different academic environment that they encountered in Australia. I became particularly concerned with the lack of support that this university offers to these overseas academics, assuming that they would easily adapt to the institution's culture.*

This event was equally as significant as Deborah's first event; however, some of the aspects were repeated. This event (involving inward academic mobility) demonstrates an assumption by an Anglophone institution recruiting academics internationally that academic careers are similar, if not the same, regardless of cultural contexts.

Another *like* event involved Ivo (a Czech academic and senior leader) who instigated unification of a credit system across his university (over 40,000 students and nine faculties). This event brought much more transparency into study for both students and academics and involved enhancement of quality at institutional level, through observation of good practices, discussions with similar overseas institutions and consultation with international experts. Thus, internationalisation in this case involved sharing international practices among senior leaders in institutions.

Richard told a story of an *other* event related to internationalisation in a large research-intensive university in the Czech Republic. He perceived internationalisation as linked to a number of aspects of quality. One aspect being debated in his institution concerned attracting international students through delivering programmes either in Czech or in English. (This aspect would not represent a quality measure in Anglophone systems, as a great majority of, if not all, programmes for international students would be in English.) Richard outlined how the language of delivery relates to offering programmes to particular groups of international students:

> 1) *Programmes delivered in Czech would be targeted at Central and Eastern European students who would be able to master Czech with the help of a short language course (as they would be mainly speakers of other Slavonic languages);*
> 2) *Programmes delivered in English would be targeted more at other overseas students mainly from the 'Western world'.*

Richard believed that English as the language of delivery was a powerful tool to 'measure' quality of programmes in his institution.

Two other Czech academics and senior leaders, Tomas and Krystyan, gave examples of *other* events concerning language. Tomas perceived the current pressure on Czech academics to publish in English to be a dangerous development. He expressed concern, for example, with the potential loss of terminology in the Czech language.

Related to teaching in Czech and other languages, but also to publishing, Krystyan, on the one hand, was supportive of delivering some programmes in English; on the other hand, he expressed a strong support for learning languages other than English.

This equally applies to students and academics in Australia and England who are largely monolingual. This issue was highlighted by James (a senior English academic mentioned earlier), who admitted that his own lack of language proficiency in other languages limited his knowledge of other European education systems. The issue of lack of foreign language proficiency among Australian-born academics and students was highlighted by Marginson (2007) and Green and Mertova (2010).

On the matter of cultural inclusivity, Anna (a senior Australian academic) highlighted the issue of regard for Indigenous knowledges and experiences in an *other* event. This event does not concern internationalisation as such, however, in the Australian higher education context, it relates to cultural inclusivity. Anna ran academic development sessions on indigenous cultures and learning and remarked that she would repeatedly encounter 'universalistic' and domineering attitudes among some academics indicating that indigenous students have only to learn from the Western ways of teaching and learning. She expressed a deep concern about such attitudes.

On a systemic level, an English academic and higher education leader, Colin, gave an example of another *other* event. He previously worked as a higher education quality auditor and felt he learnt a great deal concerning different cultural practices through visiting overseas institutions. He highlighted the significance of learning from other cultural practices, which he felt some English institutions were not prepared to do. By saying this, he hinted at the 'colonial' attitudes of some English institutions and the need to be sensitive to and learn from other practices. This event highlighted how different cultural contexts and practices can enable reflection and enhancement of practices, including internationally.

Findings and their implications for teaching practice

This chapter has brought together academic perceptions of internationalisation and its relation to quality from three higher education systems: Czech, Australian and English. It has drawn on examples of *critical events* from programme, department and faculty levels to university levels.

The preliminary findings of this research are that Czech academics perceived direct and largely positive impacts of internationalisation on quality, whereas English and Australian academics have not perceived such a direct relation between the two, and have been more critical of such influences.

In the Czech context, internationalisation has enabled a transformation of teaching style through changing teaching methods, including some changes in attitudes. Among the Australian and English academics, the importance of cultural sensitivity towards non-Anglophone cultures and inclusion of these cultures was highlighted, leading to transformation in the teaching styles employed from traditionally Anglo-centric approaches towards more culturally inclusive ones. This was perceived to be strongly connected with a significant change in academics' attitudes and values.

Another positive outcome of internationalisation was perceived in the Czech context through introducing transparency into programmes of study (in terms of requirements, outcomes, etc.). This was observed from overseas, particularly Western European systems, and introduced into Czech higher education. Introducing programmes of study in English was perceived by some Czech academics as another quality enhancement mechanism. Neither of these were of concern to either English or Australian academics. An overarching message from all the academics was the need for cautious consideration of cultural contexts, whether it was by those adopting or proposing models of practices and strategies from culturally different contexts.

These findings by no means suggest that these transformations and impacts of internationalisation on quality were happening across Czech, Australian and English higher education systems. Therefore, these findings and the academics' stories may offer some suggestions or, on the other hand, sound some warnings to others, not only in the systems covered here but also in other higher education systems dealing with similar issues.

References

Anderson, D. & Johnson, R. (2006). *Ideas of leadership underpinning proposals for the Carrick Institute: A review of proposals for the Leadership for Excellence in Teaching and Learning Program.* Occasional paper. Available at: http://www.altc.edu.au/system/files/documents/grants_leadership_occasionalpaper_andersonandjohnson_nov06.pdf (accessed March 2011).

Barnett, R. (1992). *Improving higher education: Total quality care.* Buckingham: SRHE/Open University Press.

Bell, M. (2004). Internationalising the higher education curriculum: Do academics agree? *Proceedings of the 27th Higher Education Research & Development Society of Australasia (HERDSA) Conference.* Miri, Sarawak: HERDSA.

Brown, R. (2004). *Quality assurance in higher education: The UK experience since 1992.* London: RoutledgeFalmer.

Campbell, C. & Van der Wende, M. (2000). *International initiatives and trends in quality assurance for European higher education: Exploratory trend report.* Helsinki: European Network of Quality Assurance Agencies.

Green, D. (ed.) (1994). *What is quality in higher education?* Buckingham: SRHE/Open University Press.

Green, W. & Mertova, P. (2010). *Listening to the gatekeepers: Faculty perspectives on developing curriculum for globally responsible citizenship.* Paper presented at the Internationalisation of the Curriculum Conference 2010, Internationalisation of the Curriculum for Global Citizenship: Policies, Practices and Pitfalls, Oxford.

Harvey, L. (1998). An assessment of past and current approaches to quality in higher education. *Australian Journal of Education, 42*(3), 237–255.

Harvey, L. (2004). War of worlds: Who wins in the battle for quality supremacy? *Quality in Higher Education, 10*(1), 65–71.

Harvey, L. (2005). A history and critique of quality evaluation in the UK. *Quality Assurance in Education, 13*(4), 263–276.

Harvey, H. & Green, D. (1993). Defining quality. *Assessment and Evaluation in Higher Education, 18*(1), 9–34.

Knight, J. (1999). Internationalisation of higher education. In J. Knight & H. de Wit (eds.), *Quality and internationalisation in higher education.* Paris: OECD.

Knight, J. (2004). Internationalization remodeled: Definition, approaches and rationales. *Journal of Studies in International Education, 8*(1), 5–31.

Lomas, L. (2000). *Senior staff member perception of organisational culture and quality in higher education institutions in England.* Unpublished PhD thesis, University of Kent, Canterbury.

Lomas, L. (2004). Embedding quality: The challenges for higher education. *Quality Assurance in Education, 12*(4), 157–165.

Marginson, S. (2007). Global position and position-taking: The case of Australia. *Journal of Studies in International Education, 11*(1), 5–32.

Mertova, P. (2008). *Quality in higher education: Stories of English and Czech academics and higher education leaders.* Unpublished PhD thesis, Monash University, Melbourne, Australia.

Ministry of Education, Youth and Sports of the Czech Republic (2001a). *Strategie terciarni sfery vzdelavani [Strategic development of the tertiary education].*

Ministry of Education, Youth and Sports of the Czech Republic. (2001b). *National programme for the development of education in the Czech Republic.* White Paper. Prague: Institute for Information on Education. Available at: http://aplikace.msmt.cz/pdf/whitepaper.pdf (accessed March 2011).

Morley, L. (2003). *Quality and power in higher education*. Maidenhead, UK: Society for Research into Higher Education/Open University Press.

Stoddart, J. (2004). Foreword. In R. Brown (ed.), *Quality assurance in higher education: The UK experience since 1992*. London: RoutledgeFalmer.

Van Damme, D. (2001). Quality issues in the internationalisation of higher education. *Higher Education, 41*, 415–441.

Van der Wende, M.C. & Westerheijden, D.F. (2001). International aspects of quality assurance with a special focus on European higher education. *Quality in Higher Education, 7*(3), 233–245.

Webster, L. (1998). *A story of instructional research and simulation in aviation (air traffic control)*. Unpublished PhD thesis, Monash University, Melbourne, Australia.

Webster, L. & Mertova, P. (2007). *Using narrative inquiry as a research method: An introduction to using critical event narrative analysis in research on learning and teaching*. London: Routledge.

Chapter 6

The challenges of multilingualism for international students in Denmark

Gordon Slethaug and Jane Vinther

Introduction

Braj Kachru (1988) was the first to diagram three concentric circles of English usage around the globe, suggesting that countries occupying the *inner circle* are those where English is a native language, those in the *outer or extended circle* are those where English plays a major if not dominant role in the country's judicial, educational and other institutions and those in the *expanding or extending circle* are those where English has no official status but plays an increasingly strong role as an alternative mode of social and intellectual expression. As Truchot remarks in the Council of Europe report (2002), 'in Western Europe the teaching of English has become the general rule, and all pupils now learn English' (Truchot, 2002, p. 8), so that throughout Europe the language will exist in one of the three circles.

Denmark, along with Sweden and the Netherlands, was among the first to require English of all its pupils in school, and domestic and international students who come to study in college or university increasingly expect a high standard of usage. Denmark is considered in the 'expanding' circle of usage, but students from across Europe and Asia come to study as if it were in the 'inner circle' because many courses and programmes are taught in English and because the general population is conversant in English. However, these students sometimes find the 'noise' of Danish language and culture a distraction within this environment and possibly an impediment to successful negotiation and completion of their programmes. This phenomenon is not an isolated one across Europe, where many programmes are now taught in English but where administrative frameworks and social discourse continue to be in a non-English local language. 'The scope for disturbance of communication flows as a result of language difficulties is considerable', whether in the university or international business setting, as Marschan-Piekkari, Welch and Welch find (1999, pp. 425–426).

Clearly, administrative frameworks must be in Danish so as not to discriminate against native Danish-language speakers. Similarly, Danish students have the right to expect that they need not be proficient in English in order to earn a college or university degree. Nonetheless, insofar as Danish universities want to take advantage of the large English-speaking European student population as well as international students from other parts of the world, then they must pursue a language-equitable policy that gives these students access to the same information in English as Danish.[1] This is not just in the interest of diversity or inclusiveness, but ensures that the visiting students' learning and course of study will not be impeded by inadequate teaching, learning and administrative materials in English.

Based on questionnaires and interviews with international students enrolled in an intercultural communication course in the English Studies programme at the University of Southern Denmark, this chapter will use motivational learning theory drawn from second-language learning to explore the confidence that international students feel in their studies and the challenges they face in their use of English in one location where English is not the native language – Denmark. It will also use structuration theory, drawn from Anthony Giddens (1999) among others, to help look critically at some of the negative responses of the students and what they are likely to mean in an otherwise optimistic motivational frame of reference. Our study will also offer some recommendations as a result of this exploration.

Motivation has been chosen as the primary social-psychological conceptual framework because its use with second-language learning theory is concerned implicitly, if not explicitly, with the best ways to foster a positive international language-learning environment and minimise interferences. This learning theory, begun by Gardner and Lambert in the 1950s and 1960s (though not significantly written up until 1972), developed at the same time that Edward Hall introduced theories of intercultural communications and that globalisation began to go into 'high gear', so it is implicitly associated with internationalism, interculturalism and English as a global language.

This theory, centring 'on the role of motivation as measurable cause or product of particular learning experiences and outcomes' (Ushioda, 2001, p. 95), often has been researched using quantitative methods, but, according to Ushioda, qualitative methods 'cast a different light on the phenomena under investigation and... raise a different set of issues' (Ushioda, 2001, p. 96). Pertinent issues include the 'patterns of thinking and belief' that 'underlie such activity and shape students' engagement in the learning process' as well as the students' evaluation of their pressures, limitations and achievements (Ushioda, 2001, p. 96). Ushioda has identified eight 'descriptive dimensions' with 'priority features' for the study of language, and these, minimally revised and reordered, can be adapted nicely to international teaching and learning in Denmark (Ushioda, 2001, p. 102):

- personal goals
- academic interest
- course and university-related enjoyment/liking
- desired levels of competence
- positive learning history

- personal satisfaction
- feelings about Danish-speaking people
- external pressures/incentives.

Motivation theory has as its primary goal the development of the learner's sense of achievement and pride leading to positive agency, but structuration theory looks at how social structure and ideology (mediational and ideational forms) affect agency and need to be taken into consideration (Lull, 2000, pp. 9–10). These involve sanctioned methods of university operation as well as the way that local students interact with each other and the international students.

With both motivation and structuration theories in mind, we have chosen the qualitative method in administering an open-ended questionnaire in the Spring of 2011 that asks international students to comment on their experiences in and out of the classroom at the University of Southern Denmark. Although 50 students would generally constitute the minimal sampling on a quantitative survey (Skerratt, 2008, p. 100), 20 is considered an upper limit for a qualitative survey (Ushioda, 2001, p. 97). Altogether, 10 students have been included (from Canada, China, France, Germany, Hong Kong, Iraq, South Korea and Spain), which was the majority of the dozen or so international students in this particular intercultural communications course. Where appropriate, we have followed up a questionnaire with discussions with the students.[2]

The questions themselves in the questionnaire focused on: the role of English; the satisfaction with the teaching, learning and social environment; difficulties that the students think they faced and anything else of relevance. These included:

- What role did an English-speaking environment play in your choice of studying in Denmark?
- Have you been satisfied with the English-speaking academic and social environment?
- How do you perceive the English competence level of their teachers?
- Have there been any language-related difficulties for you as a student? Please describe your perceptions and experiences.
- How has the Danish environment (Danish students among themselves and Danish students to teachers) affected you?
- Do you have anything else to add?

The 2009 student response

In 2009, we held a conference on international education at the University of Southern Denmark, Kolding, and invited four MA students to talk. They were from Moldova, Macedonia, Brazil and China. All had done undergraduate work in their home countries and then came to Denmark for a programme that consisted of both undergraduate and graduate work. As such, they had been at one university in Denmark for at least three years with one student at two different universities over five years. These four students indicated that they were pleased enough with their actual study programmes but that their experiences with other students inside and outside of class, as well as the administrative frameworks, led to serious grief. One of the students commented:

> *The most bitter, never ending experience I found concerning the educational process is the interaction/relation within students, especially between international and the local ones. Now in my five years of education I basically don't really have any contact with any of my classmates, if I don't come to school for a month or two nobody ever notices, nobody really cares. What I want to say actually it is not that the students are mean to each or such, but simply there is not any interaction, people don't know each others' names after many years especially when it comes to international students and locals students – zero interaction.... I often have the feeling that we are "Palle alene I verden" (all alone in the world), we come to university we load ourselves with critical thoughts and information and we go home but it is all like a "systemic pipeline" – nobody knows nobody and if they do it's only the faces a bit.*

The student who presented this was in every way lively and upbeat, but clearly the academic and social context pulled him down so that he could add:

> *Now I know that a lot of international students, who have been here for a longer time, for certain reasons will probably never write or say the fact that they feel lonely or that they are lost between two worlds of their country and Denmark – but this does not change the fact that the longer there is this parallelism the chances are that both sides will be filled with stupid and negative prejudices and stereotypes forever.*

A few basic questions come to mind as a result of this response. How widespread is the view that international students are not integrated into their academic and social environment? What are steps that can be taken to ensure a better relationship between visiting and local students? Most importantly, perhaps, has the situation changed between 2009 and 2011? Much has happened with programmes and opportunities for international students in the past couple of years, so we set out to see if students still feel this kind of alienation.

To test this out, an elective intercultural communications course in an English Studies programme was chosen because these students are located in one of the best possible places to build on their English background and to be in a classroom environment where interculturalism is articulated and international relationships are valued. All of this should mean that the comments about the teaching environment, student relationships and administrative assistance should be generally positive and lead to strong motivation. If they are not, then they must be taken even more seriously.

Personal goals and academic interest

Without exception, the international students' personal goals were to improve their English skills and succeed in their courses and programmes in Denmark and at home. None of them had known any Danish upon arrival (though two were in the process of trying to learn it), and all expressed a desire for a strong English-speaking academic and social environment in their study abroad: they expressed a need for English in their courses and their major as well as in university information but also as part of their general well-being. In this sense, they were highly motivated to take advantage of the strong abilities in English evidenced almost everywhere in Denmark. As one Chinese student noted:

> Before coming to Denmark, I didn't know much about the English-speaking environment in non-English-speaking European countries. After travelling to Finland, Sweden, and Norway, I feel I'm lucky to study in Denmark because Danes seem to have higher proficiency in English speaking.

For academic purposes, these students all required a high level of English language competence of their teachers, and, again to a person, they were pleased to note that the university did not disappoint them, though, as noted below, they did not always feel included. Indeed, one aspect of linguistic proficiency which is rarely mentioned is the matter of inclusiveness, as pointed out by Mertova in Chapter 5 of this volume. One French student noted that 'the English competence of the teachers is really good', and another said she was 'really impressed by that'. The German student echoed that, saying 'they talk on a high level and have a big knowledge of various types of dialect/intonation/vocabulary'. The Spanish student noted that the teachers' 'English competence level is very high', and the Korean student wondered how the Danes seemed to speak English nearly as well as their native language. The Chinese student asserted that 'the English competence level of the teachers in Denmark is much higher than in Hong Kong', especially in pronunciation and intonation, and asserted that she felt 'more comfortable here'. Surprisingly, the Canadian – one of those drawn from the inner circle of English speakers – commented that the teachers' English was 'Top notch. Some (very few) had an accent which made it hard to understand but not as bad as some I heard back in Canada'. The general praise for the teachers' abilities in English certainly has something to do with the fact that most were teaching in the English Studies Department, but many others outside this English language haven are also able to converse with relatively unaccented ease.

Course and university-related enjoyment/liking and desired levels of competence

Although generally enthusiastic and highly motivated about the classroom environment – lectures, discussions and participation – international students hinted at some problems and some dissatisfaction with their own abilities in this new environment. What students liked the most was the interactive classroom. As the Spanish student noted:

> *I have been very satisfied with the lessons as they are very active and easy to understand. I would like to say that I am really happy with the way teachers teach in Denmark. They seem motivated with what they teach and that makes the student be motivated too and makes them participate and learn much more than just listening to explanations.*

A French student made a similar comment, remarking that students in Denmark seemed to be genuinely involved in their studies and in the interactive classroom. She used the word 'implicated' to suggest this involvement:

> *Danish students are very implicated in their studies which is good. They partici-pate more in class than my classmates in France. Teachers are very implicated also and take a lot of importance in what the students think about their teach-ing. Danish students among themselves work a lot in groups. Close relationship between teachers and the students. It affected my way of being implicated in my study.*

Another of the French students shared this enthusiasm, admitting that she had been satisfied with the English-speaking environment academically, socially and administratively, but also hinting at occasional lapses:

> *In Denmark, the description of courses are in English, the University website is in English, the teachers speak English most of the time. Furthermore, Danish students speak good English. Almost each time we meet Danish people we can speak English to them.*

Her 'most of the time' and 'almost each time' tempered her enthusiasm and indicated a certain lack of universality in the English-speaking environment.

The Hong Kong student found no 'language-related difficulties' in the classroom and the Canadian student found that most students can speak English 'very well'. In his laconic manner, however, he continued, 'My English is fine and so are most of the Danish students and profs are very good', but 'some other international students, well that's a different story'. In reflecting on her place within the classroom, the Korean student clearly saw herself as one of those 'other international students' who had limitations with their English expression. She commented in an apologetic way to the instructor, taking all the blame on herself but showing a positive motivation, nevertheless:

> *I'm not that outgoing person, so I couldn't share my cultural things in class. I feel sorry a little bit to you. In addition, a lot of texts made difficulties to*

follow the class but it's my problem, of course. I just want to inform that I am sorry for just listening [to] your lecture, always. But your lecture was always excellent!

One of the French students echoed this feeling, noting that she had 'difficulties to get understood' and struggled with vocabulary, literal meaning and overall comprehension:

Sometimes, in readings I have to take into account the fact that it is in English and translate in my head. And then I also have to understand what is really said once I understand the words used.

The process, she argued, took long enough that she could not react spontaneously in the classroom and participate actively in discussion. This discrepancy in language skills, Marschan-Piekkari et al. (1999) note, is frequently cited as the most disruptive factor in 'contact', 'relationship building' and 'communication across cultural borders' (Marschan-Piekkari et al., 1999, pp. 426–427), so it is quite understandable that the students lament some inabilities to make themselves clear in class.

Another of the French students countered part of that view, saying that her own English skills had improved immensely in this new international environment so that she could participate in the discussion:

I know I improve my skills in this language, I can now think in English easier than before. I don't have to translate in French anymore.

However, she hinted at some problems with the Danish classroom veering away from all-English usage, but diplomatically muted that criticism: I 'only perceived some difficulties with the Danish language'.

Other students were much more direct about the intrusion of Danish 'noise' in the classroom in noting that, while classes within the English Studies programme were mainly taught in English, not all of the activities and information in and out of the classroom were. As pointed out by Edmead in Chapter 1 of this volume, group work in itself may pose a difficulty: if it is compounded by a language issue it may severely affect motivation. One of the Chinese students noted the tendency for students doing group work to speak sometimes in Danish to the exclusion of the international students:

In some group discussions, they may switch to Danish when they want to talk about some personal issues or when they try to explain some term to their friends. But it doesn't affect me much. I have experienced the same situations in Hong Kong. The only difference now is I can understand most of the Cantonese but none of the Danish.

Others saw a problem not so much in the groups' reverting to Danish but in the instructors' doing that, and one of the Chinese students was a little more pointed about the instructor's role in deviating from English:

> *The only experience I had is in a literature class. The lecturer's handout about an author was in Danish. But later he explained what's in the handout. So I didn't really think of it as a language-related difficulty.*

Other students confirmed this tendency, noting verbally that when information was presented in Danish, it was never accompanied by a literal translation, but rather general summarising comments so that they were never sure what they were missing in actual information or nuance. One of the French students similarly remarked that teachers would communicate informally in Danish to students, but qualified that to say that that they all spoke 'English during the lectures'. Nevertheless, she offered a word of admonition, 'but be careful of non-English PowerPoints', suggesting that this might be a greater problem within courses. If, indeed, handouts and PowerPoint presentations are not translated into English for the benefit of the increasing number of international students, then that constitutes a major lapse and structural problem within courses and programmes.

The Korean student noted that this lapsing out of English was critical outside the classroom as well, extending to information in the library and on the university website. She said:

> *Actually these days I am trying to learn Danish. Because outside lesson, everything is written in Danish, even [in the] library, [and] especially [the] Danish website.*

Students also noted that most examination information that came from the university was only in Danish, so they feared missing guidelines, dates and explanations that would be critical to their success.

These are the kind of pedagogical and administrative issues that can swamp international students in these programmes. It is certainly too much to ask that all instructions and conversations be in English throughout the university, but websites should have an English translation, and all course materials without exception should be in English in English-speaking courses. Moreover, faculty members should exercise the greatest of care in their classroom communication, so it does not appear that they tell the Danish students one thing and international students another.

Personal satisfaction and feelings about Danish-speaking people: The Danish academic and social environment

Most of the international students were quite positive about the Danes in the academic and social environment, though they did distinguish between the two, noting few problems within the academic environment, but feeling that the social environment could pose greater problems. Concerning the academic environment, the Korean student was enthusiastic about the prevalence of English usage, saying 'Yes, I've been really satisfied with those. It's really helpful to me, because I'm not used to use English before'. A French student felt the same way:

> *Actually, I am still really surprised by the social environment, lot of people are speaking English. That is really important for non-Danish speaker.*

She further notes that:

> *Danish students seem to be very seriously involved in their studies. They have really respectful but at the same time close relationship to their teacher; that appears nice, because communication is supposed to be quite easy.*

Also focusing on the social dynamics of the classroom, the Spanish student spoke glowingly about the relationship between students and teachers:

> *The Danish environment has affected me in a really positive way. I see that the relationship between them is very positive and very close to each other, what I like the most is that the teacher makes you participate and teaches in a dynamic way.*

The refrains of the prevalence of speaking English in the student body and this positive relationship among teachers and students in the Danish classroom played throughout the student comments.

The Spanish student also reflected upon the social environment, but restricted the comments to the Danes' facility with English rather than about a society that could make her feel at home:

> *I am also very satisfied with the social environment because if you don't know any Danish, people talk to you in English without problem.*

However, other student perceptions ranged from the quizzical concerning the culture in general to acceptance, if not understanding, of the initial coolness of Danes towards foreigners. The Korean student noted that the Danish culture 'is interesting because of difference' from her own. She says, 'When I heard something about their culture, I was always surprised. It's funny'. The Hong Kong student noted that the Danes are cool to outsiders but do warm up when the outsiders take the initiative on friendships:

> *Danish students are pretty friendly and helpful if I approached them, but they do not approach international students themselves. Danes are*

pretty cool to people, but they are friendly once you started to be friends with them.

The Canadian student noted the same thing:

It has made things interesting. Sometimes the Danes will keep to themselves and their groups but once you get in the 'in group' you're fine.

The German student noted her positive feelings about the Danes, but also stated that as an exception to what others thought:

Generally, Danes are very open-minded towards foreign people (in my view which apparently differs from others').

External pressures/incentives

International students were not too forthcoming in identifying external pressures that might stand in the way of motivation and high achievement, but they did take note that Danes see themselves, and are, as the Hong Kong student remarked, 'more direct and critical, and they expect me to be the same'. This student summed up what many Asian students strongly believe, that they 'usually express negative comments more indirectly' rather than directly, and that being too direct could be unsettling.

Moreover, some students felt themselves to be 'outside the pale' of social relationships. As it happens, the ones who expressed this most strongly were the students from Middle Eastern backgrounds. In commenting on the social environment, one Iraqi student said, 'There is no social environment. People mind their own business'. It is hard to tell whether this comment has the ring of an accepted truth about society or if there is also a strongly felt criticism, but it is likely the latter. Another of the Iraqi students who had come to Denmark as a refugee summed up her feelings in terms of the stranger within culture – the one who for all external appearances seems to adapt, but who on the inside sees himself as a perpetual stranger outside the values and relationships of the in-group (Rogers & Steinfatt, 1999): 'After 12 years in Denmark, I can understand/relate to the Danish environment more than my own culture. But I don't feel 100% Danish. In Denmark, I feel like I'm a stranger and in my own country I feel the same. I'm somehow caught in between'.[3]

Overall, the international students in this intercultural communications course agreed with the Canadian student that 'It's been a good time learning here. Gives you a different approach to things'. They were sufficiently motivated to overcome the academic, administrative and social lapses and inconveniences that could scuttle their enthusiasm. Clearly, students in this class were more accepting of the Danish social situation than were the 2009 students from Moldova, Macedonia, Brazil and China. However, by leaning towards structuration theory in this opinion survey, it is possible to make some recommendations that can serve Denmark as well as other countries that wish to incorporate English-speaking international students into their academic fabric.

Recommendations

- Universities need to be mindful of their total English-speaking environment.

Universities must not assume that they can simply take in students without ensuring that their teachers are capable of teaching in English and that all important administrative information on the homepage, library, Blackboard, in-house posters, memoranda, etc., is translated into English and properly disseminated to the students.

- All handouts, lecture notes and course instructions (hard copy in class, soft copy online, Blackboard, PowerPoint presentations) should be presented in English when international students are part of the class.

- Activities in class should be structured to include the international students with the local students.

That is, discussion and presentation groups should be structured to incorporate international students on a systematic ongoing basis to give the international and local students a chance to know one another more intimately in the classroom context.

- Students should be encouraged to take intercultural or other communication courses.

These could help student to learn about various intercultural theories and practices in conjunction with local students, increasing the likelihood of fostering academic and social well-being among them.

Conclusion

Finally, then, it is possible to say that motivational learning theory and qualitative surveys of international student opinion can go a long way to assisting these students in remaining highly motivated in their educational pursuits abroad and that teachers and administrators need to follow student reflections on their education at that institution. As Ushioda (2001) commented in her own learning surveys, 'These findings suggested that *effective motivation thinking* might entail filtering experience and focusing on the positive incentives, while de-emphasising the negative' (Ushioda, 2001, p.109). These University of Southern Denmark students followed the same pattern in remaining mainly enthusiastic and muting their negative feelings. In synthesising their own and other research on motivation, Cxizér and Dörnyei (2005) draw upon two opposite poles of motivation, one with a promotion focus and the other with a prevention focus. The promotion focus is 'concerned with hopes, aspirations, advancement, growth, and accomplishments', and the prevention focus with 'regulating the absence or presence of negative outcomes, concerned with safety, responsibilities and obligations (Cxizér & Dörnyei, 2005, p. 617). The proposition is that students will work towards reducing the discrepancies between these two. The student statements included in this chapter point in the same direction. Structuration theory, however, reminds us that individual mastery in overcoming these feelings does not solve social and administrative problems, and that the university must assess its international learning situation and take very precise steps to make certain that international students are not 'all alone in the world'. While it is clear that universities, indeed, have learned how better to manage their international student population over the past few years, being vigilant about the well-being of international students is still the key to the success of the programme and the students.

Notes

1 Macias (1997) gives an interesting account of the development of language-equitable policies in the US during the latter part of the 1990s. Whereas these cannot have the same force of law in Europe as they must have in the US, they do demonstrate the need for such practices.
2 The student quotes in this chapter are all from the questionnaires. Ensuing subsequent discussions with the students were pertinent to the remarks made in the questionnaires, but these discussions were primarily conducted to ensure that our understanding of the remarks in the questionnaires were in line with the intention of the students in question. As is apparent from the quotes in this chapter, not all comments made in the questionnaires were well-formed and clear in their verbal expression.
3 This concept derives from Georg Simmel's late nineteenth-century notion. Raised in Germany but Jewish, he always felt at home and at a distance from his culture – a feature that he called the stranger. This is a widely used term in intercultural communications nowadays.

References

Cxizér, K. & Dörnyei, Z. (2005). Language learners' motivational profiles and their motivated learning behaviour. *Language Learning, 55*(4), 613–659.
Gardner, R. C. & Lambert W. E. (1972). *Attitudes and motivation in second language learning.* Rowley, MA: Newbury House.
Giddens, A. (1999). 'Globalisation – London'; 'Risk – Hong Kong'; 'Tradition – Delhi'; 'Washington DC – Family'; and 'London – Democracy'. *Runaway World.* BBC Reith Lectures. Each section is 7 pages. http://news.bbc.co.uk/hi/english/ static/events/reith_99/week1/week1.htm http://news.bbc.co.uk/hi/english/ static/events/reith_99/week2/week2.htm http://news.bbc.co.uk/hi/english/ static/events/reith_99/week3/week3.htm http://news.bbc.co.uk/hi/english/ static/events/reith_99/week4/week4.htm http://news.bbc.co.uk/hi/english/ static/events/reith_99/week5/week5.htm (accessed 15 November 2010).

Kachru, B. (1988). The sacred cows of English. *English Today, 16,* 3–8.

Lull, J. (2000). *Media, communication, culture: A global approach.* Cambridge: Polity Press.

Macias, R. F. (1997). Bilingual workers and language use rules in the workplace: A case study of a nondiscriminatory language policy. *International Journal of the Sociology of Language, 127,* 53–70.

Marschan-Piekkari, R., Welch, D. & Welch, L. (1999). In the shadow: The impact of language on structure, power, and communication in the multinational. *International Business Review, 8,* 421–440.

Rogers, E. M. & Steinfatt, T. M. (1999). *Intercultural communication.* Prospect Heights, IL: Waveland Press.

Skerratt, S. (2008). Doing small-scale qualitative research on educational innovation. In R. Murray (ed.), *The scholarship of teaching and learning in higher education.* Maidenhead: Open University Press.

Truchot, C. (2002). *Key aspects of the use of English in Europe.* Strasbourg: Language Policy Division, DGIV.

Ushioda, E. (2001). Language learning at university: Exploring the role of motivational thinking. In Z. Dörnyei & R. Schmidt (eds.), *Motivation and second language acquisition.* Honolulu, HI: Second Language Teaching & Curriculum Centre, University of Hawaii.

Part 2

New ways of designing and delivering curriculum

Chapter 7

Engaging students in academic transitions

A case of two projects using student voice and technology to personalise the experience

Monika Foster

Context

The UK higher education has been attracting increasing numbers of international, non-EU students. The growth in non-EU student numbers calls for a review of our approach to the relationship with the students, where possible, reaching out and engaging the students in the academic transition to the new learning and teaching context (Pringle, Fischbacher & Williams, 2008).

It seems vital to ensure that the students blend well into the UK education system and are equipped with the right skills to make the most of their time in the UK through effective and meaningful induction. Increasingly, attention is given to a wider context of transition from one academic context to another, seen more as a process than an induction event at the start of the programme. Shofield and Sackville (2006) view induction as having three parts: academic, social and administrative. Cook, Macintosh & Rushton (2006) propose 'extended induction', which is about 'a longer assimilation of new students into the ways in which the institution operates' (Cook et al., 2006, p. 7). Similarly, Timpson (2008) recommends viewing induction as an extended process in which students are welcomed and allowed time to adapt.

Academic transition is concerned with a wider student experience, before, during and after induction. Academic transition can be a new and exciting experience, a substantial hurdle or even a traumatic experience for students coming from a very different academic culture, trying to cope with a culture shock, accommodation process and home sickness (Ballard & Clanchy, 1994). It can include feelings of being inadequately prepared and incompetent in the key academic skills expected of the students in the new place of study (Burns, 1991). Bamford (2008) reported on a study to establish students' perceptions of their educational experiences in the UK in the context of transition and possible solutions for improvements. The biggest challenges in adjusting to a new educational environment for the students in Bamford's study were English language ability, social and cultural adjustment and study methods. The students' suggestions for improving their experiences included peer mentoring, local language/study groups, more social activity and inclusive learning, teaching and assessment design.

Institutions have a role to play in supporting students in transition and generating conditions that stimulate and encourage student engagement (Davis & Murrell, 1993). Engagement is a broad phenomenon which encompasses academic as well as non-academic and social aspects of the student experience. It embraces the relationship between students and institutions in the context of internationalisation of higher education:

> *The presence of international students on university campus provides a unique social forum for embracing all students' understanding and appreciation of the richness of other cultures.... Since opportunities for inter-cultural learning are seldom taken spontaneously, tertiary institutions have a social responsibility to design learning environments which foster students' development of inter-cultural adaptability.*
>
> (Volet & Ang, 1998, p. 176)

A report on a national student survey of first-year experience in Australian universities, looking specifically at student engagement (Krause & Coates, 2008), classified the range of engagement experienced by the students in several engagement scales. This includes a transition engagement scale (TES), which captures the value of early intervention in orientation and ongoing support during study and includes issues of identity and expectations of the students. Two other scales are the academic engagement scale (AES), which measures such skills as managing one's own time, study habits and strategies for success and the peer engagement scale (PES), which captures students' interaction with peers for academic and non-academic reasons connected to the effectiveness with which students engage with the transition process.

In order to address issues involved in the academic transition and factors supporting student engagement, Robertson et al. (2000) advocate a 'whole student', in which staff and students work closely together to achieve a mutually desirable outcome. In this approach, students' views on how to overcome challenges inform the development of support on offer. In the study by Robertson et al. (2000), suggestions offered by students to overcome the difficulties include 'self-help strategies and the value of mentors as a support through the process' (Robertson et al., 2000, p. 100). Additionally, learning from peers has been reported as particularly helpful in engaging students in the learning process (Lowe & Cook, 2003).

Last but not least, technology offers opportunities to reach out to students as early as possible to help engage students and personalise the experience at the induction stage and thereafter. Palloff and Pratt (2007) believe the aim of the induction process is to maximise the educational potential for both the online classroom and online student. Web-based materials are increasingly explored to enhance induction. Pringle et al. (2008) discuss the use of web-based materials developed to support international students prior to and during the study. The main benefit for the students seemed to be an opportunity to compare expectations about learning and teaching, and the reality, as well as considering changes to students' own learning styles prior to commencing their study.

Online study skills resource SPICE

Edinburgh Napier University, like many UK higher education institutions, has a diverse student population, with international students being a majority in many of the programmes. The need for a pre-arrival induction was iden tified on the undergraduate Hospitality Management programme. The course has large numbers of direct entry Indian students (approximately 100+) who come to study in Edinburgh for one year after completing two years of college study in India as part of the 2+1 degree programme. They encounter a number of challenges related to the differences in academic cultures, different expectations of university students in the UK and living and studying in a new country.

The standard induction is too short, happens too late (post-arrival) and cannot address the breadth of the new skills and awareness that need to be assimilated by the students. Additionally, many of the students on the programme prefer to rely on peers who already study in the UK to provide academic and pastoral support.

To address the above issues, an online pre-arrival induction resource SPICE (Student Pre-arrival Induction for Continuing Education) was created. SPICE is driven by students sharing their experiences with their peers, so 'by students and for students' is very much the motto of the resource. The SPICE resource was developed for third year direct entry Indian students on the BA Hospitality Management programme. It has now been used by two cohorts of students in India (n = 387 students) studying on the Edinburgh Napier programme.

The SPICE resource includes three strands of online activities following the student journey through the university. The first strand introduces students to the roles and expectations in the university, and helps students to reflect on their current learning styles and how they can develop them to engage successfully in university study. The second strand includes activities which help develop confident and effective academic study skills such as time management, planning for assessments, independent study skills, team work, library research skills, etc. The third strand develops confident academic writing skills, as this is the single largest challenge for students, including such skills as essay, report and case study writing and referencing. The users can work their way through the strands in order of their preference. However, in order to receive a certificate of SPICE completion, the users must complete activities in all strands. SPICE is a resource designed to help the users consider their current learning skills and try out new ones, so the time taken to complete SPICE will vary depending how much time the user can dedicate to working with the resource. Depending on whether SPICE is used as an intensive induction tool or a self-study material, the user's previous educational background, level of English and commitment to use the resource, it can take two weeks or two months to complete the activities in the SPICE resource. SPICE can be used as a stand-alone self-study tool or it can be used as a basis for a face-to-face delivery in the class as part of a bridging programme. In the case of the latter, SPICE can be used over a longer period of time, integrated with other class materials and online activities.

Features of this resource include being student and task driven. Students complete the tasks online or can use a printed version of the activities to complete together in class. Upon completing an activity, students receive feedback that is generated automatically from the bank of feedback and answers. The feedback and the comments from the students are used to affirm the student's expectations of the university and explain effective study habits. Students' progress, including an overview of what activities students completed or failed to complete, can be viewed using the administrator account.

An underlying principle of the design of the SPICE resource was to work closely with the current students in preparing the strands and the activities by involving them in the choice of the topics included in SPICE, contributing to the design of the activities and even creating the feedback sections together with the resource developers to ensure the outcome is appealing to the new students. According to Edward (2003), for students to succeed in their education, they must be 'motivated, accustomed to the university culture and feel part of the university community' (Edward, 2003, p. 223). There were two ways students were involved in the design of the SPICE resource: through group and individual interviews with students already studying at Edinburgh Napier University (altogether over 70 students) and through focus groups with students in India preparing to arrive in the UK (altogether 56 students).

The process of designing SPICE began with collecting information from the current students about their experience of studying at Napier. Seventy-three current Edinburgh Napier University students took part in group interviews. In groups of six to eight, the students were asked questions about their experience of life and study at Edinburgh Napier, specifically how they found the timetable, how they planned for assessments, how they found working in groups and working individually, etc. The students pointed to a number of differences from their previous learning contexts, such as considerably fewer contact hours with the lecturers, having to manage their own time and planning for assessments (many students said they found this part very hard as they had not done this before their study in the UK because everything had been planned and structured by their teachers/college), having to decide what's important to study and how to find relevant resources. Many students discussed the novelty of working for assignments in teams and even working in groups in tutorials was quite new to them. They found their social life to be poor and not engaging very much with the university due to work commitments and relying on their immediate peer group. Quite a few students elaborated on how at the start of their studies they had found the above issues difficult, but they seemed to have overcome them by applying themselves, following the guidance from the module leaders and making friends with students out with their immediate peer group either through sports or work. These stories were recorded and used with permission to produce sound bites of student voices for the SPICE resource for the new students to listen to.

The themes from the group interviews were further explored in depth in individual interviews to substantiate the claims made by students in groups. Eight students agreed to participate in individual interviews. They represented a range of educational experiences from India as they came from all four partner colleges in India.

During the individual interviews, the students provided further, more detailed descriptions of their experiences in Edinburgh. Most of the discussions during the individual interviews explored further the three themes from the group interviews: contact hours and time management; working in groups versus working individually and assessment. Students commented on the relatively small number of contact hours on their programme of study at Edinburgh Napier University (6–9 hours a week) compared with their experience of studying at a college in India where students normally spend between 10 and 12 hours a day on classes with their teachers. Their studying week is organised for them, with little or no self-study time. The students rely on the contact time with the teacher to get all the information they need to complete the course and pass the assessments. Used to the teaching timetable filling up their week, nearly all interviewed students pointed to the lack of time management skills to deal with the 'free time' and planning their study time. They discussed how they had to work hard on this skill, often learning from their own mistakes of not planning for assessment deadlines. Another new skill students commented on a lot was working in groups. The students explained that they did not have much experience of working on an academic task in a group, negotiating team roles and working together to achieve a goal. A major challenge which the students did not expect was doing well in assessments. They were used to presenting the information from the tutor. Using knowledge from the tutorials and lectures to write essays or case studies was a new skill which they had to learn fast. Below are examples of students' comments on each of the themes which illustrate the discussion in individual interviews.

Contact hours

In India, the college starts at 8, ends by 6 pm so we have 10–12 hours of college course a day so you go on studying. But here, if students come 6–9 hours a week, that's enough, sufficient to give you knowledge, give you the basic idea to give you the degree. (In India). All we need is the knowledge you get into your head, that's it. And here, I was first confused, you should have the initiative, you should take the initiative, you should have the courage to go about it and show your knowledge.

Working in groups

About differences in working in groups. We have little experience of working in groups and, even if we do, it's quite informal only, for talking about something. Here, the groups have a specific task, they are professional, they are formally run. So that's quite different, but you need to learn how to do it, how to work in a group. Otherwise, you can be very disappointed and disappoint others.

Assessment

The first assessment here was the first time I did anything like this, writing an essay or a report, analysing literature, writing a case study. I don't know how I am supposed to go about it, and what will be the marks, and if I fail, what happens then. So, this made me very nervous and confused. In India, we didn't use the reference rule that much.

After the results of the individual interviews were matched with the results of the group interviews, a selection of the student voices as sound bites to listen to and narrative to read was included in the online study skills SPICE resource to help new students identify themselves with the new experience and to emphasise the message such as: 'this is what happened to me and I used the following strategies to overcome it, you can do it too!'.

The focus groups in India were the next stage of the process of designing the student voice into the SPICE resource. Having gathered a selection of peer voices about the experience of studying in the UK, it was interesting to see how students who prepare to study in the UK in the coming academic session would react to the peer voices. The focus groups were convened from volunteer students in Year 2 of study in each of the four colleges in India preparing to study in Year 3 at Edinburgh Napier University as part of their 2+1 degree. Altogether 56 students participated in the focus groups. During the focus groups in India, the students were presented with a selection of the peer voices from the interviews conducted in Edinburgh, as discussed above, and asked to comment. The students in India were very interested in the comments from their peers in Edinburgh and noted that the student voices were more detailed in their account of studying and living in Edinburgh, and more focused on the academic skills, than the advice they tend to get from their peers informally through social networks. The information they get from peers tends to focus on the practical aspects of studying and living in Edinburgh, such as finding a flat or a job, and less on the academic aspects, such as studying for assessments.

The students in India also described their hopes and fears about study abroad and what they think may be useful for them. Some of the comments from the focus groups are included below:

> *We know little about what is awaiting for us in Edinburgh so this is very useful for us to make us less anxious.*
> *The change from what we do now is going be very big but we know our col-leagues who are in Edinburgh now did this and they do well so it makes us feel better about trying ourselves.*
> *A lot of the examples are completely new to me, I want to know more about them and how to do well at Napier.*

It was apparent from the focus group exercise that the international students who prepare to study in the UK, although they can read about their courses and chat informally to their peers, have few opportunities to engage with the learning and teaching context of their future courses in the UK and value and benefit from the peer-told accounts of the study experience, which have as a result become the main feature of the SPICE resource. Another advantage of conducting the focus groups with the material from the interviews in Edinburgh was an opportunity to get feedback from the students abroad – in this case students in India – on the materials from their peers in Edinburgh which enabled the selection of the student voice sound bites the students found most relevant and helpful.

Benefits for the students

There are some initial findings emerging about the benefits of using the SPICE resource, which will be further asserted as part of ongoing evaluation. The SPICE resource's strength seems to be in developing a student-led perspec-tive on transition to the new learning and teaching context. This is based on the rich student stories from student interviews in Edinburgh and is guided by the choice of topics and activities in the SPICE resource made by students in India preparing to come to the UK. The two groups of students, current students in Edinburgh and students in India preparing to come to the UK as part of their 2+1 programme, who were involved in the design of the SPICE resource, were encouraged to contribute actively to the contents of SPICE by giving their opinions about what should be included, the challenges they faced and the solutions they developed. The students chose the main parts of SPICE; they were asked to sample the activities and give feedback, choose the pictures for SPICE and even the name of the resource.

The SPICE resource has been used by students as a self-study resource. Cohorts of students from colleges in India coming to Edinburgh as part of the 2+1 study programme in 2009/10 and 2010/11 had access to SPICE as a self-study resource prior to commencing their study in Edinburgh, guided by the local tutors and an online guide on how to use it. Reports from lecturers who worked with students from the colleges who used SPICE suggest that students who have used the SPICE resource are more confident about their studies, have more specific expectations about their new learning and teaching context, approach tutors for help more readily rather than wait until problems arise and show a positive attitude towards attending lectures and participating in tutorials.

The use and benefits of the SPICE resource, used on a 2+1 programme, rely to some extent on the support from the local tutors in the colleges in India who work with the students prior to continuing their studies in the UK. The SPICE resource is a stand-alone resource which can be used for a self-study but it became evident in the work with the two cohorts of students from India (2009/10 and 2010/11), that the students seek advice on some of the activities and prefer to follow SPICE as a class activity with the teacher as they find it difficult to work with the SPICE resource on their own. The Indian tutors used the SPICE resource with the students in a computer lab and assisted with any questions. The directors and tutors in all four colleges supported the design and implementation of SPICE to enhance their students' transition to the UK educational system. Informally, the tutors were asked for their opinions about SPICE and its effectiveness. All 12 tutors commented on the usefulness of SPICE to introduce students to life and study at Edinburgh Napier and pointed to the high value of students being able to consider their current study skills and develop effective skills for study at Edinburgh Napier.

The experience from the design and use of the SPICE resource developed for the Indian students on the 2+1 programme informed the work currently taking place to extend the online SPICE resource to meet the needs of all international students planning to study at Edinburgh Napier University, and call it SPICE International. SPICE International will include a wider range of the generic study skills activities of SPICE, including activities for other subject groups of students (e.g. postgraduate Engineering students), a wider range of student voices from various nationalities and programmes, to represent the diversity of the international student body at Edinburgh Napier, and an enhanced interface and functionality to be more user-friendly.

E-mentoring project

Another example of a project aiming to reach out to students and engage them in the academic transition by using peer power and technology is the e-mentoring project with direct entry Indian students. The e-mentoring project complements the SPICE resource and aims at the same group of students on the 2+1 programme. In addition to using a pre-arrival online SPICE resource, the students in four colleges in India were matched with their older peers who volunteered to act as mentors and studied on the same 2+1 programme but a year or two earlier than the mentees. The mentoring scheme offered a more individual contact, and an opportunity to ask questions and make friends with their older peers. In a way, the peer mentoring programme enabled students to get a first-hand account of the issues and skills discussed in the SPICE resource, with an additional bonus of making connections with Edinburgh Napier before arrival to study in Year 3.

Bamford (2008) reviewed international students' perspectives on their educational experience in the UK and suggested a number of strategies to improve international students' academic and cultural experiences, including:

- peer mentoring
- local language/study skills groups
- more social activity
- teaching, learning and assessment – the importance of the tutor having some knowledge of the cultural differences
- staff development.

Furthermore, a study carried out with students from India at Edinburgh Napier University in 2009 revealed a strong preference to rely on peers to provide academic and pastoral support before arrival and during study at Edinburgh Napier. It was felt this needed to be addressed, as the information and advice passed to new students may be misleading, particularly in relation to study skills and engagement with the programme and other students.

The results of the study informed the development of a pilot e-mentoring project which was set up in 2009/10. The mentoring project took place during trimester 2 and involved 18 student mentees (students in second-year Hospitality in India preparing to study in the UK) and 10 student mentors (Indian students in third-year Hospitality at Edinburgh Napier).

The ethos of the project was to engage with students' cultural preference for getting information, pastoral and academic advice from peers, while providing them with new mentoring skills, guiding them to reflect on their experience at Edinburgh Napier and passing on correct advice regarding study skills and pre-arrival information to the mentees. The project was supported by a small internal funding which enabled the coordination and management of the activities and the involvement of colleagues and students.

The project used technology to enhance student–student communication. The students communicated via Elluminate Live, which is a real-time demonstration and collaboration environment. It allows more than one user to participate at each end of the exchange so, apart from individual meetings, group meetings can be easily arranged. Elluminate's collaboration environment enables the delivery of live mentoring with live exchange text messages, display live video, share whiteboards, multimedia files and applications in an intuitive, graphical interface.

During the duration of the e-mentoring project (i.e. one trimester), there were three group meetings on Elluminate Live, followed by individual meetings. Some students opted to use Skype for individual meetings. None of the mentors had used Elluminate Live before and they all reported that they thought it was a good medium, especially for group discussion.

Additionally, students contributed materials and videos to a secure Wiki site, a shared space for the project. The mentees in India had not previously known how to use Wiki for educational purposes and found participating in setting up and contributing to the Wiki a new learning experience. Both mentors and mentees reported that they enjoyed putting up pictures and videos about Edinburgh Napier and about preparing to come to the UK and having a shared space for the project.

Benefits for the students

As is the case with the SPICE resource, the peer mentoring project is a new initiative which is due to be evaluated towards the end of the second year of running of the project, that is, Spring 2012. In the meantime, initial insights based on the comments from the mentees and mentors gathered in feedback sessions at the end of the e-mentoring project highlight a number of interesting findings, the main one being that the mentors seem to be the group that benefited most from the project. The mentors enjoyed a sense of belonging to a project which helps new students and they felt valued by the university but were at the same time doing something that is expected of them in any case in their own culture. The mentors said they benefited a lot from the training sessions on becoming a mentor facilitated by colleagues from Student Affairs. The mentors had been in Edinburgh for just over four months at the time of the training. Their first observations were that they found out more about study skills from the mentor training than they had known since their induction in September. The mentors also valued the new mentoring skills which they can add to their CVs and the top-up training in study skills.

The mentees required more support from the project team than initially expected and this area needs to be given more attention. Nevertheless, the mentees from the first round of the project have now arrived at Edinburgh Napier as third-year students, and they were very positive about the experience, remembering how much it helped to ease their worries. They praised the peer mentoring project during their induction and discussed the benefits with their tutors and programme leaders. A number of last year's mentees volunteered to be mentors in the 2010/11 round of the project.

Adapting to different contexts

Both projects aim to enhance the transition experience by building an early relationship with the new students through the use of existing students' voices to share their study experience with the new students and to advise the new students on the strategies their peers used to study effectively. Both projects employ technology to encourage better engagement of the new students with their new university, their study programme and their peers already in Edinburgh. Both projects are quite generic in their application, transgressing subjects and contexts. Although both were intended initially for students on Hospitality programmes, work is now under way to extend the online SPICE resource to all international students, and a successful version of the e-mentoring project has been adapted with Engineering students at Edinburgh Napier University.

Although further evaluation of both projects may reveal more detailed evidence, initial findings seem to point to an opportunity for colleagues working with students in academic transition from one educational context to a new one to engage with the students and gain an insight into students' 'journeys' as one of the main benefits from both projects. These insights inform programme development and enable a richer, student-driven perspective in the resources and activities on offer to support students. Both the SPICE resource and the e-mentoring projects can be adapted for diverse groups of students or focus on the needs of a specific group. The real asset of the e-mentoring project was the close teamwork with the students, which would have to be monitored if it is extended to larger groups of students, and on programmes which do not have the support of the local tutors overseas, such as the support on the 2+1 programme in India.

Support for the projects

It needs to be stressed that both projects could not have run without internal support and resources from the university. This enabled putting together a team who coordinated the projects, including staff working on the programme and colleagues from central services, such as Student Affairs, Computing and Information Technology services (C&IT) and the International College. SPICE and the e-mentoring projects involved a range of partnerships. Both projects benefited from strong support from colleagues in India. In the e-mentoring project, colleagues from Student Affairs provided the training and advice as their university-wide mentoring programme had been well established before the e-mentoring project was set up. Likewise, building and developing SPICE has involved work with colleagues from Student Affairs, C&IT, the International College and other groups to ensure SPICE relates to all aspects of the 'student journey'. This collaboration is an asset to the project but also a challenge to share the same aims and objectives with academic and non-academic departments.

Evaluation of the projects

The projects described above seemed to have benefited both the existing students at Edinburgh Napier University and those preparing to come to study in Edinburgh as part of the 2+1 programme. The process of designing the SPICE resource and work on the e-mentoring project have been very successful in involving existing students in co-developing an online SPICE resource for future

Edinburgh Napier students and collaborating in the e-mentoring project to support the new students prior to arrival in Edinburgh.

Many of the existing students who contributed to both projects often remarked on the feeling of belonging to a useful and fun initiative, being appreciated by the university and gaining experience they can include on their CV. They readily offered more of their time than required as they were keen for the projects to be successful. More importantly, although already at Edinburgh Napier University and seemingly passed the transition stage, many of the existing international students who contributed to both projects felt they had benefited themselves from evaluating their own experience to help the new students and learn more about the effective study skills.

The students who prepare to go the university, for whom both projects are designed for – in this case international students from India on a 2+1 programme – were very enthusiastic about the opportunities to learn more about the university they are going to study at and to make friends with their peers who are already at the university. The students who were preparing to come to Edinburgh remarked repeatedly that using the SPICE resource, listening to their peers describing their study experience, trying their hand at SPICE activities to develop new learning skills and talking to their mentors on Elluminate Live and on email considerably lowered their anxiety and made them feel a part of their course and the university well before arrival. Long after arrival at the university, many of the mentees referred to the SPICE resource and the peer mentoring programme as fundamentally positive and useful tasks which they would like to recommend to other international students.

As indicated earlier, it is the intention to collect further data on the benefits of the project, especially more quantitative data on any correlation between the students' academic results and the use of the SPICE resource and/or participating in the mentoring programme before arrival to Edinburgh. Also, further details may emerge on the benefits and use of the above projects, following further expansion of the SPICE resource for all international students (SPICE International) as well as further development of the peer mentoring programme to include more diverse groups of mentors and mentees, representing a range of nationalities.

It is the belief that such initiatives as the SPICE resource and the e-mentoring project, which benefit both the existing and the new students by involving them in discussing their study experience (existing students) and anticipating the new learning and teaching context (new students), are examples of initiatives which help engage students in the learning and teaching from the very beginning of the experience of studying at the university and throughout their studies. They help make the students see themselves as valued partners and contributors, whom the university wants to enjoy and benefit from the experience of studying from the very beginning of the journey.

References

Ballard, B. & Clanchy, J. (1994). *Study abroad: A manual for Asian students.* Melbourne: Longman.

Bamford, J. (2008). Strategies for the improvement of international students' academic and cultural experiences in the UK. In P. Kemp & R. Atfield (eds.), *Enhancing international learning experience in Business and Management, Hospitality, Leisure, Sport and Tourism.* Newbury: Threshold Press.

Burns, R. B. (1991). Study and stress among first year overseas students in an Australian university. *Higher Education Research and Development, 10*(1), 61–77.

Cook, A., Macintosh, K. A. & Rushton, B. S. (eds.) (2006). *Supporting students: Early induction.* Coleraine: University of Ulster.

Davis, T. & Murrell, P. (1993). A structural model of perceived academic, personal and vocational gains related to college student responsibility. *Research into Higher Education, 34,* 267–289.

Edward, N. S. (2003). First impressions last: An innovative approach to induction. *Active Learning in Higher Education, 4*(3), 226–242.

Krause, K. & Coates, H. (2008). Students' engagement in first year university. *Assessment and Evaluation in Higher Education, 33*(5), 493–505.

Lowe, H. & Cook, A. (2003). Mind the gap: Are students prepared for higher education. *Journal of Further & Higher Education, 27*(1), 53–76.

Palloff, R. M. & Pratt, K. (2007). *Building online communities: Effective strategies for the virtual classroom.* San Francisco, CA: John Wiley and Sons.

Pringle, G., Fischbacher, M. & Williams, A. (2008). *Assisting international students to manage their transition to UK academic culture.* Paper presented at Universitas Teaching and Learning Conference, University of Glasgow. Available at: http://www.universitas21.com/RelatedFile/Download/121 (accessed 11 November 2010).

Robertson, M., Line, M., Jones, S. & Thomas, S. (2000). International students: Learning environments and perceptions: A case study using the Delphi technique. *Higher Education Research and Development, 19*(1), 89–102.

Shofield, M. & Sackville, A. (2006). *Student induction – from event to entitlement.* Paper presented at 29th Annual Improving University Teaching (IUT) Conference, Duqesne University, Pittsburgh. Available at: http://www.edgehill.ac.uk/solstice/researchanddissemination/documents/Studentinduction-fromeventtoentitlement2005.pdf (accessed 12 November 2010).

Timpson, N. (2008). *Induction – Make a start with e-learning.* Available at: http://www.epic.co.uk/content/news/resources/Induction_Make_a_Start.pdf(accessed 12 November 2010).

Volet, S. E. & Ang, G. (1998). Culturally mixed groups on international campuses: An opportunity for intercultural sharing. *Higher Education Research Quarterly, 60*(1), 27–51.

Chapter 8

Business lessons without business

Can arts-based training enhance cultural competence?

Helen E. Higson and Kai Liu

Introduction

One of the striking phenomenon in contemporary Western business schools is the presence of a high percentage of international students. Students in business schools are essentially studying in the most multicultural environment of the higher education sector in comparison with their peers from other departments. Business schools are also the institutions which often put 'educating global business leaders' in their mission statements and invest heavily in developing teaching and research with international relevance. Intercultural training is, however, largely overlooked in the business school context and few schools actually take initiatives to embed intercultural training into their curriculum. This seems a rather puzzling phenomenon, as promoting intercultural learning amongst students could both benefit teaching and learning within business schools and also help students advance their future careers as effective managers or employees in an increasingly globalised and multicultural environment.

In the last few decades, intercultural training itself has become a 'growing branch of the coaching and consulting industries' (Szkudlarek, 2009, p. 975). It is widely reported that failures of expatriate employment overseas (Eschbach, Parker & Stoeberl, 2001) could seriously jeopardise a multinational's global operation and, as a result, an estimated 60 per cent of multinational companies offer some form of intercultural training (Bennett, Aston & Colquhoun, 2000). However, most training methods struggle to meet expectations and there has been a call for 'teaching to move away from focusing teaching exclusively on country-specific, predominantly cognitive cultural and linguistic knowledge, towards general cultural sensitivity skills, or "cultural intelligence", which enables managers to adapt swiftly to new cultural situations' (Blasco, 2009, p. 13). The teaching approach we present in this chapter is an innovative attempt to show how intercultural training can be delivered in an interesting and creative way. We also collect data to evaluate the outcome of our training and the initial analysis shows that training improves participants' cultural competence, although further work needs to be done to perfect our approach.

This chapter is organised as follows: the next three sections will review the literatures of intercultural training in learning and corporate contexts; arts-based methods for management education; and arts-based methods for intercultural training. Following the review, we present our training approach and how we collected data from students who participated in the training. The subsequent section presents an analysis of our data, and the final section discusses the results and draws some conclusions and thoughts for future work.

Intercultural training in learning and corporate contexts

Our review of intercultural training starts from theories developed in the learning and education field. We identify three strands of theoretical thinking which guided us to develop our own training approach. Herzfeldt (2007) investigated cultural competence amongst undergraduate students and her research shows that the effectiveness of an individual to work in international group situations increases incrementally with the number of international or intercultural experiences that person engages in. In summary, anyone who has studied foreign languages or has spent time studying or working abroad will be a more effective international learner than those who have never been abroad or studied another's culture. For this reason, it is important to increase cultural exposure opportunities for students. This may be by making extra-curricular language tuition available, arranging study trips abroad, or ensuring that students have the opportunity of experiencing the kind of innovative intervention which is piloted in this research. The theory underpinning Herzfeldt's study is the model of cultural learning developed by Yamazaki and Kayes (2004) based on Kolb's (1984) experiential learning cycle. Such development increments over time, as the participants gradually learn about different cultures, getting used to different norms and building up new forms of behaviour. This links with the second set of theories which underpin Herzfeldt's work: that of personality (Van Oudenhoven & Van der Zee, 2002). Herzfeldt (2007) suggests that individuals who have more cultural experiences not only operate more effectively in intercultural situations but also develop a greater 'multicultural personality' (specifically, open-mindedness and social initiative). Their ability to reflect on life in general is increased. Importantly for this research, Herzfeldt found that the UK students showed less cultural competence than international students. This was due to their lower number of cultural experiences and to the UK's individualistic learning culture, as compared with the communalism experienced by many international students (Waistell, 2009).

The second strand of our theoretical framework is encapsulated in the work of Ippolito (2007). Ippolito asserts that 'deficit' models are often used to frame international students' assimilation into the UK education. There is much research on how international students can be 'enabled' to succeed academically in this higher education environment, rather than acknowledging what such students can bring to the UK learning experience. In order to ensure that international students can achieve to the same extent as home students, learning and teaching must be more inclusive. The theory which underpins Ippolito's work links critical pedagogy with intercultural communications (Hellmundt, 2003) and challenges assumptions that international students should merely adjust to how learning is oriented in the UK. Furthermore, the cultural experiences of international students can be used to increase the cultural experience of their home-based peers in the classroom (Ward, 2001).

The third strand of the theoretical framework is about the importance of an inclusive approach to be used to teach both home and international students. The natural corollary of the framework which is being built up is that, as well as finding ways which increase the intercultural capital of home students and the communication skills of international students, one needs to build intercultural training that is much more flexible than has traditionally been the case (see also Kember & Gow, 1991). Welikala and Watkins (2008) suggest that such training must avoid stereotyping. The premise of their work is 'the concept of cultural script', and the importance of taking into account learners' varying scripts. These authors suggest that peer interaction is important; learning should be based on a set of interactions between participants with different cultural scripts. Welikala and Watkins (2008) suggest that these scripts are important learning resources rather than barriers and they use the discourse approach to intercultural learning espoused by Scollon and Scollon (1995).

In the corporate context, research has found a common pitfall which is that few intercultural training programmes are skill-based; instead, they are focused on building awareness of the expatriate's own culture and the culture of the host country (Littrell & Salas, 2005). Although building cultural awareness is crucial for familiarisation with the new culture, building cultural awareness alone may not be a strong enough intervention to ensure that expatriates will have the tools necessary for cross-cultural interaction. The acquisition of knowledge does not guarantee that the expatriate will apply the appropriate principles, and expatriates need to be provided with the skills that enable them to interact effectively in the host country. In addition, international managers nowadays are also facing much more complicated cultural environments than ever before; they are often required to move from one location to another, making country-specific knowledge less relevant (Earley & Peterson, 2004). This makes the challenge of cultural training increasingly difficult because conventional methods that rely on country-specific knowledge often prove inadequate. Methods that orient managers to dyadic interactions in new countries fail to prepare them for the complexity encountered in multinational teams and work settings (Earley & Peterson, 2004). Byram (1997) concurs, and maintains that assessing knowledge is only a small part of what is involved. What also needs to be assessed is an individual's ability to step outside his/her cultural boundary, to make the strange familiar and the familiar strange, and to act on that change of perspective.

Earley (2002), too, asserts that cultural knowledge and awareness are necessary, but not sufficient for performing effectively in a cross-cultural setting, because an individual must also have the motivation to use the knowledge available. Those findings naturally point out one direction, which is that intercultural training needs to be delivered in an innovative way to ensure participants gain not only the knowledge but also the skills to cope with different cultural situations.

Arts-based methods for management education

There is a growing trend of using arts-based methods for organisational and leadership development (Adler, 2006; Darsø, 2004; Nissley, 2004; Taylor, 2008). Taylor and Ladkin (2009) conclude that arts-based methods are underpinned by four distinctive processes that do not operate within conventional organisational development approaches. They are *skill transfer, projective technique, illustration of essence* and *making*. For the purpose of intercultural learning, we found two processes – *projective technique* and *illustration of essence* – are particularly relevant. Linstead (2006) suggests that aesthetic forms have an important role to play in helping to make tacit knowledge of 'invisible' concepts such as 'culture' visible. In fact, he proposes that culture can best be explored and presented through artistic forms because they make the tacit and felt experience of culture an object in the world. Cultural development is a particularly good example of where arts-based methods are useful. Any organisational phenomena such as group dynamics, leadership, or politics that is to some degree tacit and felt can be the subject of arts-based methods to be made visible and projected into the world. Grisham (2006) describes how leaders in cross-cultural settings can build trust and empathy through storytelling and the use of poetry. By sharing and highlighting the essence of something that is important to them in their sense-making of such art forms, leaders bridge cultural gaps and find common understanding and ways of connecting with one another. The purpose that illustration of essence serves, particularly in relation to leadership and the use of narrative, is further explored in Taylor, Fisher and Dufresne's (2002) theory of the aesthetics of leadership storytelling. They suggest that the power of storytelling rests in its ability to convey felt meaning directly without being 'explained' by our rationalising faculties. Furthermore, because the story is enjoyable it is remembered and retold. When art is used as illustration of essence, we get the idea of the essence of the concept being communicated directly, and much of our intellectual filtering is bypassed.

Arts-based methods for intercultural training: A promising way forward?

To date, arts-based methods are rarely applied to intercultural training settings, although the relationship between arts practice as a means of reaching out across cultures is well documented in the literature (Bailey & Desai, 2005; Liddicoat & Diaz, 2008). Wolf, Milburn and Wilkins (2008) analyse the effectiveness of moving away from traditional teaching methods and theories towards more student-centred and expressive methods of addressing culture in the classroom. They show that such a method helps students to evaluate, reflect and act in a culturally inclusive way. The reasons for these results are explained by Wesley (2007) and further emphasised by Crichton and Scarino (2007, p. 15) as 'identifying the importance of interaction as the key principle in the development of intercultural awareness'. A theme of much of this literature is that greater cultural competence comes from active learning. Through the arts, people can learn more holistically, they have a greater chance of interacting with different nationalities and cultures, and form connections with others more easily.

Through the reviews of merits of arts-based methodology for management development and intercultural learning, we think arts-based methods have great potential to be used for improving students' cultural competence. Below are a few reasons which we identified in preparing for incorporating arts-based methods into our workshops:

1. Practicing arts can make people communicate deeply, even without speaking their own language; practising arts together can have a harmonising effects for all the participants, thus allowing them to seek common ground in their communicative process.
2. It is engaging and fun; using arts-based methods often involves physical activities (e.g. theatre practice and dancing), which make the whole process interesting and entertaining experiences.
3. It plays a crucial role of 'ice breaking' and building rapport among participants. Those skills are probably the most important skills to be acquired to deal with intercultural encounters.
4. It provides a natural setting (non-academic environment) and level playing field for home and international students to interact, thus building confidence and encouraging reflections among participants.

The process of designing the training programme is based on pilot research with students and staff at a midland university. After consultation and research, we identified some key art forms and creative processes that can respond to the dynamics of the learning context, gathered specialists from a group of artists with expertise in those art forms and undertook a collaborative design process to devise the training. The key element in the design is to identify specific aspects of the artistic process that offer metaphors for developing understanding, awareness and skills around the relevant areas. This use of process as metaphor offers powerful learning and development channels and tools, which is distinct from the use of the arts as an expressive tool in themselves.

Some examples of methods used

* Working with image to develop close and attentive observation skills (art postcards).
* Drawing on the culture and processes of theatre rehearsal to explore collaborative practice that can harness diversity (working together on the creation of an art form).
* Working with the toolkit of actors and directors to develop communication skills, relationship building and feedback (statues).
* Working with theatre games and exercises to raise awareness around the dynamics of collaboration, non-verbal communication and spontaneity and idea generation (group movement games).
* Working with story and scenario to explore identity, values, choices and consequences ('scary' stories).
* Working with artistic media to map cultural preferences on key themes such as time, prioritisation, communication and relationships (art postcards).

Research design and methods

Intervention procedure

We designed two-hour workshops in collaboration with a group of artists who have a strong track record of facilitating creative development for a range of organisations. The sessions began with warm-up exercises based on movement and communication designed to break down shyness and lack of communication within the group and to encourage the students to think outside their normal sphere of understanding and comfort. The sessions involved using art postcards to open up experiences (Observation); exploring perspectives by telling scary stories (Listening) and providing tools for new ways of connecting with other students ('I see ... this suggests to me that ... I think this because ...'). The idea here was to develop further the students' mutual understanding within groups (Communication), so that they could be more effective in understanding multiple educational, multicultural and multinational backgrounds. Each group was allocated an artist facilitator, who helped the students explore aspects of learning in an intercultural context. Students worked with actors and were also encouraged to look at pictures. Then all groups worked to produce a creative piece of work. The session ended with a sharing of work and an opportunity to reflect on the distinctive ways of working that can develop cultural competence (peer interaction). The training was diverse, including visual arts, and theatre practice and movement.

Our initial idea to design a pre- and post-training questionnaire was to assess how effective our training programme was and what were the students' reflections and thoughts on the whole training process. We eventually settled on Earley and Ang's (2003) cultural intelligence framework as it provides comprehensive measures on various aspects of cultural competence. Earley and Ang (2003) defined cultural intelligence (CQ) as an individual's capability to deal effectively in situations characterised by cultural diversity. We used a 20-item intercultural intelligence scale (CQ) (see Table 8.1) with a 7-point Likert scale plus some open-end qualitative questions to measure students' cultural competence. This questionnaire was chosen because it has measures that linked the three main theoretical concepts described at the beginning of this chapter. A pre-training survey was sent out two weeks before the session and closed two days before training took place. The post-training survey which contained the same CQ items but different open-ended questions was sent out immediately after the training and closed two weeks later.

Sample

Participants were undergraduate students at a multicultural business school in the UK. The sample was a combination of survey data in two consecutive years (2009 and 2010) due to the low response rate of a post-training sample in 2009 (only 29 completed questionnaires returned). After discarding invalid responses and cases with too many missing values, we got a pre-training sample ($n = 202$) and post-training sample ($n = 84$) for the purpose of analysis.

Data analysis

We mainly used descriptive analysis to compare the pre- and post-training outcome in a range of factors provided by the cultural intelligence scale (CQ). Table 8.1 and Table 8.2 show the comparisons of results of the 20 CQ items and aggregated scores of the four factors, respectively, before and after training.

Findings

Tables 8.1 and 8.2 present our findings. From the data shown in Table 8.1 and Table 8.2, we can clearly see that there are improvements (difference is calculated by subtracting pre-training mean from post-training mean) in almost every CQ items (19 out of 20 of them, the only exception is item 'I adjust my cultural knowledge as I interact with people from a culture that is unfamiliar to me'). Within the four factors, the items associated with cognitive, motivational and behavioural factors experienced the most significant increase.

As our data also contained the demographical information of the participants, we also produced Figures 8.1–8.3 to show the relationship between training and type of students (Home/EU students vs international students, English as first language vs English is not first language, students who speak one language vs students who speak more than one language). This links with the findings of Herzfeldt (2007) discussed earlier that those who speak more than one language or work or study abroad are more effective in intercultural groups.

Table 8.1 Means and SDs of measures at pre- and post-training

CQ	Pre-training (n = 202)		Post-training (n = 84)		Difference
	Mean	SD	Mean	SD	
Metacognitive					
I am conscious of the cultural knowledge I use when interacting with people with different cultural backgrounds (Mc1)	5.19	1.43	5.33	1.54	+ 0.14
I adjust my cultural knowledge as I interact with people from a culture that is unfamiliar to me (Mc2)	5.21	1.28	5.19	1.51	– 0.02
I am conscious of the cultural knowledge I apply to cross-cultural interactions (Mc3)	4.94	1.35	5.05	1.41	+ 0.11
I check the accuracy of my cultural knowledge as I interact with people from different cultures (Mc4)	4.85	1.53	4.92	1.47	+ 0.07
Cognitive					
I know the legal and economic systems of other cultures (Cog1)	3.64	1.45	3.99	1.51	+ 0.35
I know the rules (e.g. vocabulary, grammar) of other languages (Cog2)	3.82	1.68	4.01	1.83	+ 0.19
I know the cultural values and religious beliefs of other cultures (Cog3)	4.38	1.43	4.61	1.53	+ 0.23
I know the marriage systems of other cultures (Cog4)	3.86	1.53	4.23	1.57	+ 0.37
I know the arts and crafts of other cultures (Cog5)	3.82	1.51	4.17	1.58	+ 0.35
I know the rules for expressing non-verbal behaviours in other cultures (Cog6)	3.74	1.58	3.88	1.70	+ 0.14

(Continued)

Table 8.1 (Continued)

CQ	Pre-training (n = 202)		Post-training (n = 84)		Difference
	Mean	SD	Mean	SD	
Motivational					
I enjoy interacting with people from different cultures (Mot1)	5.63	1.43	5.68	1.69	+ 0.05
I am confident that I can socialise with locals in a culture that is unfamiliar to me (Mot2)	5.06	1.51	5.37	1.66	+ 0.31
I am sure I can deal with the stresses of adjusting to a culture that is new to me (Mot3)	5.09	1.47	5.45	1.51	+ 0.36
I enjoy living in cultures that are unfamiliar to me (Mot4)	4.73	1.58	5.06	1.52	+ 0.33
I am confident that I can get accustomed to the shopping conditions in a different culture (Mot5)	5.09	1.48	5.38	1.39	+ 0.29
Behavioural					
I change my verbal behaviour (e.g. accent, tone) when a cross-cultural interaction requires it (Beh1)	4.70	1.59	4.92	1.56	+ 0.22
I use pause and silence differently to suit different cross-cultural situations (Beh2)	4.29	1.49	4.69	1.66	+ 0.4
I vary the rate of my speaking when a cross-cultural situation requires it (Beh3)	4.81	1.43	5.00	1.52	+ 0.19
I change my non-verbal behaviour when a cross-cultural interaction requires it (Beh4)	4.61	1.59	4.87	1.5	+ 0.29
I alter my facial expressions when a cross-cultural interaction requires it (Beh5)	4.31	1.62	4.80	1.55	+ 0.49

CQ: cultural intelligence scale; SD: standard deviation.

Table 8.2 Means/SDs of measures at pre- and post-training (composite score)

Measures	Pre-training		Post-training		Difference
	M	SD	M	SD	
Metacognitive	20.2	4.75	20.5	5.14	+ 0.3
Cognitive	23.27	7.01	24.9	7.92	+ 1.63
Motivational	25.61	6.12	26.9	6.72	+ 1.29
Behavioural	22.72	6.26	24.27	6.65	+ 1.55

SD: standard deviation

Figure 8.1 shows that the international students have higher CQ scores than the UK/EU students before the training, but the training seems to have greater effect on the UK/EU students, as their CQ score improved significantly after the training. The training seems to show less impact on international students, as their score remains the same or slightly lower than the pre-training score. The same patterns also applied to the students who have English as their first language and only speak one language in Figures 8.2 and 8.3.

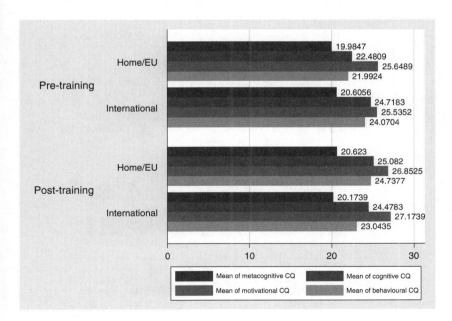

Figure 8.1 Four-factor CQ of home/EU and international students in pre- and post-training settings

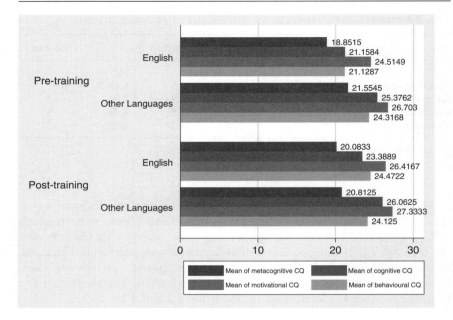

Figure 8.2 Four-factor CQ of English as first language in pre- and post-training settings

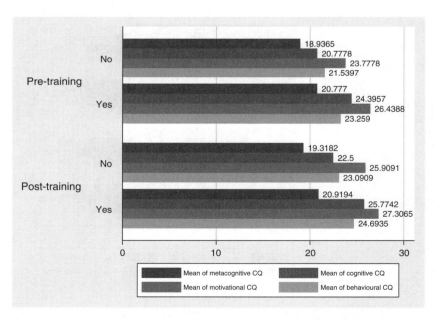

Figure 8.3 Four-factor CQ of students who speak only one language (No) or more than one (Yes) in pre- and post-training settings

The questionnaire also gave students an opportunity to make comments. Our open-ended questionnaires provide us some useful information on students' expectations before training and feedback after training. It allows us to take into account the theories of Welikala and Watkins (2008), which suggest that training must be accessible to a wide range of participants. Below are some interesting viewpoints from students regarding whether pre-training expectations and post-training evaluation of their training outcome has been met or not.

What are you expecting to get from intercultural training? Most of the students who replied were aware of the importance of cultural skills to their studies and future career, so they hope to get more information or skills through the training:

> *I hope to learn more about different cultures and ways that make it easier to interact with people from a different cultural background.*

> *I want to develop skills in interacting better when (I) am in a multi-cultural environment.*

Were expectations met? A large majority of those who replied agreed that the training exceeded expectations, although some started by saying that they had no expectations! The approach was praised variously as interesting, unexpected and fun.

> *It was quite different to my original expectations; however, it did address the issue of how different people view the same situation in a different manner.*

> *I came out with a better understanding of group work involving team members whose first language was not English.*

Several students reported that they found that they learnt something about themselves:

> *I also learnt things about myself at the training, e.g. my preferences regarding the way I think and work etc. [which] will allow me to adopt strategies that best complement my personal preferences.*

Discussion and conclusion

This chapter studies the impact of using arts-based methods to improve undergraduate students' cultural competence in a multicultural business school in the UK. Unlike traditional intercultural training approaches which emphasise country-specific knowledge and business etiquettes of different cultures, we recognised the diverse nature of our student community and design our training approach based on using arts-based methods to create an interactive learning environment for all the students.

The unique feature of our workshop is about creating a level playing learning for students to engage with each other; the art forms we use, such as visual arts and theatre practice, act as medium to facilitate the exchange among them. Although our ultimate aim is to help students to improve their cultural awareness and competence, there was no mention of cultural knowledge of any kind during the training process. Rather, we use arts practices as a 'bridge' or 'focal point' to enable students to go through a self-discovering cultural journey by interacting with other students from different backgrounds. The analysis of pre- and post-training surveys also confirms one interesting fact: this innovative method works best at the behavioural aspect of cultural competence, which is often regarded as the most difficult part of intercultural training, as traditional 'lecturing' people about country-specific cultural knowledge can do little to alter real behaviour of people in the cross-cultural encounter.

The pre- and post-training surveys reported in this chapter were carried out to gauge the change in students' cultural intelligence scales, and the results show improvements in almost every items of the four factors, with motivational and behavioural measures increased most significantly. The results also show home/ EU students, students with English as the first language and students who speak only one language gained most in terms of training effectiveness. This is generally in line with the theory we reviewed at the beginning of the chapter, which is that home students require more intercultural skills than international students due to less cultural exposure. The qualitative analysis of participating students' expectation and feedback also shows this innovative training approach has been received well by students, and many participants think the training approach is unique and it would be more effective if it is delivered at the onset of student life. The chapter contributes to a growing body of literature regarding intercultural training but also connects to an increasingly popular approach which is using arts-based methods for organisational and management development. The survey results gave strong evidence that such an approach is a promising way forward for intercultural training. Our research is the first step to evaluate the training outcome based on this new method, but some limitations remain (e.g. the research design contains no control group who undertake a different type of training, and our response rate for the post-training survey is low). However, our research is ongoing and we will incorporate considerations on those issues in our future research.

The approach taken in this research was successful because it is not context specific. The lessons learnt go beyond this module and ensure that students go away from the experience armed with something that they can use in a range of situations. The workshops encourage deep and active learning in a way which is fun and far reaching.

References

Adler, N. (2006). The arts & leadership: Now that we can do anything, what will we do? *The Academy of Management Learning and Education*, 5(4), 486–499.

Bailey, C. & Desai, D. (2005). Visual art and education: Engaged visions of history and community. *Multicultural Perspectives*, 7(1), 39–43.

Bennett, R., Aston, A. & Colquhoun, T. (2000). Cross-cultural training: A criti cal step in ensuring the success of international assignments. *Human Resource Management*, 39(2–3), 239–250.

Blasco, M. (2009). Cultural pragmatists? Student perspectives on learning culture at a business school. *The Academy of Management Learning and Education*, 8(2), 174–187.

Byram, M. (1997). *Teaching and assessing intercultural communicative competence.* Clevedon, England: Multilingual Matters Ltd.

Crichton, J. & Scarino, A. (2007). How are we to understand the'intercultural dimension'? An examination of the intercultural dimension of internationalisation in the context of higher education in Australia. *Australian Review of Applied Linguistics*, 30(1), 1–21.

Darsø, L. (2004). *Artful creation: Learning-tales of arts-in-business.* Copenhagen: Samfundslitteratur.

Earley, P. C. (2002). Redefining interactions across cultures and organizations: Moving forward with cultural intelligence. In B. M. Staw & R. M. Kramer (eds.), *Research in Organizational Behavior: Vol. 24.* Oxford: Elsevier.

Earley, P. C. & Ang, S. (2003). *Cultural intelligence: Individual interactions across cultures.* Stanford, CA: Stanford Business Books.

Earley, P. C. & Peterson, R. (2004). The elusive cultural chameleon: Cultural intelli gence as a new approach to intercultural training for the global manager. *The Academy of Management Learning and Education*, 3(1), 100–115.

Eschbach, D. M., Parker, G. E. & Stoeberl P. A. (2001). American repatriate employees retrospective assessments of the effects of cross-cultural training on their adaptation to international assignments. *The International Journal of Human Resource Management*, 12(2), 270–287.

Grisham, T. (2006). Metaphor, poetry, storytelling and cross-cultural leadership. *Management Decision*, 44(4), 486–503.

Hellmundt, S. (2003). *The internationalisation of the tertiary curriculum: Linking international communication theory with teaching and learning practices.* York: The Higher Education Academy. Available at: http://www.heacademy.ac.uk/assets/ York/documents/resources/resourcedatabase/id_The_internationalisation_ of_the_tertiary_curriculum.RTF (accessed 1 March 2011).

Herzfeldt, R. (2007). Cultural competence of first-year undergraduates. In H. E. Higson (ed.), *Good practice guide in learning and teaching,* Vol. 4. Birmingham: Aston University, pp. 23–29.

Ippolito, K. (2007). Promoting intercultural learning in a multicultural university: Ideals and realities. *Teaching in Higher Education*, 12(5–6), 749–763.

Kember, D. & Gow, L. (1991). A challenge to the anecdotal stereotype of the Asian student. *Studies in Higher Education*, 16(2), 117–128.

Kolb, D. A. (1984). *Experiential learning: Experience as the source of learning and development.* Englewood Cliffs, NJ: Prentice-Hall.

Liddicoat, A. J. & Diaz, A. (2008). Engaging with diversity: The construction of policy for intercultural education in Italy. *Intercultural Education*, *19*(2), 137–150.

Linstead, S. (2006). Exploring culture with The Radio Ballads: Using aesthetics to facilitate change. *Management Decision*, *44*(4), 474–485.

Littrell, L. N. & Salas, E. (2005). A review of cross-cultural training: Best practices, guidelines, and research needs. *Human Resource Development Review*, *4*(3), 305–334.

Nissley, N. (2004). The 'artful creation' of positive anticipatory imagery in appreciative inquiry: understanding the 'art of' appreciative inquiry as aesthetic discourse. *Constructive Discourse and Human Organization: Advances in Appreciative Inquiry*, *1*, 283–307.

Scollon, R. & Scollon, S. W. (1995). *Intercultural communication: A discourse approach*. Oxford: Blackwell.

Szkudlarek, B. (2009). Through Western eyes: Insights into the intercultural training field. *Organization Studies*, *30*(9), 975–986.

Taylor, S. S. (2008). Theatrical performance as unfreezing. *Journal of Management Inquiry*, *17*(4), 398–406.

Taylor, S. S. & Ladkin, D. (2009). Understanding arts-based methods in managerial development. *The Academy of Management Learning and Education*, *8*(1), 55–69.

Taylor, S. S., Fisher, D. & Dufresne, R. L. (2002). The aesthetics of management storytelling: A key to organisational learning. *Management Learning*, *33*(3), 313–330.

Van Oudenhoven, J. P. & Van der Zee, K. I. (2002). Predicting multicultural effectiveness of international students: The multicultural personality questionnaire. *International Journal of Intercultural Relations*, *26*(6), 679–694.

Waistell, J. (2009). Building a future in a global world: Managing individual and communal knowledge at university and work. In *Proceedings of the Centre for International Curriculum Inquiry & Networking Conference*. Oxford: CICIN.

Ward, C. (2001). *The impact of international students on domestic students and host institutions: A literature review*. Export Education Policy Project, New Zealand Ministry of Education. Available at: http://www.educationcounts.govt.nz/publications/international/the_impact_of_international_students_on_domestic_students_and_host_institutions (accessed 3 August 2010).

Welikala, T. & Watkins, C. (2008). *Improving intercultural learning experiences in higher education: Responding to cultural scripts for learning*. London: Institute of Education, University of London.

Wesley, S. (2007). Multicultural diversity: Learning through the arts. *New Directions for Adult and Continuing Education*, *116*, 13–23.

Wolf, K., Milburn, T. & Wilkins, R. (2008). Expressive practices: The local enactment of culture in the communication classroom. *Business Communication Quarterly*, *71*(2), 171–183.

Yamazaki, Y. & Kayes, D. C. (2004). An experiential approach to cross-cultural learning: A review and integration of competencies for successful expatriate adaptation. *The Academy of Management Learning and Education*, *3*(4), 362–379.

Chapter 9

Towards the global citizen

Utilising a competency framework to promote intercultural knowledge and skills in higher education students

Stuart Reid and Helen Spencer-Oatey

Introduction

The aspiration to provide an international experience for undergraduates in the UK higher education institutions has been defined in different ways and has been implemented to radically varying degrees in different institutions. There is no single or simple answer to how one achieves the goal of developing students with a global perspective or the qualities of a global citizen. Conventional approaches have been highly reliant on strategies such as international exchange and study abroad programmes. However, it cannot be assumed that such programmes automatically enhance the participants' intercultural effectiveness. Indeed, some studies have shown contrary impacts on students' perceptions and behaviour (Bennett, 1993; De Nooy & Hanna, 2003; Greenholtz, 2003). There is a danger that initiatives under the general banner of 'internationalisation' introduce curriculum content, exchange schemes or extra-curricular activities that are assumed to promote greater intercultural awareness without any proven link between the aspiration and the outcome.

In our view, this is due, in part, to the conceptual gap that currently exists between, on the one hand, strategic aspirations and, on the other, activities at grass-roots level. In this chapter, we argue for an approach that involves grounding any activities in a well-defined framework of personal and professional competencies. By identifying the competencies that support effective intercultural behaviour it is possible to define the broader aspiration to internationalise in terms of specific competencies and, in turn, demonstrate how those competencies will contribute to the development of more capable (and employable) students. However, we believe the work presented here goes beyond much of what currently exists in terms of competency-based approaches to developing student skills or capability. We not only describe a specific and research-based framework of intercultural competencies but also demonstrate how this might be used as part of a targeted and supported learning process for undergraduates.

The core of the chapter provides an overview of the framework of competencies developed by the Global People team in the Centre for Applied Linguistics at the University of Warwick (www.globalpeople.org.uk). The framework is grounded in empirical research from both the academic and commercial sectors. The stimulus for this chapter was the authors' involvement in a joint research project between the University of Warwick and King's College, London aimed at identifying ways in which undergraduates at research-led universities would 'experience a truly distinctive education' (http://kingslearning.info/kwp). The authors undertook comparative and primary research as part of the project strand focused on increasing the 'global connectedness' of the student experience (King's–Warwick Project, 2010; Reid, 2010; Reid et al., 2010).

In this approach, competencies specific to working and communicating in an intercultural context may be targeted through the introduction of new activities or through the provision of specialist support elements to existing activities. To be most effective, intercultural activity also needs to be located in a context of experiential learning where the participants are properly prepared and where they have the opportunity to reflect on their experiences and consciously develop new knowledge and skills. Students can thereby develop a greater awareness of their actual and potential competencies and extract more value from the intercultural experiences that they encounter.

This chapter is divided into four main sections. Sections 1 and 2 provide a brief summary of how our work relates to the broader debate on internationalisation and on the use of competencies within internationalisation strategies, respectively.[1] Section 3 then describes the specific approach taken by the Global People team and presents some of the competency material developed for use at the University of Warwick. Finally, Section 4 outlines actual and potential applications of this approach to developing strategies for internationalisation through the development of student capability and employability.

Internationalisation strategies and their limitations

Internationalisation and globalisation have become buzzwords in the higher education sector and internationalisation has become a priority at the highest strategic level at most institutions (Knight, 2003; Middlehurst & Woodfield, 2007; Toyoshima, 2007).

> *Changes in government policies and the social and economic context within which universities operate have resulted in increasing pressure for them to... internationalise their curricula*

> (Leask, 2000, p. 1).

However, according to the most extensive review of the internationalisation literature (Caruana & Spurling, 2007), this policy arena is fraught with mixed messages, potential contradictions and inconsistencies. Aims are often unclear, interpreted in numerous different ways and there is a clear gap between the announcement of ambitious schemes and actual change in education practice. As a consequence, the internationalisation of the curriculum is often more rhetoric than reality. Bourn, McKenzie and Shiel (2006, p. 38) also stress that current practice reveals a lack of initiative, stating that 'a historical review of policy initiatives...reveals a history of emphasising the criticality of the issues, followed by periods of complete inaction, particularly on the part of Higher Education'. It seems evident from the literature that many institutions have lacked a clear direction in the implementation of meaningful and sustainable policies. Meanwhile, a vigorous debate has developed within the academic community on both the meaning and the implementation of internationalisation strategies (Jones, 2010; Jones & Brown, 2007).

The presence of international students is often seen as a key to internationalisation (as well as having obvious commercial benefits), but the actions taken to accommodate and integrate those students are often inadequate or inappropriate. The UK higher education institutions compete fiercely for fee-paying overseas students without always guaranteeing a proper infrastructure to support those students or to integrate them into the local student culture in a way that is beneficial to them as well as to local students. Also, there may not be a clear strategy for reviewing the pedagogical approaches that are taken to instruct those students. What appears to be required are concrete activities that meet the needs of both home and international students, enabling the latter to function better in the UK context and the former to develop the intercultural understanding necessary to interact with overseas students in the UK as well as to prepare to work in an intercultural setting for overseas sojourns or future employment. Indeed, an ideal strategy would find ways of optimising the co-learning between all students from different cultural backgrounds.

The competency approach in internationalisation

The competency approach constitutes a pragmatic response to the need for internationalisation, emphasising the development of intercultural practices, knowledge, skills, values and attitudes. The focus has been on adding value both to the student experience and to the employability of graduates leaving the UK higher education institutions. In this respect, it is closely aligned with other strategies designed to improve graduate capability such as personal development plans and the building of transferable skills (Leggott & Stapleford, 2007).

Employing a competency-based approach has been presented by a number of writers as the most meaningful step towards internationalisation, especially with regard to integrating internationalisation at home into the curriculum (Bourn, n.d.; Caruana & Hanstock, 2003; Caruana & Spurling, 2007; Leask, 2000; Tan, 2008). It is seen as offering a more profound strategy as it focuses on embedding intercultural knowledge and skills rather than focusing on more superficial measures such as student mobility or international recruitment. A number of pioneering schemes at the UK universities have identified appropriate sets of competencies which would contribute towards intercultural 'capability' in students and have addressed the challenge of integrating these into the student experience (Caruana, 2010; Killick, 2007). Nevertheless, there remains a lack of clarity about what actually constitutes a 'global citizen' (Bourn, 2010) and a perception that there is still relatively little concrete evidence of how intercultural competencies might be identified, acquired and recognised in the practice of student experience.

There is a natural fit between the concerns of those in higher education institutions and the wider study of intercultural interaction on which our Global People work draws. A well-established strand of literature exists referring to the personal competencies, skills or personality traits relevant to effective communication across cultures.[2] Although this work comprises contributions from a range of academic disciplines (e.g. Applied Linguistics, Business Management and Psychology), all contributions tend to focus on what an individual should ideally know before embarking on intercultural collaboration and on what personal competencies an individual should possess in order to perform effectively. Typically, these competencies are divided into categories such as awareness (Barham & Devine, 1991; Bennett, 1993; Fantini, 2000); attitudes and emotions (Hammer, Gudykunst & Wiseman, 1978); communication skills (Berger, 1998; Schneider & Barsoux, 1997; Ting-Toomey, 1999); cultural knowledge (Byram, 1997; Gudykunst, 2004; Motteram et al., 2007) and language proficiency (Ewington, Lowe & Trickey 2007; Fantini, 2000; Smith, 2001).

The work of the Global People team extends the competency literature in relation both to the identification of intercultural competencies and to its application in the development of graduate capability. The aim has been to take the best insights from intercultural research and – refined by original research – to generate a set of clearly defined intercultural competencies that are sufficiently generic to be applied to a range of personal and professional development contexts. With regard to developing graduate capability, this full set of competencies can be tailored (through selection and contextualisation) to produce frameworks within which productive student development can take place.

The Global People competency framework

Bridging the gap between aspiration and grass-roots activity

The key to developing intercultural awareness and effectiveness among undergraduates is to be able to understand what this means in terms of actual behaviour. With this understanding, it might be possible to practise, support and develop those behaviours through the curriculum, where curriculum is understood in its widest sense to include the overall learning experience of the undergraduate while at university. The Global People competency framework identifies key competencies shown to be of value in underpinning intercultural performance and links these to activities that would exercise and develop those competencies within a process of supported learning. The intention is to provide a coherent vision of student development that links the aspiration (creating graduate capability), the personal goals (intercultural competencies), the means of achieving those goals (learning activities within the student experience) and the evidence of capability.

A research-based set of generic competencies

The set of competencies generated for the King's–Warwick Project was based on a much larger set of competencies developed for the Global People project (Spencer-Oatey & Stadler, 2009; www.globalpeople.org.uk). That full set of intercultural competencies was developed from earlier research, notably the eChina–UK Programme (www.eChinauk.org; Spencer-Oatey, 2007) and by the competency set created by WorldWork Ltd. (WorldWork, n.d.) as a tool for the training and development of international managers. As such, the constituent elements in the competency framework have emerged out of both academic research and commercial practice; they have common elements with other classifications of intercultural competencies but have the advantage of being grounded in real-life experience.

The competency framework developed for the King's–Warwick 'Graduate Pledge' project is set out in full in Table 9.1.[3] The aim was to produce a set of competencies which would be manageable in number and able to be tailored for local activities, had observable behaviours and could be related to recognisable stages in the undergraduate career.

The framework was circulated to colleagues at Warwick and at King's College, London for comments and then used as the basis for discussion with key stakeholders at Warwick when identifying potential areas for intervention.

The framework as it is set out here is basically a matrix setting selected intercultural competencies (Column 1) against three basic stages (or experiential contexts) in the undergraduate journey (Columns 2, 3 and 4). The competencies selected and adapted from the larger Global People competency framework are the 10 which the project team regarded as being the most appropriate and meaningful for undergraduates participating in any intercultural interaction. Some of these are primarily about knowledge and skills (information gathering; language learning; attentive listening); others are focused on the art of building relationships (flexible behaviour; rapport building) and others emphasise the development of personal qualities (spirit of adventure; self-awareness).

The three 'stages' (transition; participation; employability) represent critical situations in which intercultural competencies might be of particular value and might be effectively developed. They are not intended to be strictly chronological but could be used this way: for example, as part of a student personal development programme. Their main function is to provide a more accessible framework for thinking about building intercultural competencies by encouraging users

Table 9.1 Intercultural competency framework for the King's–Warwick 'Graduate Pledge' project

	CRITICAL SITUATIONS IN WHICH INTERCULTURAL COMPETENCIES MIGHT BE NEEDED		
Value	Transition	Participation	Employability
Relevance for...	Sojourns in another country: ✓ Preparing ✓ Entering & coping ✓ Returning	Integration in an academic community: ✓ Collaborating in multicultural learning groups ✓ Sharing social & leisure activities with peers ✓ Managing administrative transactions	Future employment: ✓ Preparing CV ✓ Interacting with careers advisors ✓ Job seeking ✓ Undertaking interviews
Of benefit to...	• International students and staff entering Warwick • Warwick students and staff preparing for periods of time abroad for one term or longer • International staff and students interacting with service providers and support staff	• Students participating in mixed ethnicity classes and group work • Teachers working with students of mixed ethnicity • Staff engaging in international collaborations • Students engaging with diversity in local communities	• Students wanting to enhance their employability by demonstrating intercultural awareness • Students preparing for jobs that require any form of interaction with people from other cultures

	DEVELOPMENT & USE OF THE COMPETENCIES IN EACH CRITICAL SITUATION		
Competencies	Transition	Participation	Employability
Information gathering	• Identify sources of cultural data	• Learn about unfamiliar cultures, using a range of strategies to gather relevant information	• Able to show evidence of independent research activity to gather information for practical and academic purposes

Flexible thinking	• Foster a sense of curiosity • Be open to new ideas • Be willing to challenge stereotypes & modify assumptions	• Actively seek to understand unfamiliar behaviour • Avoid judging people from other cultures on the basis of stereotypes • Acknowledge that different practices are sensible and meaningful in their cultural context and can add value to your own way of thinking	• Able to show evidence of drawing on diverse thinking and actively modifying assumptions in the face of unfamiliar thinking and behaviour
Flexible behaviour	• Be prepared to adjust your behaviour when sharing facilities • Flex your behaviour not to offend • Be ready to adopt the behaviour of locals, and experiment with different ways of behaving	• Learn how and when to adapt by observing other people's behaviour • Build a repertoire of behaviour to suit different purposes, contexts and audiences	• Able to show evidence of increased effectiveness through adaptive behaviour
Rapport building	• Initiate contact and show interest in people from unfamiliar cultures • Develop connections with locals on a personal level	• Exhibit warmth & friendliness • Maintain and extend working relationships • Be willing to focus on long-term trust-building	• Able to show evidence of establishing sustainable relationships across cultures
Language learning	• Invest in learning words and phrases in other languages • Try out expressions and words when communicating with locals • Practise your language skills with native speakers	• Do not rely on the others' language skills • Do not feel too self-conscious about your language proficiency • Do not let your language proficiency hold you back from contributing	• Able to show evidence of acquisition and use of (new) language skills for performance
Making yourself understood	• Adapt use of language to the proficiency level of the recipient(s) to maximise comprehensibility • Explain clearly to local people what you need and why you need it	• Actively clarify your own contribution • Be prepared to share the thought process behind your intentions • Adjust speed, complexity and selection of language to suit needs of interlocutor	• Able to show evidence of successful modification of communication to achieve understanding in a challenging context

Table 9.1 (Continued)

DEVELOPMENT & USE OF THE COMPETENCIES IN EACH CRITICAL SITUATION

Competencies	Transition	Participation	Employability
Attentive listening	• Listen actively to what the other is trying to say • Double-check that you have understood what local people want you to do • Pay attention to non-verbal signals	• Check and clarify rather than assuming understanding • Pay close attention to how people from other cultures differ in their body language • Develop ability to anticipate and handle potential misunderstanding	• Able to show evidence of active listening and to provide examples of successful and more challenging interactions
Self-awareness	• Recognise that others may see you and treat you as a foreigner • Be aware of how you come across to others	• Use diversity as a mirror to explore your own cultural identity • Observe how your style impacts on group dynamics • Reflect on how you may be perceived by people from other backgrounds when you are behaving 'normally'	• Able to show evidence of what you have learnt about yourself from working internationally
Personal strength	• Develop strategies to cope with difficult situations and the stress that comes with living in a foreign environment • Remember the benefits and opportunities for personal growth that come with overcoming adversity	• Remain positive even when you encounter problems or failure • Retain a sense of inner purpose – try to be flexible, but 'stand your ground' when it is necessary • Adhere to your values and provide a sense of direction for yourself and others	• Able to show evidence of resilience in adversity • Able to maintain a balance between flexibility and personal values
Spirit of adventure	• Develop a positive attitude to new experiences • Be adventurous and try something new on a regular basis	• Be ready to deal with ambiguous situations • Develop tolerance of ambiguity • Enjoy the opportunity to work in diverse groups with different perspectives	• Able to show evidence of successful risk-taking in uncertain, unpredictable or challenging situations

to focus attention on the most important challenges in any given context. These contexts are given more definition in the first two rows of the table, which suggest the value of the competency: both its relevance to a particular situation ('Relevance for…') and the potential benefits of exercising that competency ('Of benefit to…').

Each cell of the table then provides a short list of behaviours which exemplify the exercise of the given competency in the particular context. To demonstrate the use of the framework in a simple way, look at the cell that has been highlighted in Table 9.1. It is in Column 2, representing Participation, a context where intercultural competencies will be useful to support 'Integration in an academic community'. This would be of benefit to a number of constituencies, including 'students participating in mixed ethnicity classes and work groups'. The highlighted competency is that of Flexible Thinking and the observable behaviours suggested in the cell are:

- Actively seek to understand unfamiliar behaviour.
- Avoid judging people from other cultures on the basis of stereotypes.
- Acknowledge that different practices are sensible and meaningful in their cultural context and can add value to your own way of thinking.

The level of detail here is intended to encourage staff, students and facilitators to use the competency framework as a means of informing and supporting intercultural challenges in the normal activity of student life. The table's contents provide guidance to the appropriate context, the potential benefit and the proposed behaviour. The framework thus aims to provide not only a prompt to the user but also a means of monitoring observed behaviour.

The role of active learning

Central to the utilisation of a competency framework is the integration of a process of active learning for the participants in any intercultural activity. This has been acknowledged by many of the contributions to the debate on graduate capability, especially in relation to the role of reflection on experience as a means of facilitating self-awareness (Jones & Killick, 2007). The concept of reflection is at the heart of modern theories of learning (Argyris & Schön, 1974; Greenwood, 1998; Kolb, 1984; Mezirow, 1991; Schön, 1983; Wallace, 1991) and has become a core element in contemporary teaching and learning processes such as action learning (Revans, 1998) and problem-based learning (Boud & Feletti, 1998; Ratiu, 1983; Savin-Baden & Major, 2004). The application of the Global People Competency Framework assumes the provision of support to participants that enables them actively to reflect on their own intercultural experience and to identify their competency needs.

In practical terms, this kind of reflection, either individually or in group discussion, may focus on a case, a practical problem or an incident; valuable learning may be produced from a consideration of 'failures' or mistakes as usefully as from obvious successes (Hunfeld, 1997). Belz and Muller-Hartmann (2003) employ the term 'rich points' to describe 'instances of communicative behaviour' where participants from one culture do not understand, or misunderstand, the members of another culture (Belz & Muller-Hartmann, 2003, p. 73). A similar practice is used in educational programmes and in inter-professional learning where learners are encouraged to select 'critical incidents' – elements of practical experience where perceived success or failure can be analysed in order to extract useful learning (Ayas & Keniuk, 2004; Barr, 2002; Poell Tijmesen & van der Krogt, 1997; Reid, 2007; Wallace, 1991). Within the literature on internationalisation, a number of similar examples already exist where structured reflective practices have been employed to encourage student learning from international experience (Russell & Vallade, 2010).

Originality of the Global People approach

What is distinctive – and especially practical – about the Global People approach is, first, the explicit linking of *competencies* to *behaviours* and then to *opportunities for intervention*. That linking is frequently absent from other competency-based approaches which do not go far enough beyond the aspirational level. The Global People framework is grounded in research and practical application and offers a guide to how these desired competencies can actually be observed and acquired. Second, this model explicitly locates the acquisition and practice of intercultural competencies within a *process of learning*; the student's acquisition of competencies is supported and facilitated by attention to their learning process and to a conscious reflection on experience. Again, the value of integrated learning has been frequently acknowledged but less frequently linked to an identified set of competencies and activities.

There is, in other words, a specific emphasis in the current work on both the context of competency acquisition and its active facilitation. The participants – and those supporting them – can identify, structure and support the process of identifying, acquiring and refining intercultural competencies. Furthermore, they can do this through explicitly identifying behaviours that enact (and thus offer evidence of) that learning process. This, we believe, deepens the competency approach to developing students' intercultural knowledge and practice while offering a generic model that can be tailored to the needs of specific contexts.

Application of the framework in the internationalisation process

Using the competency framework presented above, the Global People project team worked with colleagues across the Warwick campus to identify opportunities to use the framework to improve the intercultural awareness and competence of students and staff. As the remit and resources of this phase of the King's–Warwick 'Graduate Pledge' project extended only to conducting a feasibility study, the aim of the team was to identify a number of areas where potential for the use of the competency framework could be agreed with colleagues. In practice, one opportunity led to immediate implementation and two further opportunities for intervention were identified and have been developed. These were as follows.

Undergraduate personal development

In collaboration with the Student Careers and Skills Centre, the project team produced a (further) tailored version of the competency framework aimed at students keen to develop their intercultural performance and to have this achievement recognised. The modified framework has been used in the creation of a new award for Warwick undergraduates – the Warwick Global Advantage Award – available through the University intranet (www.warwicksu.com/globaladvantage). Competencies from the Centre for Applied Linguistics model constitute the criteria against which achievement is to be judged. The award was launched by the Careers Centre in February 2010, was sponsored by Deloittes and immediately attracted considerable student interest. The essence of the Global Advantage Award process is its stimulus to students to reflect on past and current intercultural experience and to record their learning from that experience, using the competency framework. It also supports them in using the framework to prepare for new intercultural experience. This process then becomes forward-looking as participants are encouraged to recognise – and record – the enhanced knowledge and skills they have acquired as a contribution to their personal development and employability.

Support for study abroad schemes

Material from the Global People Resource Bank (www.globalpeople.org.uk) is already being made available by the University of Warwick International Office (IO) both to overseas students taking foundation courses prior to the UK study and to current undergraduates preparing for study abroad. IO staff see further potential for using competency-based material both in preparing students for participation in the Erasmus programme and in producing questionnaire surveys for incoming international students. They have recently initiated a project with the Centre for Applied Linguistics to develop just such support materials. These materials should be available to the sector as a whole by 2013.

The Global People competency framework is also being used by staff in the Centre for Applied Linguistics, in collaboration with the British Council in Japan, to develop a suite of online resources for university students wanting to improve their intercultural skills for the global workplace. The materials, entitled *TIES for Work (Training in Intercultural Effectiveness for Work)* are being piloted in the autumn of 2011 and will be available to the sector in late 2012.

Contribution to the international curriculum

The project team, in consultation with the Warwick Business School, has targeted an undergraduate module in International Business where the competency framework could be used to extend the current teaching of intercultural awareness. At present, the approach is limited to exploring the cultural challenges in particular countries; the proposal is that the competency framework is used as a teaching tool to introduce the concept of generic intercultural competencies that can enhance business performance in all situations of cultural diversity.

Conclusion: Building the global citizen

In terms of higher education internationalisation, the competency-based approach can be employed in a number of different settings. For example, it can be used as a personal development tool by students wishing to develop their global competencies and build their employability profile. More specifically, it can be used to prepare students for international visits or to 'debrief' them on their return, and it can be used with incoming international students to help them identify competencies that will help them to manage cultural transition. By working with this framework – or with selected competencies drawn from it – individuals can develop greater self-awareness and can thus build some of the attitudes and skills needed to work more effectively in any intercultural situation. This, in turn, enhances the employability of the student on graduation. The competencies are regarded as generic but the selection of prioritised competencies will be driven by the specific needs of the student group in question.

The limitations of the Global People competency framework relate primarily to the extent of its empirical testing within a specifically undergraduate environment. Although the concepts and definitions have been utilised within commercial and academic environments, the activities at the University of Warwick described in Section 4 constitute the first trialling of the model with students at a higher education institution. Our intention, at this stage, has been to contribute to the debate on internationalisation and student capability by presenting what we believe constitutes a coherent framework for addressing the challenges of developing our students as global citizens.

Notes

1 This chapter is not intended to be a literature review but a summary presentation of recent work within the context of other research in this field. A fuller discussion of the internationalisation literature can be found in Reid et al. (2010). A detailed literature review is available in Caruana and Spurling (2007); a recent overview can be found in De Vita (2007).
2 For a review of this literature, see Reid, Stadler and Spencer-Oatey (2009, pp. 38–45).
3 The authors gratefully acknowledge the funding provided by the Higher Education Funding Council for England, both for the King's–Warwick Project, within which

this specific work was carried out, and for the eChina–UK Programme, which constituted the basis of the current Global People Resource Bank.

References

Argyris, C. & Schön, D. A. (1974). *Theory in practice: Increasing professional effectiveness*. San Francisco, CA: Jossey-Bass.

Ayas, K. & Keniuk, N. (2004) Project-based learning: Building communities of reflective practitioners. In C. Grey & E. Antonacopoulou (eds.), *Essential readings in management learning*. London: Sage.

Barham, K. & Devine, M. (1991). *The quest for the international manager: A survey of global human resource strategies. Special Report No. 2098*. London: Ashridge Management Research Group/Economist Intelligence Unit.

Barr, H. (2002). *Interprofessional education: Yesterday, today and tomorrow*. London: UK Centre for Advancement of Interprofessional Education, University of Westminster.

Belz, J. & Muller-Hartmann, A. (2003). Teachers as intercultural learners: Negotiating German–American telecollaboration along the institutional fault line. *The Modern Language Journal, 87*(i), 71–89.

Bennett, M. J. (1993). Towards ethnorelativism: A developmental model of intercultural sensitivity. In M. Paige (ed.), *Education for the intercultural experience*. Yarmouth, ME: Intercultural Press.

Berger, M. (1998). Going global: Implications for communication and leadership training. *Industrial and Commercial Training, 30*(4), 123–127.

Boud, D. & Feletti, G. I. (1998). *The challenge of problem-based learning*. London: Kogan Page.

Bourn, D. (2010). Students as global citizens. In E. Jones (ed.), *Internationalisation and the student voice: Higher education perspectives*. London: Routledge.

Bourn, D. (n.d.). *Global perspectives in higher education: The contribution of development education*. Unpublished paper.

Bourn, D., McKenzie, A. & Shiel, C. (2006). *The global university: The role of the curriculum*. London: Development Education Association. Available at: http://www.dea.org.uk (accessed 2 September 2009).

Byram, M. (1997). *Teaching and assessing intercultural communicative competence*. Clevedon, England: Multilingual Matters Ltd.

Caruana, V. (2010). The relevance of the internationalised curriculum to graduate capability. In E. Jones (ed.), *Internationalisation and the student voice: Higher education perspectives*. London: Routledge.

Caruana, V. & Hanstock, J. (2003). Internationalising the curriculum: From policy to practice. In *Proceedings of the Inaugural Learning and Teaching Research 'Education in a Changing Environment' conference*, 17–18 September 2003, University of Salford.

Caruana, V. & Spurling, C. (2007). *The internationalisation of UK higher education: A review of selected material*. York: Higher Education Academy. Available at: http://www.heacademy.ac.uk/assets/documents/tla/internationalisation/lit_review_internationalisation_of_uk_he_v2.pdf (accessed 2 September 2009).

De Nooy, J. & Hanna, B. E. (2003). Cultural information gathering by Australian students in France. *Language and Intercultural Communication*, *3*(1), 64–80.

De Vita, G. (2007). Taking stock: An appraisal of the literature on internationalising HE learning. In E. Jones (ed.), *Internationalisation and the student voice: Higher education perspectives*. London: Routledge.

Ewington, N., Lowe, R. & Trickey, D. (2007). Being international: What do international managers and professionals really think is important – and do the experts agree? WorldWork. Available at: http://www.tco-international.com/download. aspx?FileUid=%7B5d498af0-4b66-4b20-a6b4-9111b9d854d0%7D   (accessed 20 March 2008).

Fantini, A. E. (2000). A central concern: Developing intercultural competence. *World Learning*, *1*, 25–42.

Greenholtz, J. (2003). Socratic teachers and Confucian learners: Examining the benefits and pitfalls of a year abroad. *Language and Intercultural Communication*, *3*(2), 122–130.

Greenwood, J. (1998). The role of reflection in single and double loop learning. *Journal of Advanced Nursing*, *27*, 1048–1053.

Gudykunst, W. B. (2004). *Bridging differences: Effective intergroup communication* (4th edn). Thousand Oaks, CA: Sage.

Hammer, M. R., Gudykunst, W. B. & Wiseman, R. L. (1978). Dimensions of intercultural effectiveness: An exploratory study. *International Journal of Intercultural Relations*, *2*, 382–392.

Hunfeld, H. (1997). *Principles of intercultural learning – for better knowledge of the LIFE concept*. BMW Group Corporate Communications. Available at: http:// www.bmwgroup.com/e/nav/index.html?http://www.bmwgroup.com/e/0_0_ www_bmwgroup_com/verantwortung/gesellschaft/lifeaward/lifeaward2011. shtml (accessed 12 September 2011).

Jones, E. (ed.) (2010). *Internationalisation and the student voice: Higher education perspectives*. London: Routledge.

Jones, E. & Brown, S. (eds.) (2007). *Internationalising higher education*. London: Routledge.

Jones, E. & Killick, D. (2007). Internationalisation of the curriculum. In E. Jones & S. Brown (eds.), *Internationalising higher education*. London: Routledge.

Killick, D. (2007). World-wide horizons: Cross-cultural capability and global perspectives – guidelines for curriculum review. In E. Jones & S. Brown (eds.), *Internationalising higher education*. London: Routledge.

King's–Warwick Project. (2010). *Creating a 21st century curriculum: The King's–Warwick project*. Available at: http://kingslearning.info/kwp/attachments/134_ KWP-Creating_a_21st_Century_Curriculum_Final_Report.pdf.pdf (accessed 31 August 2011).

Knight, J. (2003). *Internationalisation of higher education practices and priorities: 2003 IAU survey report*. Paris, France: International Association of Universities.

Kolb, D. A. (1984). *Experiential learning: Experience as the source of learning and development*. Englewood Cliffs, NJ: Prentice Hall.

Leask, B. (2000). Internationalisation: Changing contexts and their implications for teaching, learning and assessment. In L. Richardson & J. Lidstone (eds.), *Flexible learning for a flexible society. Proceedings of ASET–HERDSA 2000 Conference*, Toowoomba, Queensland, 2–5 July 2000. ASET and HERDSA.

Leggott, D. & Stapleford, J. (2007). Internationalisation and employability. In E. Jones, & S. Brown (eds.), *Internationalising higher education*. London: Routledge.

Mezirow, J. (1991). *Transformative dimensions of adult learning*. San Francisco, CA: Jossey-Bass.

Middlehurst, R. & Woodfield, S. (2007). *Responding to the internationalisation agenda: Implications for institutional strategy*. Higher Education Academy Research Report 05/06. York: Higher Education Academy.

Motteram, G., Forrester, G., Goldrick, S. & McLachlan, A. (2007). Collaborating across boundaries: Managing the complexities of e-learning courseware production in a joint international project. In H. Spencer-Oatey (ed.), *e-learning initiatives in China: Pedagogy, policy and culture*. Hong Kong: Hong Kong University Press.

Poell, R., Tijmesen, L. & van der Krogt, F. (1997). Can learning projects help to develop a learning organisation? *Lifelong Learning in Europe, 2*, 67–75.

Ratiu, I. (1983). Thinking internationally: A comparison of how international executives learn. *International Studies of Management and Organization, 13*, 139–150.

Reid, S. (2007). Learning partnerships for partnership learning: A case study of the postgraduate certificate in cross-sector partnership. In *Proceedings of the 37th Annual Conference of the Standing Conference on University Teaching and Research in the Education of Adults*. Belfast: Queen's University.

Reid, S. (2010). *The impact of intercultural experience: A survey of undergraduates at the University of Warwick*. Warwick: The Centre for Applied Linguistics, University of Warwick. Available at: www.globalpeople.org.uk (accessed 31 August 2011).

Reid, S., Stadler, S. & Spencer-Oatey, H. (2009). *The Global People landscaping study: Intercultural effectiveness in global education partnerships. Warwick occasional papers in applied linguistics #1*. Warwick: The Centre for Applied Linguistics, University of Warwick.

Reid, S., Stadler, S., Spencer-Oatey, H. & Ewington, N. (2010). Internationalisation in the UK higher education sector: A competency-based approach. *Warwick occasional papers in applied linguistics #7*. Warwick: The Centre for Applied Linguistics, University of Warwick. Available at: www.globalpeople.org.uk (accessed 31 August 2011).

Revans, R. (1998). *The A.B.C. of action learning* (new edn). London: Lemos and Crane.

Russell, M. & Vallade, L. (2010). Guided reflective journalling: Assessing the international study and volunteering experience. In E. Jones (ed.), *Internationalisation and the student voice: Higher education perspectives*. London: Routledge.

Savin-Baden, M. & Major, C. H. (2004). *Foundations of problem-based learning*. Milton Keynes: Open University Press.

Schneider, S. C. & Barsoux, J. L. (1997). *Managing across cultures*. Englewood Cliffs, NJ: Prentice Hall.

Schön, D. A. (1983). *The reflective practitioner: How professionals think in action*. Aldershot: Gower.

Smith, P. G. (2001). Communication holds global teams together. *Machine Design*, 70–74. Available at: http://www.europa.com/~preston/MD3-00/MD7-01.pdf (accessed 3 April 2008).

Spencer-Oatey, H. (ed.) (2007). *e-Learning initiatives in China: Pedagogy, policy and culture*. Hong Kong: Hong Kong University Press.

Spencer-Oatey, H. & Stadler, S. (2009). *The Global People competency framework: Competencies for effective intercultural interaction. Warwick occasional papers in Applied Linguistics #3*. Warwick: The Centre for Applied Linguistics, University of Warwick. Available at: www.globalpeople.org.uk (accessed 31 August 2008).

Tan, P. L. (2008). *Working paper on internationalization at King's College London*. London: The Learning Institute, King's College. Unpublished paper.

Ting-Toomey, S. (1999). *Communicating across cultures*. New York: The Guilford Press.

Toyoshima, M. (2007) International strategies of universities in England. *London Review of Education*, 5(3), 265–280.

Wallace, M. (1991). *Training foreign language teachers: A reflective approach*. Cambridge: Cambridge University Press.

WorldWork (n.d.). Available at: http://www.worldwork.biz/legacy/www/downloads/Sources.pdf (accessed 1 April 2008).

Chapter 10

Exploring stakeholder perspectives regarding a 'global' curriculum

A case study

Sharon Slade, Fenella Galpin and Paul Prinsloo

Introduction

Since the Bologna Declaration of 19 June 1999, the internationalisation of higher education has been embedded in the broader discourses on global citizenship, the competencies of graduates, curriculum development and pedagogy. The Policy Brief (2004) of the Organisation for Economic Cooperation and Development (OECD) clearly states that:

> *Higher education has become increasingly international in the past decade as more and more students choose to study abroad, enrol in foreign educational programmes and institutions in their home country, or simply use the Internet to take courses at colleges or universities in other countries.*
>
> (OECD, 2004, p. 1)

It also states that the 'four leading English-speaking countries alone (the United States, the United Kingdom, Australia and Canada) account for more than half (54 per cent) of all foreign students in the OECD area' (OECD, 2004, p. 2).

Various authors (e.g. Altbach & Knight, 2007; Britez & Peters, 2008; Callan, 2000; Dell & Wood, 2010; Haigh, 2002; Hudzik, 2011; Kehm & Teichler, 2007; Morey, 2000; Schoorinan, 1999, 2000; Söderqvist, 2007; Torres, 1998; Westwood, 2006) have explored the implications of the internationalisation of higher education on curriculum development, pedagogy and delivery beyond the issues of funding, policy and access.

There is an urgent need to take into account the differing frames of reference (epistemologies and ontologies) for international students and 'local' students. A number of authors (such as Torres, 1998) would agree that even 'local' or indigenous students are increasingly not homogeneous. However, it is not only the student body that is becoming increasingly diverse. Faculty, administrators and tutors are mirroring the diversity of the student population, and they have their own perceptions, stereotypes, epistemologies and ontologies.

This chapter shares the analysis and findings of a survey which considers the viewpoints of students, administrators, faculty, tutors and employers regarding what it means to offer an MBA (Master of Business Administration) in an increasingly internationalised context.

Problem statement

While the internationalisation of higher education is well-accepted, the impact on curriculum development and delivery is less clear. Even more unclear are the perceptions of stakeholders such as students, faculty, tutors and employers regarding the meaning of internationalised curricula. These stakeholders play a crucial role in the design, development and delivery of the curriculum – and their views and perceptions regarding what students and employers want crucially influence the curriculum and its realisation.

How do curriculum design, development and delivery address these perceptions and the broader strategic aim of preparing our business graduates for an internationalised, networked and increasingly globalised world? What do students 'want' from a qualification such as an MBA? Do they have need for a curriculum that addresses international issues and provides them with the necessary competencies to act in an increasingly international environment?

Literature review

In this literature review, we provide a brief overview of the discourse regarding the internationalisation of higher education, before specifically exploring literature regarding the broader context of internationalisation and globalisation.

It is easy to embrace uncritically the internationalisation of the curriculum without interrogating its claims against the backdrop of globalisation trends and practices (Yang, 2003). In the light of the increasing transnational and cross-border operations of multinational organisations and their accompanying impact on the composition of workforces, diversity and issues of multiculturalism are pertinent (Banerjee & Linstead, 2001) and require careful consideration in any discourse on the internationalisation of the curriculum. Perhaps then, the internationalisation of the curriculum is in response, inter alia, to the increasing diversity of students and the roles of multi- and transnational corporations that may operate across geopolitical borders (Miyoshi, 1993).

Callan states that 'A reading of the literature on the internationalization of education, both European and worldwide (particularly North American), shows that ... the concept has been understood and applied in *a highly variable fashion*' (Callan, 2000, p. 16) [emphasis added] (see also Söderqvist, 2007). The different scopes and definitions of the term 'internationalisation' continue to shift according to 'varying rationales and incentives for internationalization, the varying activities encompassed therein, and the varying political and economic circumstances in which the process is situated' (Callan, 2000, p. 16). Varying interpretations and claims also result from different 'regional differences' and 'historical associations' (Callan, 2000, p. 16). There are also variations and overlapping meanings between the terms internationalisation, globalisation, cross-border, transnational and Europeanisation (Callan, 2000; Knight, 2004, 2007). It falls outside the scope of this chapter to interrogate these differences, but we agree with Callan (2000) that there are multiple juxtapositions between these terms and that, under the influence of new technologies and geopolitical formations (Appadurai, 1990), the notion of internationalisation will continue to be contested and the surrounding discourse will grow and be redefined (Kehm & Teichler, 2007). For the sake of this chapter, we accept Knight's (2004) proposition that: 'Internationalisation is changing the world of higher education, and globalisation is changing the world of internationalisation' (p. 5).

Van der Wende (1997) states that the internationalisation of the curriculum 'is intended to improve foreign language proficiency, enhance understanding of other countries and cultures, and strengthen intercultural competence and cross-cultural communication skills' (p. 55). McFadden, Merryfield and Barron (1997) propose that an internationalised curriculum should promote equity and social justice; improve inter-group relations and the promotion of intercultural competencies; reduce prejudice, stereotyping and discrimination; support the acquisition and the imparting of knowledge of human diversity and commonality as well as the acquisition of knowledge for cultural consciousness regarding one's own and other cultures and develop skills in the critical understanding of the processes of knowledge construction (see also another approach to achieve this described by Morey, 2000). Schoorinan (1999) proposes the internationalisation of the curriculum as 'an ongoing, counter hegemonic educational process that occurs in an international context of knowledge and practice where societies are viewed as subsystems in a larger, inclusive world' (p. 21). An internationalised curriculum that is counter-hegemonic calls for the representation of multiple cultural perspectives, a variety of pedagogical styles and multidirectional, dialogic communication as well as an examination of the rationale for an internationalised curriculum.

Despite the growth in research into internationalisation, it remains 'fuzzy' (Kehm & Teichler, 2007, p. 261), and research into internationalisation outside of the English language is generally not accessible. Despite these drawbacks, internationalisation has become part of the mainstream focus, a priority issue and a 'normative topic with strong political undercurrents' in higher education (Kehm & Teichler, 2007, p. 262). These authors identify seven broad themes: namely (1) mobility of students and academic staff; (2) mutual influences of higher education systems on each other; (3) internationalisation of the substance of teaching, learning and research; (4) institutional strategies of internationalisation; (5) knowledge transfer in which the notion of 'employability' is pertinent; (6) cooperation and increasing competition and (7) national and supranational policies regarding the international dimension of higher education (Kehm & Teichler, 2007, p. 266).

It is clear from the literature review that perspectives on internationalisation within higher education range from acceptance of it as factual (e.g. Söderqvist, 2007) to counter-hegemonic practice (Schoorinan, 1999).

Research context

This study was undertaken in the context of two modules comprising the first stage of the MBA programme at the Open University Business School in the UK. The research focused on surveying students, tutors, faculty, administrators and employers involved with these modules regarding their perceptions and expectations of the content and delivery of an MBA programme.

MBA students could study one of two modules at Stage 1: one provided a direct entry route onto the MBA for graduates with some middle/senior management experience; the other module provided an entry route for students who had worked through a previous entry qualification and were assumed to be aspiring managers. Both modules were available for delivery in two formats: one provided tuition contact time via an online medium; the other provided direct tuition face-to-face. The online tuition versions were available to students globally and attracted a wide range of international students, while the face-to-face tuition versions were available only to students in the UK and mainland Europe. As well as seeking an improved understanding of student and other stakeholder perceptions, we wanted also to ascertain whether there were any differences between students, based largely on known characteristics, such as educational background or country of study. Some characteristics, such as occupational status and ethnicity, were self-declared on registration.

Methodology

The survey was sent to over 2,000 recipients from five stakeholder groups – students, tutors, faculty academic staff, faculty support staff involved in the production and presentation of the MBA and employers/sponsors. Questions were largely identical across all stakeholder groups, rephrased as appropriate, with the aim of obtaining comparable data for analysis. They sought to identify reasons that students would register for an MBA; the challenges that managers face; the knowledge, skills and values which managers need to face these challenges; the advantages and disadvantages of working in multicultural and international groups and the challenges in working in such groups. Each group was also requested to list topics they felt should be included in an MBA and their perceptions regarding the meaning of an 'international' degree.

The student survey was tested on a small pilot group. It was then sent to all students registered within a single year across both Stage 1 MBA modules (direct graduate route and non-graduate entry route) and for both face-to-face and online tuition versions. Tutor, faculty and administrator contact details of those involved with these modules were provided by the business school.

Employers were selected as those having sponsored students on the modules for whom clear contact details were available.

The surveys were sent via a URL link in an explanatory email invitation to all stakeholder groups between 13 and 20 September 2010. Two weeks later, a reminder was sent to those who had not responded, or who had started and not yet completed the survey. The survey was live for four weeks.

The surveys attracted the response rates shown in Table 10.1.

The researchers undertook a thematic analysis, as described by Braun and Clark (2006). After studying the responses, we agreed what might constitute a theme and whether to focus on a rich description of the data set, or a detailed account of any one particular aspect. In choosing between semantic or latent meanings, we opted for semantic meanings as described by Braun and Clark (2006), identifying themes within the text at face value: that is, we did not attempt to interpret further the possible meanings of the entries. We followed Braun and Clark's 'guided process' and became familiar with the data before generating initial codes. These were cross-checked between the three researchers and agreement sought, before being used to generate themes. Themes were subsequently cross-checked between the researchers, and consensus sought on the scope of each.

Outcomes

Due to the volume of the data set, we have not attempted to describe the outputs from our analysis of all of the survey questions here. We therefore present and analyse our findings with regard to stakeholder perceptions on the reasons for study and the challenges and skills required by managers today, and any resultant impact on the internationalisation of the MBA curriculum.

Reasons for studying for an MBA

The survey asked respondees to provide reasons why students register for an MBA (registered students from their own perspectives and the other stakeholders responding in general). A total of 1,492 responses of students (n = 506) were coded and classified into themes given as career progression; sponsored by

Table 10.1 Overview of the response rates of the surveyed stakeholder groups

Stakeholder groups	Potential responses	Actual responses	Response rate (%)
Students	2,123	506	23.9
Tutors	79	43	54.4
Faculty	14	10	71.4
Administrators	17	8	47.1
Employers	63	12	19.1

employer; personal development; the status of the MBA; to improve management skills; increase in knowledge; for the qualification; adding value to their organisations; networking; and 'other'. 'Career progression' included all responses referring to aspiring for promotion after completion of the MBA; job security; changing jobs; increasing chances of finding a different job and/or seeking more responsibilities based on studying for an MBA. The category 'personal development' included responses referring to self-improvement; personal fulfilment; improving personal skills, etc. The 'other' category included responses such as 'boredom while on maternity leave'; 'interested in learning'; 'I wanted to spend my spare time constructively' and 'understanding of the world'.

The most commonly provided reasons by *students* were clustered under career progression (28%); personal development and self-improvement (17%); increase in knowledge/expertise (15%) and improving management skills (9%). All stakeholders listed career progression most frequently. However, tutors, faculty, administrators and employers listed 'improve management skills/acquiring specific skills' as the second most provided reason, as opposed to 'personal development and self improvement' most often listed by students. There was no substantive difference between the different student responses registered on the different modules/versions, or when the data set was reviewed regarding gender, race, educational background or occupation.

Challenges faced by managers

This question asked each of the stakeholder groups to list three main challenges faced by managers today. In asking this question, we sought to understand the context for studying a 'global' or 'international' MBA. What were the issues that the various stakeholders assumed that (future) managers would face, and how might the MBA prepare them for those issues?

Students ranked their answers in order of significance. The reasons provided by the student groups were analysed and thematically clustered. Table 10.2 provides an overview of the perceptions of the different stakeholders regarding the challenges that managers face, and demonstrates the differing perspectives of students versus other stakeholder groups.

As a whole group, students ranked the 'changing context' as the fourth most important challenge that managers face, while the other stakeholders considered it to be the most important. This is crucial for our exploration (and understanding) of the impact of internationalisation on curriculum design and delivery. It would seem that students were either unaware of the impact of the changing context on managers, or tend to focus on more immediate issues such as people management (e.g. conflict resolution; staffing issues; performance management, etc.) and strategic planning in their day-to-day operational function as managers. It may be that dealing with the changing context is possibly the prerogative of senior and executive management, while Stage 1 MBA students are working at a more operational level.

Table 10.2 Overview of stakeholder views on the challenges managers face

Students	Tutors	Faculty and administrators	Employers
1 People management[1]	The changing context[2]	The changing context	The changing context; people management
2 Developing as a manager/becoming a leader [3]	Developing as a manager	Developing as a manager	Resource management[4] Developing as a manager
3 Sustaining growth/ strategic planning/ leadership[6]		People management Personal[7] Sustaining growth	Ethics[5]

These categories included:

1 Conflict management and resolution; performance management; motivation; communication and organisational culture.
2 Organisational change; economic downturn and changes; budget cuts; political changes; uncertain future and internationalisation.
3 Continuous professional development; delegation; keeping abreast with change; multitasking; work–life balance; job security; knowledge transfer; confidence in decision making; organisational politics and social skills.
4 Financial management; budgets and limited resources.
5 Doing the right things in the right way; values and environmental sustainability.
6 Leadership in changing times; innovation; planning for restructuring/adaptation; doing the right thing for the company; deciding on priorities; strategy implementation and anticipating crises.
7 Own identity; work–life balance and own personal dreams and insecurities.

Other categories mentioned were stakeholder/shareholder and network management; project and operation management; information and knowledge management; relationship with seniors/hierarchy and multicultural and diversity issues and other.

The responses of the student group could be further categorised under a number of characteristic headings: for example, gender, age, occupational status, educational background, country of study and ethnicity. When refining the student group, we noted the differences described below.

Country of study

The majority of students were UK-based ($n = 313$), with a further 174 students based in mainland Europe and 19 students in other parts of the world.[1] The smaller 'rest of the world' group gave a much greater prominence to the changing context than the other two groups. The challenge most frequently cited by the UK and European students was people management.

---

1 Canada (4); Chile (1); Ghana (1); Japan (2); St Lucia (1); Morocco (1); Mexico (1); Qatar (1); Sudan (1); Somalia (1); Tunisia (1); Turkey (1); US (4).

Ethnicity

In this category, students were grouped (self-selected) into 'White' (n = 364), 'Black' (n = 16), 'Asian' (n = 17), 'Chinese and other' (n = 6) and 'mixed' (n = 11). There were some interesting differences between the groupings, although it should be noted that the number of students in some groups were small. Most of the student groupings looked at internal challenges: that is, they focused on current operational issues such as difficulties in managing staff, projects and resources. Students in the 'Asian' ethnic grouping were the only group to highlight challenges presented by the changing context, and this was cited twice as frequently (making up 38% of the responses) as the next highest challenge (for this grouping, developing as a manager). The changing context formed less than 1 per cent of the responses made by 'Black' students.

Occupational status

In this category, students were grouped (self-selected) into: 'modern' professional (n = 104), senior managers or administrators (n = 121), middle or junior managers (n = 94) and 'traditional' professional (n = 36). There were other groupings, but the numbers were too small to be meaningful. Modern professional included, for example, software engineer, area sales manager or consultant, and traditional professionals included occupations such as solicitor, army officer or accountant.

People management was the most frequently cited response for all groups. Traditional professionals gave a much narrower range of responses, focusing mostly on people management and strategic planning. Middle or junior managers mentioned developing as a manager more frequently than the other occupational groups.

Age

The changing context was mentioned most frequently by the most mature students, with the number of citings decreasing generally with age. Younger students had a greater focus on strategic planning and, unsurprisingly, developing as a manager.

There were no substantive differences in response according to the students' educational background, and very little difference overall between gender groupings, with the exception that the changing context was seen as much more relevant to male students than females.

Skills needed by managers

A follow-up question required stakeholders to list the three most important skills that managers need (in response to the challenges already listed). The responses of all groups were analysed and thematically clustered. Table 10.3 provides an overview of the responses.

People skills and leadership and strategic thinking were frequently mentioned by all groups. It was interesting that whereas both student and employers frequently cited communication skills as important, neither the tutor or faculty/administrator groups ranked this highly. Perhaps this reflects their focus on skills that can be *taught* within a standard curriculum as opposed to practical skills gained through work experience.

In terms of student characteristics, there were no substantive differences in response between genders or educational status.

Ethnicity

Differences between ethnic groups are mainly reflected in the responses for country of study, although it was interesting to note that students describing themselves as 'White' provided a wider range of skills. All ethnic groups selected people management skills as the most important, with the exception of students in the 'Chinese and other' grouping ($n = 6$), for whom this was relatively unimportant. The most important skill declared in this group was leadership, closely followed by financial acumen (a skill which ranked low in all other ethnic groupings). Leadership skills also ranked highly for other groupings, although students

Table 10.3 Management skills needed by stakeholder group

	Students	Tutors	Faculty and administrators	Employers
1	People skills[1]	Leadership and strategic thinking[2]	Leadership and strategic thinking	Leadership and strategic thinking People skills
2	Leadership and strategic thinking	People skills Other	People skills	Communication skills[3] Willingness to learn[4] Plan, organise[5]
3	Communication skills	Financial and numeracy skills Emotional intelligence[6]	–	–

1 Facilitating consensus, listening and motivating; managing performance
2 Political skills; influencing; charisma
3 Clearly, often; language ability
4 Adaptable; flexible
5 Prioritising; work allocation; project management skills
6 Self-awareness; ability to reflect

Other skills mentioned were: delegation; analytical and critical thinking; networking with different and between different stakeholders; knowledgeable/expertise/understanding; time management; change management; integrity/credibility; creativity and emotional intelligence.

in the 'Black' group were the only grouping to rank communication skills as more important.

Age

The oldest group of students were much less likely to mention leadership skills than other age groups, perhaps reflecting their existing positions within organisations. They were also the only age group to suggest the importance of financial and numeracy skills to any real degree.

Occupational status

All occupational groups, except traditional professionals, suggested that leadership, strategic thinking and decision-making skills were most important. This was most apparent amongst the senior manager group. Traditional professionals opted for people management as most important – this category was deemed second most important by all other occupational groups.

Unsurprisingly, traditional professionals mentioned knowledge and expertise more frequently than other groups. Other groups thought planning, organising and managing processes were more important.

Country of study

The non-UK/European students rated communication skills more highly than other nationalities – perhaps not surprising in this context, as it may be presumed that they include students with English as a second language. The UK and European students also referred to a broader set of management skills, although there were small changes in emphasis, with the UK students focusing more keenly on people management and European (non-UK) students mentioning leadership skills more frequently. The UK students also flagged planning and organisational skills to be more important than other student groups. Students from outside of Europe mentioned far fewer skill categories. People management was still cited more often than other categories – in fact, it was given by a higher proportion of these students than for the UK/European students. For the non-European students, the only other significant skill categories mentioned were leadership, communication and business expertise.

Findings

It is clear there are differences in perceptions between the challenges and skills required for today's managers across a range of stakeholders, and so also clear that any curriculum developed in response should take account of those differences. Other work would seem to confirm that responses to this question do depend on the perspective of the respondent. For example, a study by Andrews and Tyson (2004) of 100 executives in over 20 countries to identify the knowledge, skills and attributes which young business leaders need to succeed suggested that the primary requirement is to provide an executive education which is 'global in its outlook and content ... to prepare business leaders with global business capabilities'. Although this view was largely reflected by employers and faculty staff in this study, the main focus of students surveyed tended to be internal and short term, looking to develop skills which would be more immediately of use.

Within the student group itself, there were differences in perspective across a range of characteristics, with, for example, the non-European students placing a greater emphasis on the changing context and communication skills than students based in Europe. It seemed clear that students could also have different perspectives based on their existing career path.

Should universities then develop curricula which provide students with what they (think they) need? This apparent mismatch between student expectations and those of tutors, faculty and sponsors might result in disengagement and frustration on the side of students. Conversely, if the curriculum does not deal with the reality of what managers may face, students may be even less prepared for what awaits them as they progress in the organisational hierarchy. Caruana (2011) discusses the tensions between creating a curriculum which reflects and responds to the diversity of students' backgrounds and cultures and the need to be seen to retain academic rigour. Clearly, both are needed to ensure that a curriculum delivers maximum benefit to the student (and employer) while also meeting important accreditation standards.

Although we are still struggling with 'the fuzzy notion' of internationalisation of the curriculum (Kehm & Teichler, 2007, p. 261), this research shows some clear implications for future curriculum development that aims to meet the requirements of students in an international work context.

Implications for curriculum development and implementation

How can curriculum design, development and delivery address these findings, satisfy stakeholders and equip our students for the challenges of an internationalised future?

Issues of people management are cited as the most important challenge faced by managers, by all student groupings. With increased internationalisation/globalisation of the workforce, these issues become more challenging as employees increasingly work across cultures. However, although people management skills were universally cited as important by students, what is good practice in one cultural context may not be appropriate in another. Curriculum developers must decide whether a single context – whether Western or not – is more appropriate or attractive than a multiple context. If the preference is to attempt a balance of perspectives, other issues around the composition of both a curriculum development team and the appointment of tutors to support an 'international' curriculum arise. Is this best achieved by further recruitment of staff from a wide range of national contexts, or does this simply introduce fresh differences (between social background and organisational experience, say)?

There are, perhaps, other means of addressing context. For example, students may be formed into groups which reflect their own contexts and have tutor support which further enhances their own national, cultural or professional requirements. Alternatively, students may be deliberately mixed to ensure that a curriculum developed to suit a range of contexts remains prevalent, and collaborative work then serves to enhance a wider understanding and appreciation beyond their immediate experiences. This latter accords to an extent with work drawn from a study by Caruana and Ploner (2010) looking at managers, staff and students from six universities located in England, Wales and Australia which suggests that an internationalised curriculum should take account of students' diverse backgrounds and prior learning experiences and provide curriculum space to discuss and reflect on transitions.

Much of this can be supported with an appropriate use of technology, to better support dispersed groups. For instance, asynchronous and synchronous communication technologies allow for student and tutor meetings across geographical boundaries: what used to have to be delivered face to face in a physical location can now take place online, and thus reach a much wider audience. However, it is important not to assume that all students have equivalent access to those technologies, and also to recognise that there are cultural variations in how students engage with them. Similarly, most business schools increasingly ask students to reflect and engage with the curriculum in different ways – Are there similar national/cultural issues relating to student willingness or interest to do this?

Although online education is often celebrated as an environment where race, culture and gender do not matter, there is ample evidence (e.g. Bell, 2001; Gunn et al., 2003; Jones, 2001; Jordan, 1999; Leaning & Pretzsch, 2010; Suler, 2002) that cyberspace, in general, and online learning communities are not neutral spaces but embedded in socio-economic, gender, racial and geopolitical power relations. Not only do culture, gender and race play a role in determining access to online learning environments (especially in the developing world) but also they determine the unofficial rules of engagement: for example, number of postings, the freedom to critique, respect for educators or facilitators of learning and raising dissenting views.

Further analysis of the survey responses will indicate whether the 'international' perspective is indeed as relevant or interesting to students and sponsors as we have assumed. Any curriculum will have a range of focus areas, and it would be foolish to adjust the emphasis of any programme without sufficient evidence to support that. Furthermore, any significant change in curriculum content or delivery may have implications for existing accreditation bodies and the general need to retain accreditation. For example, the AMBA (Association of MBAs) accreditation body demands that a distance-learning MBA programme should have no less than 120 contact hours. Any adjustment to the delivery mechanism which hopes to facilitate improved access for international students must be set against this and other criteria. It is hoped that further examination of the data yielded by this study will provide a clearer insight into those aspects of the study experience and curriculum content.

Further work

We acknowledge that we have barely skimmed the surface of the data contained in the questionnaire. Not only is there a substantial amount of analysis still to be done but also a number of the above findings and analyses need to be triangulated with focus group interviews, individual interviews and further exploration of other variables such as ethnicity.

Acknowledgements

We acknowledge the input of Jan Jones, IET and the Open University in supporting the survey design and management of the survey process. We also acknowledge the Open University Business School for funding the fellowship which allowed this study to take place.

References

Altbach, P. G. & Knight, J. (2007). The internationalisation of higher education: Motivations and realities. *Journal of Studies in International Education*, *11*, 290–305.

Andrews, N. & Tyson, L. D. (2004). The upwardly global MBA. *Strategy + Business*, *36*, 1–10.

Appadurai, A. (1990). Disjuncture and difference in the global cultural economy. *Public Culture*, *2*(2), 1–24.

Banerjee, S. B. & Linstead, S. (2001). Globalization, multiculturalism and other fictions: Colonialism for the new millennium? *Organization*, *8*(4), 683–722.

Bell, S. (2001). *Introduction to cybercultures*. New York: Routledge.

Braun, V. & Clark, V. (2006). Using thematic analysis in psychology. *Qualitative Research in Psychology*, *3*, 77–101.

Britez, R. & Peters, M. A. (2008). Internationalisation and the cosmopolitan university. In D. Epstein, R. Boden, R. Deem, F. Rizvi & S. Wright (eds.), *Geographies of knowledge, geometries of power: Framing the future of higher education. World yearbook of education, 2008*. New York: Routledge.

Callan, H. (2000). Higher education internationalization strategies: Of marginal significance or all-pervasive? The international vision in practice: A decade of evolution. *Higher Education in Europe*, *25*(1), 15–23.

Caruana, V. (2011). *Internationalising the curriculum – Exploding myths and making connections to encourage engagement*. York: The Higher Education Academy. Available at: http://www.heacademy.ac.uk/assets/York/documents/ourwork/internationalisation/Viv_Caruana_leeds_Met.pdf (accessed 17 March 2011).

Caruana, V. & Ploner. J. (2010). *Internationalisation and equality and diversity in higher education: Merging identities.* Equality Challenge Unit. Available at: http://www.ecu.ac.uk/publications/internationalisation-and-equality-and-diversity-in-he-merging-identities (accessed 17 March 2011).

Dell, C. & Wood, M. (2010). Internationalisation and the global dimension in the curriculum. *Educational Futures, 2*(2), 56–72.

Gunn, C., McSporran, M., Macleod, H. & French, S. (2003). Dominant or different? Gender issues in computer support learning. *JALN, 7*(1):14–30.

Haigh, M. J. (2002). Internationalisation of the curriculum: Designing inclusive education for a small world. *Journal of Geography in Higher Education, 26*(1), 49–66.

Hudzik, J. K. (2011). *Comprehensive internationalisation.* Washington, DC: NAFSA, Association of International Educators. Available at: http://www.nafsa.org/uploadedFiles/NAFSA_Home/Resource_Library_Assets/Publications_Library/2011_Comprehen_Internationalization.pdf (accessed 26 February 2011).

Jones, A. (2001). Cross-cultural pedagogy and the passion for ignorance. *Feminism & Psychology, 11*(3), 279–292.

Jordan, T. (1999). *Cyberpower: The culture and politics of cyberspace.* Available at: http://www.isoc.org/inet99/proceedings/3i/3i_1.htm (accessed 23 November 2011).

Kehm, B. M. & Teichler, U. (2007). Research on internationalisation in higher education. *Journal of Studies in International Education, 11*, 260–273.

Knight, J. (2004). Internationalisation remodelled: Definition, approaches, and rationales. *Journal of Studies in International Education, 8*(1), 5–31.

Knight, J. (2007). Internationalization brings important benefits as well as risks. *International Higher Education, 46* (Winter), 8–10. Boston, MA: Boston College Center for International Higher Education.

Leaning, M. & Pretzsch, B. (2010). *Visions of the human in science fiction and Cyberpunk.* Oxford: Inter-disciplinary Press.

McFadden, J., Merryfield, M. M. & Barron, K. R. (1997). *Multicultural and global education: Guidelines for programs in teacher education.* Washington, DC: American Association of Colleges for Teacher Education.

Miyoshi, M. (1993). A borderless world? From colonialism to transnationalism and the decline of the nation-state. *Critical Inquiry, 19*(4), 726–751.

Morey, A. (2000). Changing higher education curricula for a global and multicultural world. *Higher Education in Europe, 25*(1), 25–39.

Organisation for Economic Cooperation and Development (OECD). (2004). Policy brief: Internationalisation of higher education. Paris: OECD. Available at: http://www.oecd.org/dataoecd/33/60/33734276.pdf (accessed 17 March 2011).

Schoorinan, D. (1999). The pedagogical implications of diverse conceptualizations of internationalization: A U.S. based case study. *Journal of Studies in International Education, 3*, 19–46.

Schoorinan, D. (2000). *How is internationalization implemented? A framework for organizational practice.* Boca Raton, FL: Florida Atlantic University.

Söderqvist, M. (2007). *Internationalisation and its management at higher education institutions. Applying conceptual, content and discourse analysis.* Helsinki: Helsinki

School of Economics. Available at: http://hsepubl.lib.hse.fi/pdf/diss/a206.pdf (accessed 27 February 2011).

Suler, J.R. (2002). Identity management in cyberspace. *Journal of Applied Psychoanalytic Studies*, 4(4), 455–459.

Torres, C. A. (1998). Democracy, education, and multiculturalism: Dilemmas of citizenship in a global world. *Comparative Education Review*, 42(4), 421–447.

Van der Wende, M. (1997). Internationalising the curriculum in Dutch higher education: An international comparative perspective. *Journal of Studies in International Education*, 1, 53–72.

Westwood, R. (2006). International business and management studies as an orientalist discourse. A postcolonial critique. *Critical Perspectives on International Business*, 2(2), 91–113.

Yang, R. (2003). Globalisation and higher education development: A critical analysis. *International Review of Education*, 49(3–4), 269–291.

Chapter 11

Socrates in the low countries

Designing, implementing and facilitating internationalisation of the curriculum at the Amsterdam University of Applied Sciences (HvA)

Hans de Wit and Jos Beelen

Introduction

Amsterdam is an international and multicultural hub. The higher education institutions in the city therefore aim to equip their students with the competences to function successfully in such a setting. However, how successful they are is not easy to define. This is mainly due to the fact that intercultural competences of students are not defined and assessed in a systematic and consistent way and that the professional field is not particularly explicit about the exact nature of these competences. The Amsterdam University of Applied Sciences (HvA) faces challenges that differ from those of a research university. In this chapter, the internationalisation policy of HvA, and the issues it faces with respect to its implementation, are placed in the global and Dutch contexts of internationalisation of higher education.

Contexts

Over the past 25 years, the international dimension of higher education has risen on the agendas of international organisations and national governments, institutions of higher education and their representative bodies, student organisations and accreditation agencies. This process is also described as *mainstreaming* of internationalisation. Internationalisation has moved from a reactive to a proactive strategic issue, from added value to mainstream, and also has seen its focus, scope and content evolve substantially. Increasing competition in higher education and the commercialisation and cross-border delivery of higher education have challenged the value traditionally attached to cooperation: exchanges and partnerships. At the same time, internationalisation of the curriculum and the teaching and learning process (also referred to as 'Internationalisation at Home' or IaH) has become as relevant as the traditional focus on mobility (both degree mobility and mobility as part of the home degree).

Some *implicit* notions of internationalisation are firmly shared across the field of higher education; the word 'internationalisation' is being used as if we all mean the same thing in using this term. Except for the understanding that it relates to including an international/global dimension into the functions of a university, everybody uses the term on his or her own conditions. Mobility is an important part of international activities but increasingly this holds true for curriculum development as well.

Over the years, international educators have focused too much on activities such as mobility, study abroad and international classrooms as goals in themselves. But a shift from activities to competences is evolving in the policies with respect to the internationalisation of higher education. We have assumed for a long time that these activities or instruments were good in themselves and, that by undertaking them, students would automatically develop competences related to these activities, without any proof that they have. For that reason, the shift in focus from the *how* (instruments) to the *why* (objectives) is a positive development.

Internationalisation at Home

In Europe, this shift was driven by the IaH movement at the end of the 1990s. This movement has similarities to developments in the US (*internationalising the campus*), Australia (*internationalising the curriculum*) and also developed momentum elsewhere. The IaH movement – although relevant for the shift in focus from the how to the what – has the risk of evolving from a movement into a dogma and, by that, in losing its function to inspire change. We see signs that it also becomes more instrumental: focusing on international classrooms and teaching in English, as if these were aims in themselves rather than on tools that generate learning outcomes and competences.

The shift in focus from activities and instruments to outcomes and competences is an important one, but in this new focus we see a risk of inflation of terminology and of unclear and vague notions: global competence, intercultural competence, intercultural sensitivity, international competence, multicultural competence, transnational competence, global citizenship, etc. These terms, like the traditional terms in international education, are used as synonyms for internationalisation of the curriculum and IaH, and without clear definitions and ways how to assess them.

The notion of 'Internationalisation at Home' (IaH) does not purport to come up with a new definition (Beelen, 2007). The addition 'at Home' indicates that the process is not something that takes place 'far away' but that indeed takes the local, multicultural conditions as a focus and point of departure. It places institutional (educational) developments in internationalisation in a broader context by linking the international and the intercultural dimension. Moreover, IaH claims that everyone, both mobile and non-mobile students, are entitled to an education that prepares them for a globalised living and working environment. And last, but not least, it raises the question of how to benefit from local diversity. Developing strategies to address these questions is an important and challenging ambition and the success of a university in reaching these goals an important benchmark of quality (Nilsson & Otten, 2003).

Intercultural learning not only concerns students but also requires encouragement for interaction with the local community. 'Internationalisation at Home' has put diversity issues more clearly on the agenda within the context of the international tasks of a university. Global conditions will require global learning and different knowledge, skills and attitudes in people. One can only be a 'global citizen' at Home. Universities need to prepare students to become a global citizen. In this context, the initiative by the American Council on Education (Olson, Evans & Shoenberg, 2007) to bridge the current divide between internationalisation and multicultural education is also important.

This focus on internationalisation of the curriculum and intercultural competences for students is at the centre of the strategic policy plan for internationalisation 2010–2014 of HvA, and also plays a central role in the internationalisation policy of its School of Economics and Management (SEM). To better understand the case of HvA, it is important to position that case in the context of the Dutch universities of applied sciences.

Internationalisation at the Dutch universities of applied sciences

Little systematic study has been carried out on the internationalisation of universities of applied sciences in Europe and in the Netherlands. The one and only extensive European analysis dates from over 12 years ago: *Internationalisation in European Non-University Higher Education* (Waechter, 1999). In their introduction to this study, Bremer and Waechter (1999) state that the relatively young age of this sector, the lack of a research tradition, its more practical and professional orientation as well as the 'schoolish' nature of it, and the more local mission and orientation of the sector, can all be considered major explanations for the arrears in internationalisation of the European non-academic higher education. The picture of the Dutch sector, as described by Arjen Van Staa, did not deviate much from the above (Van Staa, 1999).

Thirteen years later, steps forward have been made in the internationalisation of Dutch universities of applied sciences (UAS). But a pilot from NVAO on 'distinguished feature internationalisation' also demonstrated, amongst other things, that arrears compared with the research universities have barely been made up, and that the programmes of universities of applied sciences scored relatively lower than the academic programmes, especially on the points vision/mission/policy and intercultural and international learning goals (NVAO, 2011).

An important dimension is the relation with the professional fields for which universities of applied sciences prepare their students. Even more than for research universities, this relation with the professional field should be the underlying motive for internationalisation for universities of applied sciences (Leggott & Stapleford, 2007) However, in particular the SMEs (small- to medium-sized enterprises), where the greater part of the graduates of universities of applied sciences end up, are insufficiently prepared for the worldwide knowledge economy. Furthermore, universities of applied sciences have an increasing intercultural student population – 14 per cent of the student population in 2010 (against 13 per cent in research universities). In the cities of Holland, universities of applied sciences like HvA have considerably more than 14 per cent, which, on top of the requirements from the professional field, also has consequences for the management of intercultural and international competencies.

Summarising, this implies that internationalisation in Dutch UAS should be driven primarily by their relation with the professional field and the worldwide knowledge society.

The internationalisation policy of the HvA

HvA has a long experience of international activities, based on initiatives from individual teaching staff, departments and schools. At the same time, the international dimension is rather fragmented, lacks internal communication, coherence and structure, is low in incoming and outgoing mobility, as a whole is better in intention than in implementation, is lacking brand recognition abroad and, being a university of applied sciences, is not known for its research. The challenges facing HvA are those that have been described by Söderqvist (2007). She cites the challenges formulated by Van der Wende (1999) with regard to developing an international dimension without a strong basis in international research cooperation, cooperating internationally with comparable institutes that have a different status, and responding to the requirements of the international labour market.

In this context, the board of HvA decided that it was time to develop a long-term vision, which among others would be based on the *OECD/IMHE Review of Higher Education in Regional and City Development* of Amsterdam (OECD/IMHE, 2009), and which recommended the following: more efforts to integrate immigrants into higher education, an adequate offer of higher education for the knowledge-based economy, more attention for lifelong learning, make Amsterdam more attractive for global talent, develop Amsterdam into an educational hub and more focus on applied research and an internationalisation policy based on the international potentials of the city and its higher education sector.

The review is set against a background of a city in which more than half of the population is of non-Dutch origin. Working in the city and the region therefore involves working with and for people with diverse cultural backgrounds. HvA had already started profiling itself as an urban institution, forging close links with the city of Amsterdam. An increasing number of the students have a non-Dutch background and come from middle vocational education. In addition, Amsterdam houses a considerable number of international companies that form an important part of the world of work in the city.

Given the choice to focus on international and intercultural competences for all students, the curriculum moves into the centre of the new policy. Internationalisation of the curriculum has been operationalised in three layers:

- A **basic** layer to provide *all students* with a minimum of 30 European Credits (EC), focused on European and global developments in their profession, plus basic skills in English and intercultural communication.
- A **plus** option, in which an additional 25 per cent of their curriculum is interculturally and internationally oriented: at least one foreign language, at least one semester abroad for study and/or placement, one study visit abroad and options for international classroom experience.
- A complete **international** variety, in which the whole programme is delivered in English in international classrooms with international students and staff, a semester abroad, two foreign languages and two study projects and/or study visits abroad.

The rationale behind this policy was that, so far, attempts to internationalise had a tendency to focus on the two upper layers, as it was assumed that students are inclined to be internationally oriented. The reality is that only a limited number of students will actually go abroad for study or internship. By giving priority to the basic layer and making that a compulsory part of the curriculum for all students, HvA now implements a strategy that provides all its students with basic intercultural competences, at the same time allowing those students who want to be more internationally focused with two more layers (Hogeschool van Amsterdam, 2010). Labelling the basic layer *'learning and working in a metropolitan international environment'* demonstrates the link between local and global.

The School of Economics and Management

The School of Economics and Management (SEM) had already adopted a policy for an international and intercultural dimension in all its Dutch-medium programmes. This happened in 2008, two years ahead of the rest of the university. The policies of HvA and that of SEM have a number of similarities. They both have three layers, of which the basic one is compulsory for all students, but there are marked differences in this basic layer, which have considerable impact on the implementation process. The school policy went beyond the university-wide policy described above. The 30 EC internationally oriented education would be concentrated in one (full) semester and that semester would be entirely in English. The rationale was that such semesters would accommodate incoming international exchange students. This implied that the most appropriate position of the international semester would be in the third or fourth year of the four-year (240 EC) bachelor curriculum. An additional consideration for the international semesters was the wish to immerse all students in 30 EC English-medium education. The decision to have full semesters in English would have far-reaching consequences for the implementation process, as would become evident during the monitoring phase (see below).

Monitoring the implementation of international semesters

This section of the chapter describes how the implementation of the international dimension at the SEM was monitored. The outcomes of the monitoring yielded important insights for the coaching process described in the next section of this chapter.

One of the research groups at the SEM focuses on internationalisation of higher education. The management team of the SEM assigned the task of monitoring and analysing the process of setting up international semesters to this research group. The aim of the analysis was to make an inventory of the progress, but also to see if there were specific issues or obstacles that would need attention. The research group chose to interview all 19 managers of the 32 Dutch-medium programmes at the school. The interviews focused on two main dimensions: the internationalisation of the curriculum in the first two years and the international semester in Year 3 and Year 4.

Most programmes offer English language courses ranging from 6 to 22 EC. The level that is aimed for is either B2 or C1 (Common European Framework of Reference for Languages). In many cases, the curricula do not provide opportunities for students to practise their language skills by writing papers or giving presentations in English. Many students have problems with the level of English, especially those entering the university from middle vocational education and those with a non-Dutch background.

Courses in a second foreign language, still obligatory in the international programmes, in the Dutch programmes over the years have been eliminated or reduced to 6 EC.

A number of programmes contain courses on intercultural communication or intercultural sensitivity. These do not make use of the considerable diversity of the student population, are not sufficiently integrated into the programme as a whole and learning outcomes are not clearly defined. In their present state, most programmes contain about 15 EC internationally oriented courses (including English, intercultural communication and international subject content).

Some managers questioned the choice for a full international semester and remarked that they would prefer to spread international modules across the whole four-year programme. Others remarked that the obligation to teach in English would lead to a very artificial situation as long as there would be no incoming international students. Yet others remarked that an international semester would be desirable but impossible in their case, since the profile of their programme is determined by national rules and regulations: for example, in the case of accountancy and fiscal economics.

On the basis of the outcomes above, the research group made the following recommendations:

- Provide students with the opportunities to practise their English language skills and encourage them to pass a British Council exam: Certificate in Advanced English (CAE) or Certificate of Proficiency in English (CPE).
- Create options for honours programmes in second foreign languages and include the teaching of a second foreign language in minors focused on business, language and culture of a specific region (e.g. a minor Doing Business in Germany).
- Train teaching staff for the Cambridge International Certificate for Teaching in Bilingual Education.
- Give part-time programmes and some full-time programmes the liberty to spread the compulsory 30 EC internationally oriented education across the whole four-year programme.
- Make other programmes provide 30 EC internationally oriented courses, spread out over the two upper years, in addition to the existing 15 EC in the lower years.
- Drop the obligation to deliver all international modules in English.
- Enforce teaching full semesters in English only when programmes connect this to the ambition of incoming mobility students.

A support system for internationalisation of the curriculum

SEM adopted its new policy in 2008, started implementing it in 2009 and reviewed the implementation process in 2010. The review revealed the need for a structured support system for the development of internationalised curriculum elements. This support system would have to address the specific obstacles to the implementation of internationalisation of the curriculum. The 3rd Global Survey of the International Association of Universities provides some clues to those obstacles. The survey distinguishes external and internal obstacles to advancing internationalisation in general. Insufficient financial resources come out as the main internal obstacle on a global level, as well as in all the regions (Egron-Polak & Hudson, 2010, p. 81, Fig. I.C.6). On an aggregate level, 'limited faculty interest' and 'limited experience and expertise of staff and/or lack of foreign language proficiency' rank 'fairly high' among the internal obstacles to internationalisation in the perspective of higher education institutions (Egron-Polak & Hudson, 2010).

The authors of the survey consider the lack of interest of academic staff 'worrisome' and mention that institutions 'need to focus far more on mobilizing, training and providing support to faculty members and staff to build up "internationalisation knowledge and readiness" if they are to reach their internationalization goals' (Egron-Polak & Hudson, 2010, pp. 77–78).

At HvA, teaching staff involved in the development of the international semesters was clearly motivated, since many of them volunteered for the task. There was no 'limited faculty interest', at least not within this group. The other obstacle, 'limited experience and expertise of staff and/or lack of foreign language proficiency' was certainly one that needed addressing.

The usual practice at HvA is that the central unit for educational research and development offers staff development courses. The courses on internationalisation of the curriculum had attracted a mixed crowd of managers, academic staff and policy advisors from across the institution. As Caruana and Hanstock (2008) note, this type of professional development courses attract converts and leads to fractured and unsystematic outcomes. The courses at HvA may have carried across the key notions of internationalisation of the curriculum but were not effective in answering needs at programme level or supporting academic staff during the process of implementing an international dimension. The same was true for the half-day kick-off sessions that had been organised at school level.

The research group therefore decided to offer the developers of international semesters the possibility of following up the kick-off session with coaching sessions in smaller groups of four to five developers per programme. It was felt that the policy decision to mainstream internationalisation through the teaching and learning process implied an emphasis on the support of academic staff at programme level. The approach chosen for the coaching sessions was Socratic. The role of the coach would be that of a 'midwife', as Socrates defined his own role: assisting in the birth of insights that were already present but needed to be activated and articulated. The developers would be considered specialists in terms of both subject content and the teaching and learning processes related to that content. The responsibility for internationalising the curriculum would be placed on their shoulders.

The first step in the coaching process would be to discuss concepts and address misconceptions, such as the notion that education with an international focus should necessarily be in English. There would be discussion on the way individual modules would contribute to the (international) competence framework of the programme as a whole and how this should be assessed in order to see if students would have acquired these competences. How would these competences relate to those that the world of work expects from graduates? Would other major elements (outside the international semesters) also be expected to contribute to the acquisition of international competences? If so, would there be a logical sequence in the shaping of the international dimension rather than an overlap?

The second step would be to contextualise the programme in terms of local, regional, national, European and global settings. Being an institution for higher vocational education means that the world of work provides the most important focus for graduate attributes. Where would graduates work? In the city or region or abroad? Would they work for Dutch or international companies? What do employers consider relevant competences? Does the programme have a mission or ambition that goes beyond what employers need?

Tools for a 'zero measurement' (assessment of the present situation) would have to be available, and developers would be encouraged to use them in order to link existing international activities to the new international semesters. In subsequent sessions, the developers discussed the choice of international literature and case studies, assignments and exams for students, portfolios and didactical issues.

When discussing the relation between individual internationalised modules and the programme as a whole, many developers remarked that the development process would 'indeed be more far reaching' than they had anticipated. In most cases, the world of work is not very outspoken about the international competences it requires from graduates. This lack of external validation was sorely felt. The institutional alumni monitor is too general to give much guidance here. There was a general need for clarification of concepts and terms in the widest sense: 'What is internationalisation?'

Issues around teaching and learning in English were paramount. The developers foresaw problems when Dutch teaching staff would lecture to Dutch students in English and said they feared that such learning environments would be 'artificial'. Another issue raised was the command of English of both teaching staff and students, especially of students who would have entered higher vocational education from middle vocational education and/or those students with a non-Dutch background.

Another major point of discussion, and insecurity, would be the number of hours required for the process and the question of whether management would be willing to supply these hours. Some developers identified funding as a main obstacle to success, without being able to specify what that money should be spent on. Later on in the development process, attention shifted to issues around (comparative) didactics, teaching methodology, the choice of literature and case studies to allow international comparisons to be made and to formulating assignments, exam questions and portfolio guidelines. It was at this stage of the process that the developers had the strongest feeling of being supported. They attributed this to the fact that they saw their efforts rewarded when they started the 'construction work' on their modules. The issues they brought to the sessions became more focused after the initial discussions on concepts and aims.

Academic staff felt particularly supported in the field of didactics and teaching methodology. It became apparent that in many cases they considered themselves subject specialists but not educationalists. What they felt lacking was a range of strategies to design learning environments with an international dimension. Most of them have little experience in working with colleagues abroad and therefore do not have examples from international practice available. The language issue added to their insecurity. It seems that these issues are the core of the obstacles to internationalisation of the curriculum and are highlighted in the 3rd Global Survey under 'limited experience and expertise of staff and/or lack of foreign language proficiency' (Egron-Polak & Hudson, 2010).

Although the presence of managers at kick-off sessions was appreciated, academic staff felt most comfortable working without them in the development teams. They discussed at length how they should present their plans to their managers and what could be expected from them in terms of resources and training.

The development teams were keen to meet others involved in the same process and exchange experiences and ideas with them. This keenness persisted, even after it had become clear to them that the international dimension of a programme is context-specific and that they should not count on finding examples of practice that could be directly transferred to their own. The exchange of experiences to some extent counteracts the effect noted by Caruana and Hanstock (2008): namely, that of the isolated project that has difficulties connecting to alternative strategies for internationalisation of the curriculum.

While the approach chosen at HvA is clearly 'diffusionist', it may not be considered project-based. The coaching strategy is not based on a top-down notion of projects as drivers for internationalisation but rather on supporting the needs of development teams. It is therefore teams that are in the lead rather than the project manager. Still, the danger of fragmentation when working with teams at module level is real. The relation between individual modules and the programme as a whole should be carefully guarded. Working in the contextualised setting of a programme and modules promises most chances of success, since teaching and learning can only be addressed at that level.

Based on the experiences at SEM, the system of kick-off with subsequent coaching sessions was requested by other schools of HvA as well as by another university of applied sciences: the HAN University of Applied Sciences. Here, too, fundamental issues around the concept of internationalisation (of the curriculum) would spring up and there was a wide demand for definitions and for examples of good practice. Leask's definition of internationalisation of the curriculum as 'the incorporation of an international and intercultural dimension into the preparation, delivery and outcomes of a programme of study' provided a workable option (Leask, 2009, p. 209). Examples of good practice served as means of orientation and inspiration but rarely provided the ready-to-use elements that the developers had hoped to find. There was a demand for meeting development teams outside their own schools to compare results and experiences from the development process.

The experiences with the support model showed that there are several factors that are important for success:

- Clarity about the roles of the staff members involved. Managers, teaching staff, international officers and quality assurance staff all have different stakes in the process and this needs to be clear from the outset.
- The developers need to realise that they are the specialists, both in terms of subject knowledge and teaching and learning processes. Examples from other contexts will not necessarily work.

- There needs to be ample time for discussion on competences for individual courses in relation to those of the programme as a whole.
- The development process needs to be contextualised at programme and at module level.
- There need to be opportunities for exchange of ideas and plans across wider sections of the university, including very different fields of study. Therefore, sessions that facilitate this exchange are an integral part of the process.

Profile of a coach

The coaching processes described above are work in progress, and it is too early to draw conclusions. It is clear that a fundamental choice for internationalisation of the curriculum for all students requires support. The HvA model provides a channel for questions of teaching staff that would otherwise remain unanswered and may, as such, add to the quality of educational development. The model requires a clear profile of the coach in the support process.

Coaches need to have a good working knowledge of pedagogy and teaching methodology, including the methodology of teaching and learning in a second language, where necessary. They need to be able to ask questions first and not immediately suggest solutions. Coaches need to be able to support developers in the articulation of student learning aims and competences. Another requirement is knowledge of instruments that can support the learning process, such as incoming mobility of staff and students. Coaches need to be able to relate the internationalisation of the curriculum to the programme's plans for outgoing mobility since an internationalised curriculum can serve to prepare students for study by placement abroad. This requires coaches to be familiar with international cooperation and to be able to suggest suitable potential partner institutions. They need to have a range of tools available, for example, for scanning the present curriculum for international content. Finally, they need to be able to articulate the developers' need for further professional development.

Conclusion

HvA has chosen to aim for a basic level of intercultural and international competencies for all of its over 40,000 students while giving those who want the opportunity to go beyond that the chance to do so. This case study shows the interaction between university policy and implementation by individual schools. The pattern is replicated when it comes to school policy and implementation by individual programmes. The monitoring by the research group on internationalisation has made these processes visible. With a top-down policy that has such far-reaching implications, support systems for bottom-up implementation are indispensable. It is a major step that institutional policy is followed up by support that leads right down to course development at module level. Coaching is an important instrument to assist the teaching staff in this process. The different ways the research group is providing coaching to teaching staff provide insight in how teaching staff can be actively involved in the internationalisation of the curriculum.

References

Beelen, J. (ed.) (2007). *Implementing internationalisation at home*. EAIE Professional Development Series for International Educators. EAIE: Amsterdam.

Bremer, L. & Waechter, B. (1999) Introduction. In B. Waechter (ed.), *Internationalisation in European non-university higher education*. ACA papers on international cooperation in education. Bonn: Lemmens, pp. 11–17.

Caruana, V. & Hanstock, J. (2008). Internationalising the curriculum at the University of Salford: From rhetoric to reality. In C. Shiel & A. McKenzie (eds.), *The global university: The role of senior managers*. London: DEA.

Egron-Polak, E. & Hudson, R. (2010). Internationalization of higher education: Global trends, regional perspectives (IAU 3rd global survey report). Paris: IAU.

Hogeschool van Amsterdam (2010). *Strategisch beleidsplan internationalisering 2010–2014 [Strategic policy plan internationalisation]*. Amsterdam: Hogeschool van Amsterdam.

Leask, B. (2009). Using formal and informal curricula to improve interactions between home and international students. *Journal of Studies in International Education, 13*(2), 205–221.

Leggott, D. & Stapleford, J. (2007). Internationalisation and employability. In E. Jones & S. Brown (eds.), *Internationalising higher education*. Oxford: Routledge.

Nilsson, B. & Otten, M. (eds.) (2003). Internationalisation at home [Special issue]. *Journal of Studies in International Education, 7*(1), 3–119.

NVAO (2011). *Evaluating internationalisation: The NVAO pilots assessments of internationalisation*. Report on the pilot project 'distinguished feature internationalisation'. The Hague: NVAO.

OECD/IMHE (2009). *OECD/IMHE reviews of higher education in regional and city development, Amsterdam*. Paris: OECD/IMHE.

Olson, C., Evans. R. & Shoenberg, R. (2007). *At home in the world: Bridging the gap*. Washington, DC: American Council on Education.

Söderqvist, M. (2007). *The internationalisation and strategic planning of higher-education institutions*. Helsinki: Helsinki School of Economics and Business Administration.

Van der Wende, M. (1999). An innovation perspective on internationalisation of higher education institutionalisation: The critical phase. *Journal of Studies in International Education, 3*(1), 3–14.

Van Staa, A. (1999). The Netherlands. In B. Waechter (ed.), *Internationalisation in European non-university higher education*. ACA papers on international cooperation in education. Bonn: Lemmens, pp. 117–132.

Waechter, B. (1999). The country reports. Some first observations. In B. Waechter (ed.), *Internationalisation in European non-university higher education*. ACA papers on international cooperation in education. Bonn: Lemmens, pp. 181–190.

Part 3

New ways of thinking and acting

A future curriculum for future graduates? Rethinking a higher education curriculum for a globalised world

Catherine Montgomery

Introduction

This chapter aims to raise issues relating to the relevance of current university curricula to the twenty-first century globalised world. Here I consider the relationship between a university curriculum and the social and cultural practices of the world beyond the university and ask what sorts of curricula might be appropriate for an increasingly complex technological world where we are more strongly connected with our global neighbours. In particular, the work initiated by the 'New London Group' (1996), including further work by Kalantzis and Cope (2005) and Kress (2000), is discussed as a way of rethinking approaches to designing a university curriculum for a globalised world. This work developed a new pedagogical framework which was encompassed, amongst other ideas, by the idea of 'multiliteracy' and aimed to reflect some of the complexities of contemporary society.

This chapter will present some important aspects of this work, which was undertaken with a focus on the secondary school sector, and discuss the relevance for developing a globalised curriculum in higher education. The aim of considering these ideas in depth is to present a framework that clarifies a way of thinking about a future international curriculum that is often muddied by confusions over terminology and contested ideas.

Why do we need to rethink our ideas about a future curriculum?

Internationalisation of the curriculum has become a strong and recurring imperative in higher education, not just in the UK but also in countries across the globe, including the US, Australia, New Zealand, China, Vietnam, South Africa and Europe. However, progress in achieving internationalised curricula seems to be slow and to be advancing unevenly, and in the UK it tends to be focused in particular universities. A lack of financial support for initiatives relating to internationalisation of the curriculum means that progress is often as a result of commitment and enthusiasm of particular individuals or groups of staff. Perhaps it is this lack of strategic and uniform direction that leads Edwards to note that as far as internationalisation is concerned we are 'still having the same conversation we were all having in the 1970s' (Edwards, 2007, p. 373).

In addition, there seems to be confusion over ideas, meanings and terms that may also be impeding progress with internationalisation in teaching and learning. Many questions surround internationalisation and, while it is not within the scope of this discussion to answer these questions, I intend to list some questions here to illustrate the contested nature of this field. Confusions include the following:

- What does internationalisation mean? Does my institution have a strategy for internationalisation and how does this relate to what happens in the curriculum?
- What do we mean by curriculum? Is this solely what happens in the classroom or does it include the informal curriculum, the extended curriculum and student interaction on and off campus?
- Does internationalisation of the curriculum relate to relationships between international students and 'home' students?
- What does cultural diversity really mean and how is it significant in learning? Is it about philanthropy or learning and knowledge?
- Is internationalisation about developing students for employment?
- What is a global citizen and how do we link internationalisation in the curriculum with developing ethical and responsible graduates?
- What about the influence of different disciplinary contexts?

There are many other concerns and confusions around internationalisation and the curriculum that often mean that discussions between staff may get no further than agreeing on terms or coming to a consensus on the reasons why we may need to internationalise. When discussions reach the stage of considering the curriculum, they tend to focus on 'learning outcomes' relating to 'graduate attributes' that are to do with personal skills and lifelong learning. Even at this stage there is a wealth of Australian research that indicates that universities' endeavours to describe generic attributes of graduates continue to lack a clear theoretical or conceptual base and are characterised by a plurality of viewpoints (Barrie, 2004).

The aim of the discussion in this chapter is to put to one side issues of internationalisation, as such, and concentrate on the nature of the modern curriculum. In addition, the idea of learning outcomes, global citizenship or graduate attributes will also be sidelined for the moment to concentrate on the idea of 'literacy'. The purpose of doing this is to have some exploratory discussions that can focus on what future curricula should be like and what sorts of 'literacies' graduates may need. The idea of literacy suggested here is not simply a replacement for graduate attributes, however. It is a qualitatively different idea that relates to graduates' competences with the wider variety of sources and modes of information, texts, discourses and knowledge that the modern world provides access to, often as a result of technology. This discussion will present the work of the New London Group (1996) and of Kress (2000) who worked on a theoretical overview of the connections between the changing social environment facing students and teachers and a new approach to literacy pedagogies that the New London Group called 'multiliteracies'.

What is the New London Group and why is their work important?

In 1994, the Centre for Workplace Communication and Culture at James Cook University of North Queensland, Australia, invited an eminent group of academics to get together in a small town called New London in New Hampshire (USA) to consider the future of literacy teaching in schools. They considered what would need to be taught in a rapidly changing near future, and how it would be taught. The work of this group became known as the New London Group and their work has continued and developed over the last 15 years. Although their brief was to consider needs for literacy in the twenty-first century, the composition of the group (including eminent linguists and educationalists Norman Fairclough, Gunter Kress, Bill Cope and Mary Kalantzis) and their diverse interests and backgrounds led to the development of ideas that have a much wider interest and application.

The group's starting point was to consider the influence of technology (in its broadest sense) on literacy and meaning-making in learning contexts. In earlier twentieth-century times the sorts of modes or genres that young people learned through and were schooled in were less diverse and relied mainly on written or oral 'texts'. The group felt that this was changing and that the 'emerging world of meaning-making would be more multi-modal ... in which written, oral, visual, spatial, gestural and tactile modes of representation would be more closely intertwined' (Kalantzis & Cope, 2010, p. xiii). As a result of this change in the way, 'meanings' are made or represented in the worlds beyond schools, in work, in citizenship and personal life, the group suggested that new approaches were needed for literacy teaching and learning (Cope & Kalantzis, 2009).

In addition to addressing the concern of 'the multiplicity of communications channels and media', the group also saw the 'increasing salience of cultural and linguistic diversity' which is a result of this and a crucial factor in future learning contexts (New London Group, 1996, p. 60). The group argued that young people and learners are involved in many more divergent communities in contemporary life, including work teams, professional groups, voluntary organisations, neighbourhood groups and social groups, and these may be local and physically co-located or dispersed, virtual and global (Cope & Kalantzis, 2000). It is more common in a technologically enhanced world that individuals may belong to multiple lifeworlds made accessible to them by electronic communication and the Internet. The increase in the variety and range of these groups means a much more salient and active interface with other social, linguistic and cultural groups. This increased immediacy of diversity and interconnectedness with global neighbours demands new sorts of literacy and wider sets of competences that the group called 'multiliteracies'. In summary, then, the group saw a need for change in ways of thinking about designing literacy and learning and presented 'the centrality of diversity ... the significance of multimodality and the need for a more holistic approach to pedagogy' as crucial considerations (Cope & Kalantzis, 2009, p. 167).

The principles emerging from the work of the New London Group have implications for thinking about internationalisation and the curriculum in higher education. Much recent literature and research in this field has suggested that the professional, personal and learning contexts that students are currently in and are aiming for are changed. Business, design and engineering industries are global in nature and staff may work in distributed teams with colleagues from across the world. People are more mobile for work and in their personal lives and are in immediate contact with social networks all over the world. These new global contexts require different sorts of literacies, a wider portfolio of literacies that range from the ability to work with a wide range of sources, media and images to intercultural understandings and an ability to adapt linguistically and socially. It is important to note that the motivation to adapt the curriculum for future graduates should not be predicated on fitting students for employment alone. As Kress (2000) notes:

> the fundamental aim of all serious education: [is] to provide those skills, knowledges, aptitudes and dispositions which would allow the young who are experiencing that curriculum to lead productive lives in the societies of their adult[hood].

(p. 134)

The development of multiliteracies needs to be an integral part of higher education and part of the process of graduates developing their social, cultural and linguistic capital.

This discussion will now move on to examine the work of the New London Group in more detail and consider the pedagogic framework they developed, and the relevance of this to a future university curriculum.

What sorts of curricula do we need in the future?

As noted above, the ideas begun in 1996 by the New London Group progressed over the following decade and led to the development of a new pedagogical framework called 'Learning by Design', which aimed to address learning in the context of the complexities of contemporary society (Kalantzis & Cope, 2005). The framework recast teachers as 'designers' of learning, with the idea of design representing work within different forms of meaning, text production and any other semiotic activity involving knowledge transformation and the construction of 'reality' in different ways (Rennie, 2010). The pedagogical framework of the New London Group had four main phases: Situated Practice, Overt Instruction, Critical Framing and Transformed Practice. Situated Practice involves experiencing the new and the known. Overt Instruction involves conceptualising or naming. Critical Framing involves developing an understanding of the cultural and social implications of what is learned and Transformed Practice results in new meaning and some kind of application (Kalantzis & Cope, 2005; Rennie, 2010).

The pedagogical model suggested above is underpinned by two important principles that are crucial for successful learning (Kalantzis & Cope, 2005). The first of these is that students need to feel a sense of belonging in relation to the content being learned, ways of knowing and the learning community itself (Rennie, 2010). This has links with work that suggest that connections with students' life-worlds are crucial to profound learning experiences (Beard, Clegg & Smith, 2007; Haigh, Chapter 14 in this volume) and also with research that argues for 'authenticity' in learning (Gullikers, 2004; Montgomery, 2009). The importance of the emphasis on this need for a sense of belonging is not only that it incorporates students' individual subjectivities but also that it suggests that differences such as race, gender and socio-cultural backgrounds are only the starting point for working with diversity in the classroom. Kalantzis and Cope (2005) argue for a further level of difference which includes values, social orientations, world experiences and ways of learning and knowing. This suggests that it is this higher level of difference that should inform the design of learning (Rennie, 2010).

The second principle that underpins successful learning in the New London Group model of pedagogy is the idea that learning should be transformative. Teaching and learning in a context where there is difference or plurality is a useful place to start because engagement with difference can be unsettling. Learning at university is not a binary of self and other (Pierce, 2003) but a complex site of struggle, tension and conflict and this 'troublesome space' in which intercultural interaction occurs is problematic but useful and transformative (Meyer & Land, 2005; Montgomery, 2011; Savin-Baden, 2008). In recent years, teaching about diversity in universities (for both students and staff) has tended to just recognise and affirm difference. The pedagogy of the New London Group suggests that students and staff must actually engage with difference despite the risk involved and the troublesome nature of this. Rennie (2010) notes that:

> *A multiliteracies pedagogy and place-pedagogy approach both suggest that truly engaging with 'difference' is a necessary, dangerous and a transformative business.*

> (p. 87)

The framework and principles outlined above have many resonances with work in the area of internationalisation of the curriculum but fewer of the confusing tensions that surround internationalisation versus globalisation; curriculum versus policy or strategy and 'international' versus 'home'. But what would the curriculum look like in practice?

Designing a future curriculum

Gunther Kress, one of the New London Group's founding members, noted that the current idea of curriculum is largely inherited from the nineteenth century and 'still assumes that it is educating young people into older dispositions, whereas the coming era demands an education for instability' (Kress, 2000, p. 133). Current design of a curriculum in higher education is sometimes bounded by quality procedures and constrained by policy rather than practice. This section presents three approaches to rethinking curriculum for a globalised world, based on and adapted from the work of the New London Group. The categories were also informed by a recent exploratory survey focusing on engineering students' perceptions of what it means to be a 'global engineer'.[1] This discipline-specific survey taken from first- and second-year engineering students supported the development of the following three approaches to curriculum design. The study will not be covered here, however, as it is reported in Montgomery et al. (2011).

Breaking down boundaries between university and community

Kress (2000) suggested the need for a curriculum with a shifting locus of site (where knowledge is delivered), time (when learning occurs) and authority (what counts as knowledge). He noted an already emerging change in the boundaries between formal institutions providing education and the community, and he identified 'processes of the dissolution of former frames and the emergence of new framings' (Kress, 2000, p. 134). Kress suggested that we need a new sort of curriculum for the modern world which blurs the boundaries between curriculum and community. He notes:

> *The curriculum in any locality will have to be attuned to [these] global demands; what is taught and how it is taught will need to take the globe not just as the relevant but as the necessary domain of thinking and practice.*

> (p. 141)

As mentioned above, meanings are grounded in real-world patterns of experience, action and subjective interest (Killick, Chapter 13 in this volume). This is what the New London Group describes as the 'pedagogical "weavings" ... between school learning and the practical out-of-school experiences of learners'. They note that these kinds of cross-connections between school and the rest of life are also 'cultural weavings' (Cope & Kalantsiz, 2009, p. 184–185). The crossing of the boundaries between the university and the community may be a way forward in making university learning meaningful and enabling students to develop learning that is fit for a complex modern world. As Kress (2000) suggests, this may require a shift in the locus of control of learning and a dissolution of the frame around the university and community and 'a change in relation between institution and community, from making the community "come to you", to going out to the community' (Kress, 2000, p. 136). Thus, in future university curricula there is a need for knowledge to be 'contextualised, applied, transdisciplinary and not necessarily carried out in universities' (Manathunga, 2009, p. 131).

Disciplines in an interconnected world

Sipos, Battisti and Grimm (2008) suggest that understanding how the world functions in the twenty-first century increasingly requires an interdisciplinary approach to using knowledge. The world is more interconnected than it has ever been. Mobility not just of people but of material products is extensive when an electric toothbrush is sourced, made and marketed in six different countries (Hoppe, 2005) and when waste from a discarded computer from a London college can end up in Ghana on a landfill where children scavenge for metal to make a living (BBC, 2010). Razbully and Bamber (2008) note that the contemporary interconnected and globalised world requires interconnectivity to be reflected within the curriculum. A future curriculum may need to provide students with a more interdisciplinary education and the boundaries between the traditional disciplines may need to be rethought. Students should be encouraged to explore interdisciplinary solutions to complex and interconnected global issues.

However, it is against this background of the need for disciplines to reflect an interconnected world that university curricula are currently for the most part fragmented into disciplines and these disciplines are taught in discrete modules that compartmentalise knowledge. Sipos et al. (2008) note that:

> *Higher education in Western societies overwhelmingly fragments knowledge into disciplines and often leads to conflict between individuals, ideologies and nations, thereby furthering the conquest of nature and the industrialization of the planet.*
>
> (p. 70)

Entwistle (2009) suggests the development of 'throughlines' in enquiry-based tasks that develop a deeper engagement with knowledge. These 'throughlines' of enquiry should perhaps encompass different disciplinary perspectives. This suggests that a future curriculum may need to have links beyond itself in order to prepare graduates for full participation in the society of their adulthood: 'Pedagogy is a teaching and learning relationship that creates the potential for building learning conditions leading to full and equitable social participation' (New London Group, 1996, p. 1).

A recent example of the introduction of interdisciplinary approaches to curricula consists of the innovations at the University of Melbourne. In 2008, the University of Melbourne made radical changes in its whole undergraduate curriculum and the resulting 'Melbourne Model' initiated global debates about the type of degree needed to prepare students for life and work in the twenty-first century. The new curriculum introduces interdisciplinarity in order that students are exposed to alternative knowledge domains, methods of investigation and enquiry and different ways of knowing. Undergraduate students are required to study one-quarter of their subjects outside their core curriculum, a requirement known as 'breadth' (Devlin, 2008). The model also emphasises academic depth through students also studying a core programme in a major discipline. The aim of the Melbourne Model is to 'ensure graduates can negotiate their way successfully in a world where knowledge boundaries are constantly shifting and reforming to create new challenges' (Devlin, 2008, p. 5). Although the Melbourne initiative has been criticised for simply adopting the American model of undergraduate study, and it remains a contested approach, it is an example of a university's attempts to develop throughlines across disciplines at an institutional level.

Developing multiliterate graduates

The idea that a future curriculum needs to educate multiliterate graduates has been discussed above in the context of the work of the New London Group. The important aspect of this is the shift away from the idea that learning revolves around written or oral 'text' alone. In traditional learning contexts, like the nineteenth-century curricula that Kress (2000) describes above, learning was through a transmission model where information was unidirectional from teacher to student mostly via text. In the future curricula advocated in this chapter, learning becomes much more multimodal, both in the sorts of sources of knowledge and in its acquisition. In order for students to learn the sorts of multiliteracies discussed here, they must do something with transmitted information: 'analyse the message, ask questions about it, discuss it with others, connect it with prior understanding and use this to change future actions' (Nicol, 2010, p. 503). This wider portfolio of literacies may not be available within the formal university curriculum and new curricula may need to draw on learning experiences beyond what is seen as 'the classroom'. Thus, authentic and 'live' curricula where students are engaging in 'real-world' activity as part of their learning and assessment are crucial.

The New London Group views multiliteracy pedagogy as a development from the earlier forms of literacy pedagogy that taught skills and competence. Pedagogy for multiliterate graduates acknowledges the role of social context and of agency in learning and seeks to create a more productive, relevant, innovative and 'emancipatory' pedagogy (Cope & Kalantzis, 2009). The approach to this is outlined in the four phases mentioned above (Situated Practice, Overt Instruction,

Critical Framing and Transformed Practice). Cope and Kalantzis (2009) reframed these ideas and transformed them into the more recognisable pedagogies or 'knowledge processes' of Experiencing, Conceptualising, Analysing and Applying. To give an example of these, 'analysing' assumes that powerful learning requires a critical capacity where a learner interrogates the interests behind a meaning or action and their own processes of thinking (Kalantzis & Cope, 2005). This sort of process enables both a cultural self-knowledge and the furthering of disciplinary knowledge (Haigh, Chapter 14 in this volume).

Overall, in order to develop multiliterate graduates, the curriculum itself needs to be multimodal, drawing on varied sources and types of information. A curriculum for multiliteracy would also employ different modes of communicating, learning and seeking out different sources for communication, ensuring in particular that teaching is dialogic and involves 'coordinated teacher–student and peer-to-peer interaction as well as active learner engagement' (Nicol, 2010, p. 503).

Conclusion

This chapter has focused on a particular strand of work initiated by the New London Group and developed by individuals from the group over the last decade. It is interesting to note that internationalisation of the curriculum initiatives have not (up to now) drawn on this work, which has such strong parallels with internationalisation. It sometimes appears that work in internationalisation of the curriculum runs on a separate track from other theories and approaches in teaching and learning (such as assessment for learning, which also has useful parallels) and, indeed, in other disciplines, notably linguistics. To move forward with the internationalisation of the curriculum agendas we will need to adopt creative ways of thinking about new curricula in order to navigate through a complex and contested landscape of terms and ideas. In addition, as this discussion has suggested, an effective future curriculum for a globalised world cannot simply be added on to the current curriculum. Fundamental and fairly daunting changes are needed. To allow Kress (2000) the final word:

What is required is a thoroughgoing review of what the features of this new world are likely to be and what curricular and pedagogic responses are likely to be possible and most useful.

(p. 140)

Note

1 The project is called 'Educating the global engineer: Staff and student perspectives on embedding sustainable development practices into the engineering curriculum' and is funded by the Higher Education Academy, Engineering Subject Centre. The project began in March 2010 and is led by Catherine Montgomery.

The project team comprises Dr Roger Penlington, Jenna Tudor and Noel Perera from Northumbria University.

References

Barrie, S. C. (2004). A research-based approach to generic graduate attributes. *Policy Higher Education Research and Development*, 23(3), 261–275.
BBC (2010). Blood, sweat and luxuries. Television documentary series, June 2010.
Beard, C., Clegg, S. & Smith, K. (2007). Acknowledging the affective in higher education. *British Educational Research Journal*, 33(2), 235–252.
Cope, B. & Kalantzis, M. (2000). *Multiliteracies: Literacy, learning and the design of social futures*. New York: Routledge.
Cope, B. & Kalantzis, M. (2009). 'Multiliteracies': New literacies, new learning. *Pedagogies: An International Journal*, 4(3), 164–195. Available at: http://newlearningonline.com/multiliteracies/files/2009/03/pedagogiesm-litsarticle.pdf (accessed 20 November 2010).
Devlin, M. (2008). *An international and interdisciplinary approach to curriculum: The Melbourne Model*. Keynote address at the Universitas 21 Conference, Glasgow University, Scotland.
Edwards, J. (2007). Challenges and opportunities for the internationalisation of higher education in the coming decade: Planned and opportunistic initiatives in American institutions. *Journal of Studies in International Education*, 11(3), 373–381.
Entwistle, N. (2009). *Teaching for understanding at university: Deep approaches and distinctive ways of thinking*. Basingstoke: Palgrave Macmillan.
Gullikers, J. (2004). *Perceptions of authentic assessment*. Paper presented at the Second Biannual Joint Northumbria/EARLI SIG Assessment Conference, Bergen.
Hoppe, R. (2005). The global toothbrush: International divisions of labour. *SPIEGEL Special Edition, Globalization: The New World*, 7, 130–135.
Kalantzis, M. & Cope, B. (2005). *Learning by design*. Melbourne, Australia: VSIC, Common Ground.
Kalantzis, M. & Cope, B. (2010). Foreword. In D. L. Pullen & D. R. Cole (eds.), *Multiliteracies and technology enhanced education: Social practice and the global classroom*. Hershey, PA: Information Science Reference.
Kress, G. (2000). A curriculum for the future. *Cambridge Journal of Education*, 30(1), 133–145.
Manathunga, C. (2009). Post-colonial perspectives on interdisciplinary researcher identities. In A. Brew & L. Lucas (eds.), *Academic research and researchers*. Maidenhead, UK: Open University Press.
Meyer, E. F. & Land, R. (2005). Threshold concepts and troublesome knowledge: Epistemological considerations and a teaching and learning framework for teaching and learning. *Higher Education*, 9, 373–388.
Montgomery, C. (2009). A decade of internationalisation: Has it influenced students' views of cross-cultural group work at university? *Journal of Studies in International Education*, 13(2), 256–270.
Montgomery, C. (2011). Developing perceptions of interculturality: A troublesome space? In B. Preisler, I. Klitgard & A. Fabricius (eds.), *Language and learning in*

the international university: From English uniformity to diversity and hybridity. Clevedon, England: Multilingual Matters Ltd.

Montgomery, C., Chakulya, M., Ndoumin, J. P. & Sedgwick, C. (2011). Being and becoming a global citizen: Student perspectives on engagement, interdisciplinarity and boundary crossings. In V. Clifford & C. Montgomery (eds.), *Internationalising the curriculum for global citizenship.* Oxford: Oxford Centre for Staff and Learning Development.

New London Group (1996). A pedagogy of multiliteracies: Designing social futures. *Harvard Educational Review, 66*(1), 1–27.

Nicol, D. (2010). From monologue to dialogue: Improving written feedback processes in mass higher education. *Assessment and Evaluation in Higher Education, 35*(5), 501–517.

Pierce, A. (2003). *What does it mean to live in-between?* Paper presented at the 4th Annual IALIC Conference, Lancaster University, 16 December 2003.

Razbully, S. & Bamber, P. (2008). *Cross curricula planning and the global dimension at Liverpool Hope.* Seminar given at Education for Sustainable Development and Global Citizenship ITE Network Inaugural Conference.

Rennie, J. (2010). Rethinking literacy in culturally diverse classrooms. In D. L. Pullen & D. R. Cole (eds.), *Multiliteracies and technology enhanced education: Social practice and the global classroom.* Hershey, PA: Information Science Reference.

Savin-Baden, M. (2008). *Learning spaces: Creating opportunities for knowledge creation in academic life.* Maidenhead, UK: Open University Press.

Sipos, Y., Battisti, B. & Grimm, K. (2008). Achieving transformative sustainability learning: Engaging head, hands and heart. *International Journal of Sustainability in Higher Education, 9*(1), 68–86.

Chapter 13

Global citizenship and campus community

Lessons from learning theory and the lived-experience of mobile students

David Killick

> *Learning is the process of being in the world. At the heart of learning is not merely what is learned, but what the learner is becoming (learning) as a result of doing and thinking – and feeling.*
>
> (Jarvis, 2006, p. 5)

Introduction

Across reports, anecdotes and much of the research literature around international outbound student mobility (study abroad, volunteering, work placements and the like) references to a 'life-changing' experience are common (e.g. several papers in Savicki, 2008). Much of the learning which contributes to such radical claims relates to the development of attributes we can associate with cross-cultural capability and global perspectives; which I consider key *act-in-the-world* capabilities of the global citizen. In this chapter, I move beyond theoretical considerations based solely in the literature on intercultural 'competencies', and the like, and relate such personal transformation back to more foundational theories of learning and development, indicating how a model of learning as change in the lifeworld is of relevance to the global citizen constructed as a way of *being-in-the-world*. I then explore findings from a research study of the UK students engaged in international mobilities that highlight particular aspects of their learning experience. An important move is then to reflect upon how home campus communities might similarly contribute to profound learning for home and international students alike.

Learning as change in the lifeworld

Much of the literature concerning the impacts of outbound international mobility is based within, or seeks to develop, theoretical models associated with intercultural/cross-cultural sensitivity, awareness and so forth (Bennett, 2008; Deardorff, 2008; Deardorff & Hunter, 2006) or is based uniquely among languages students (Byram & Feng, 2006). More isolated examples can be found of researchers linking outcomes to transformative (Bamber, 2008) or social learning (McLeod & Wainwright, 2009) theories, or to the development of critical and comparative thinking (Yershova, DaJaeghere & Mestenhauser, 2000); these each offer valuable perspectives on specific learning within the context of study abroad. However, there is some advantage in looking to more foundational learning theories in relation to lifeworld change. In this section, I briefly present a number of perspectives from learning theorists as background, and indicate particular resonances between philosophical constructs of socialised/unexamined existence and Bennett's (1993, 2008) influential ethnocentric–ethnorelative continuum. Learning as lifeworld change is argued to be holistic, and integral to self- and other-construal.

Piaget (1972) modelled learning as a process of change in the cognitive *schemes* which constitute our interpretations of the world, and Mezirow's (1991, 2000) theory of transformative learning is concerned principally with 'perspective transformation', which we might interpret as leading to such pervasive changes in our understanding/worldview as to constitute a reformulation of cognitive 'meta-scheme(s)'. Where both theories might be extended is in the dimensions of learning which they recognise, since in both cases the affective and the behavioural dimensions get scant acknowledgement. Among others, specific work on the affective dimension can be found in Krathwohl, Bloom and Masia's (1964) affective taxonomy and Goleman's (1995, 1998) construct of Emotional Intelligence. And, although much neglected today, the third, cognitive, dimension was given significant prominence in Skinner's (1953) work on behaviourist learning, and is implicit within models of experiential learning from John Dewey's (1916/1966) foundational work onwards. However, a more holistic account of learning, or development, is to be found in Rogers' (1969) work on *significant learning*, where we find learning as a journey towards becoming a *self-actualized* person through holistic development rather than what he calls 'meaningless' purely cognitive processes. In Piaget's (1972) terms, we might interpret such an account as the (re)formulation of meta-scheme(s) across all three dimensions. If we re-present these psychological models in a more phenomenological light, we can envision learning as change to the representations of the world, which constitute the *lifeworld* – a construct variously described and developed (Ashworth, 2003; Heidegger, 1998/1962; Husserl, 1936/1970), and which is taken here to encapsulate the totality of that which is known-to-me/experienced-by-me. Lifeworld *is* world-to-me, and that which is my lifeworld today drives my going forward, the ways I grasp at each new experience and my openness to lifeworld change itself.

Significantly, transformative learning theory is particularly concerned with the 'habits of expectation' which shape our understanding. These prisms and lenses, constructed in our biographies, largely for most of us through participation in the norms and rituals of our socio-cultural world, frame how we read and interpret the goings on along our lifeworld horizons. They resonate with Heidegger's (1998/1962) fundamental claim for our being as a naturally unexamined flow among the *ready-to-hand* products and practices of our lives, and with Bourdieu's (1986; 2006/1986) constructs of *habitus* and *doxa*, that:

> *way of thinking and feeling about our everyday world, the way in which we perceive it as given. It refers to that which we think from rather than that which we think about.*

(Charlesworth, 2000, p. 30)

These theoretical constructs offer socio-philosophical accounts for the unquestioning ethnocentrism much discussed in the literature on aspects of interculturality (Bennett, 1993, 2008), and often used in the US, particularly to frame research into domestic *outbound* students on international mobility, and which is equally relevant, though much less commonly cited, to international students on their *inbound* journeying. In both cases, it may be the experience of having an unexamined existence challenged among the unready-to-hand norms and practices of a new milieu which throws up the 'dilemmas' which stimulate the learning process, since 'comparatively little change occurs ... in "situations of equilibrium"' (Gmelch, 1997, p. 487), and 'harmony is a non-learning situation' (Jarvis, 2006, p. 26). Important to recognise, as Brookfield (1987, p. 31) unusually does, is that triggering 'dilemmas' may include 'positive, joyful incidents' – 'events that are fulfilling rather than distressing'.

Experiential and constructivist learning theories underpin much recent work on good practice in learning and teaching in higher education. When we look at the sites of learning, and the potential sources of learning, much emphasis is placed on the importance of inter-subjective experience of some kind – learning as socially situated. In constructivist theories, it is (variously) through our interactions with others in the world that we co-construct our understandings, whether that be through expert guidance across Vygotsky's (1962, 1978) *zone of proximal development* or through the inward-spiralling as we move from *peripheral participation* in Lave and Wenger's (1991) *communities of practice* (COP). Similarly, intercultural learning theories, variously, place emphasis on the importance of factors in the social experience of the intercultural sojourner – such as the socio-cultural distance between host and home cultures, the amount of social contact with host culture peers and an individual's intercultural sensitivity/capability as an attribute to facilitate successful host culture contact. Ward (1996), Ward, Bochner and Furnham (2001) and Ward and Kennedy (1993) sought to synthesise these various factors into 'psychological' and 'socio-cultural' domains, with psychological adjustment referring to 'feelings of well-being or satisfaction during cross-cultural transitions' and socio-cultural adaptation 'in the behavioural domain' referring to 'the ability to "fit in" or execute effective interactions in the new milieu' (Ward, 2001a,b, p. 414). In a model of learning as change to the lifeworld, I represent the 'triggers' of learning as the figures and features which present themselves in the borderlands of lifeworld horizons, at times leading us to (re)formulate aspects of the lifeworld in ways which are so significant as to lead to 'profound' changes in one or more dimensions of being (affective, behavioural, cognitive). These lifeworld horizons can be represented as borderlands with one's self and with the 'outer' world; in the contexts of global citizenship and student mobilities, I find it helpful to present the outer world as that with which we are most familiar (our ready-to-hand socio-cultural world), and that which is less familiar (the extended world). It is relevant to note here, also, that learning as lifeworld change need not imply change *for the better*; we also learn things which may be less 'true' or unrepresentative – or unwelcome.

In the exploration of the lived-experience of the UK undergraduates on international mobilities, which forms the research focus of this chapter, then, learning is considered to be a largely socially enacted process of change across three interlinking dimensions through which our representations of ourselves and the world, that is, our lifeworld, are (re)formulated, at times with profound impact upon our self-view and/or worldview. Within that process our biographies go forward, continuously on a journey of becoming. This model of learning as lifeworld change is represented in Figure 13.1.

Global citizenship as a way of being-in-the-world

Much of the literature on global citizenship is concerned with those capabilities which such a person *should* exhibit – the knowledge they *should* hold, the skills they *should* possess and the ethics they *should* espouse – and in many cases, the acts they should *perform*. These are given various emphases by different commentators, and there are quite radically different perspectives on some (particularly when it comes to questions about the universalism of ethical positions

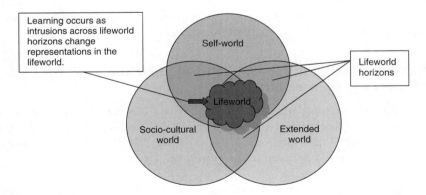

Figure 13.1 Representation of learning as change to the lifeworld across horizons with the self-world, the socio-cultural world and the extended world

or how we might *enact* our global citizenship). The model adopted in this chapter shifts the discussion and represents the global citizen as a way of *being-in-the-world* which requires primarily a sense of how I *am* among those with whom I share the planet – my sense of *self-in-the-world*, and a set of capabilities which *then* enable me to *act-in-the-world*. These, respectively, are present as life-world representations to myself of *who I am* and *what I can do*. This model gives primacy to my sense of self, or what Rogers (1959) refers to as my 'self concept', seen as:

> *the organized consistent conceptual gestalt composed of perceptions of the characteristics of "I" or "me" and the perceptions of the relationships of the "I" or "me" to others and to various aspects of life, together with the values attached to these perceptions.*

(p. 200)

I propose *self-in-the-world* as a sense of self dwelling among alterity, where difference is recognised as legitimate, a characteristic of human being in a globalising world. Whereas the literature on interculturality has things to say about both global identity and agency, the tendency to focus on the particular circumstances of the international sojourner, and upon the relevance 'in other countries' (Hunter, White & Godbey, 2006, p. 283) are limiting in the context of global citizenship as an aspiration for all students and for contexts at home or away.

Taken together, the argument thus far is that three-dimensional learning – learning as change in the lifeworld – is the process by which I might become more (or less) of a global citizen as self- and act-in-the-world meta-schemes are (re)formulated; a constant process of 'becoming' as I journey through my biography. Outbound student mobility, as a potentially rich site of new intersubjective experience among cultural others, immersion in alterity, may enable global citizen becoming in respect of both of these lifeworld meta-schemes. The research which I draw upon below revealed stories of students making precisely such journeys. The focus of this chapter is aspects of the learning *processes* they experienced rather than the outcomes of those processes.

Aspects of learning in the lived-experience of students on mobility

> *[T]he biggest thing with the experience that I had was that my experience would have been a tenth, a twentieth as good if … or I might not have enjoyed it at all – if I hadn't made such brilliant friends. Like, friends were the foundation from which I built everything up around (Tiff).*

Taking a broadly phenomenological stance, I sought to investigate the lived-experience of 14 undergraduate students across of range of outbound mobility experiences through pre-, during and post-experience interviews, and a short period of shadowing during their period abroad, and to set their narratives within the models of learning as lifeworld change and global citizenship as being-in-the-world. All participants were full-time undergraduate students studying various subjects at a large UK university. Purposeful sampling of mobility types sought to ensure a range of mobility variables were included across the sample. Table 13.1 summarises the locations and types of experience of each participant. The objective was not to obtain any sort of 'representative' sample, but to look at the lived-experiences of international mobility *per se*, rather than within a particular mobility type.

In this section, I draw directly from my research thesis to explore how participant narratives illuminated particular aspects of the learning processes which brought once dim features and figures across their lifeworld horizons, and in so doing contributed to a more global sense of self. Important is the fact that their learning was *situated* (Lave & Wenger, 1991) in a particular milieu, though I will go on to argue that some of the significant factors within that milieu might be brought into the home campus.

Open to learning and open to challenge

Several participants in the study referred to being newly open to learning during their sojourns. For example, Betty found that, in contrast to her self in Leeds, she 'would like to understand' the perspectives of others and 'definitely' wanted 'to know more about the Australian culture and, and all that sort of stuff'. As 'the outsider', Deborah was 'open-minded about things'. Belinda was someone who was not going to judge 'the way they live' and Tanya identified the importance of her determination to be not 'too judgemental' if she was to learn from her Romanian experience.

Such openness was often accompanied by a sense of a *will* to engage. Stimulated by her new environment, and by a new-found sense of self-confidence, Gill narrated how:

> *I feel like I have to experience it, so I'm going to …. I'm getting out there and doing more because I'm in another country.*

Because she was 'interested' in Andalusian culture, Paula 'was always asking questions to virtually anybody'. Lisa found she 'wanted to get to know' Melbourne, meet its people and 'have a life' there. Something which profoundly changed her view of how she could take in or take on the world at large:

> *I do want to go and see more, I want to learn more about other cultures and see different places – just increase my knowledge of the world.*

This *will* to learn also showed in how participants identified pushing themselves in some way. For Lisa, the experience of 'putting myself out there' took her

Table 13.1 Participant variables considered at the sampling stage

	Anne	Deborah	Belinda	Tanya	Rita	Paula	Joan	Margaret	Christine	Clare	Lisa	Betty	Gill	Tiff
Destination	France		Romania		Spain				Australia					
Mobility type														
Volunteering		✓	✓											
Working	✓			✓	✓	✓								
Studying							✓	✓	✓	✓	✓	✓	✓	✓
Duration (weeks)	4	4	2	2	30	30	30	30	15	15	15	15	15	15
Realistic to travel home in mobility	✓	✓			✓	✓	✓	✓						
Foreign language users	✓	✓			✓	✓	✓	✓						
Credit-bearing & directly assessed	✓	✓							✓	✓	✓	✓	✓	✓
Credit-bearing & not directly assessed					✓	✓	✓	✓						
Self-funded (whole or part)			✓	✓		✓	✓	✓	✓	✓	✓	✓	✓	✓
Found individual accommodation					✓					✓			✓	
Shared 'international' accommodation									✓		✓	✓		✓
Shared peer accommodation	✓	✓	✓	✓										

'outside of my comfort zone'. Betty had gone 'out of her way' to 'go off' and make her own friends aside from her housemates, and Clare had overcome the 'massive challenge' and 'thrown myself into it' to integrate from the start. Margaret found taking up her new life 'definitely more daunting', and felt 'like a fish out of water' as she identified as challenges things which she 'would probably not have given a thought to' in Leeds. Gill also noted how different her experience was to staying in Leeds, where 'I wouldn't have had to push myself out of my comfort zone', and as a consequence, she 'got to go out, see new places, meet new people, form better friendships', all of which opened up learning opportunities.

Learning triggers and dilemmas

The most significant learning triggers running through the student narratives were found in contact with cultural others. In some cases (participants in Romania and France, and variously those in Spain), such contacts were with members of the host community; in Australia and some cases in Spain, contacts were predominantly with other travellers. I have noted the importance of entering new international communities and of forging particular friendships with unanticipated others elsewhere (Killick, 2011). The examples below are relevant to those particular forms of contact, but also illustrate a more general point about learning as socially enacted.

'Meeting people from different backgrounds' (Betty) stimulated learning for the majority of participants. Lisa found cultural learning came from her social activities with friends from different national roots in Australia, specifically the experience of 'seeing their families'. Gill learned 'so much' through meeting 'countless amounts of people, and from all the different places'. Margaret found 'constantly being around people from here [Spain]' enabled her to learn 'how they interact with each other, and how much more relaxed they are in … with physical contact'. Lisa attributed the development of tolerance to her experiences of 'mixing with' and meeting 'different people from different … cultures and communities'. The richness of experience among a culturally diverse community was prominent in Tiff's experience:

> *I became much more culturally aware of other cultures, especially because I was an international student, like – with all the Mauritians, and [the] Americans, and the Italians … . Like all the different type of people that I met.*

Experiencing more intimate friendship development with cultural others drove learning for some participants. Clare learned the weakness of impressions 'picked up from the media' through meeting people and coming 'to know them properly'. Similarly, Rita was 'made' to 'shrug off most of my stereotypes' because she 'met Spanish people and got to know them as individuals'. And it was 'through having a lot of different friends, from sort of, like, even different continents' that she learned 'to get on with people' and 'not to take certain things offensively'.

In Montpellier, Anne did not have much opportunity to socialise with people beyond her group of fellow students on the short teaching placement, but she did have to live quite intensively with peers with whom she felt little in common. Experiencing this led to new perspectives and a generally more open attitude:

> *I did things that I didn't think I'd enjoy, and I became able to enjoy things that obviously other people enjoyed as well. And I could see things from different points of view.*

Joan developed a new found assertiveness because of the experience of having 'to come forward and say things' when 'living in a shared flat with people who are more outspoken'.

It was the intimacy of contact which brought a strong affective dimension to Tanya's learning among Romania Gypsies, through the almost visceral experience of being 'in the thick of it', experiencing: 'the smells and the clothes, and the skin'. Her learning was stimulated through 'seeing actually how people live' and 'listening to the stories', and through a direct, community experience: 'We've eaten here. We've drunk here – you know'. And it was, in particular, the 'shock factor' of seeing 'the way people live within the EU', contesting the ready-to-hand schemes of 'poverty' and 'Europe', which Belinda found 'really difficult'. The classic 'dilemma' of sojourner experience is that of culture shock (Oberg, 1960). However, although some participants did narrate experiences which echoed the stages of culture shock, this did not appear to be a significant feature of their mobilities. Tiff, Clare and Paula all referred directly to the excitement of a 'honeymoon period', arguably blocking learning because of the 'romantic' light shed on everything encountered (see Nussbaum, 1988, p. 118 for discussion on chauvinistic and romantic responses), but in each case this was followed not by an inhibiting period of anxiety, but by 'a very easy process' (Paula) of 'getting used to it' (Tiff) and it feeling 'like it's a home' (Clare).

Virtuous circles of becoming

I present virtuous learning circles as instances when learning in one dimension is seen to impact upon others. Across the participants' narratives we particularly find examples of them identifying confidence-through-action – affective learning stimulated through observations and reflections of themselves behaving in positive ways, exemplifying, personal development (or 'self-actualisation') washing through learning processes. Bandura's (1997) construct of *self-efficacy* points to the importance of a self-belief that one can complete what lies ahead; self-efficacy promotes confidence and optimism even when goals may appear difficult to attain. What surfaces in these narratives incorporates this, but extends beyond it, as *experience* of success feeds back into and extends self-efficacy and confidence, and pushes learning outwards into new experience.

For Clare, the experience of adapting and learning successfully in a new environment gave a new sense of confidence; now she can think 'I've done this before, ... what's the problem?', a positive stimulus to future learning: 'it's fed my ambition .... I want to go and see as much as I can'. Anne saw her growth in confidence as 'one of the main' impacts of her experience in Montpellier. While this was tied up in part with linguistic and classroom confidence, her experience of success in those areas made her 'more confident in working with new people generally and in speaking in general'. Although already feeling she was confident before her mobility, Margaret found herself 'not as daunted by new and unfamiliar situations'. Paula felt a similar transformation; through making face-to-face contacts amongst other sojourners, she shifted from an earlier reliance on social networking sites to form friendships, experiencing herself as more 'outgoing', 'assertive' and 'open' with other people. Clare's self-confidence was accompanied by losing her sense of inferiority among more worldly others at home; through seeing herself succeed in Melbourne she became 'as good as anybody else now'. So profound was Gill's transformation to becoming 'just so much more outgoing, so much more confident' that she came to feel her earlier self was 'a completely different person'. For Lisa, too, the change was transformational. Whereas before she was 'a lot more timid', now she is 'quite fearless':

> [I]t's increased my independence. I'd probably say almost a hundred per cent. I feel a hell of a lot more confident and independent within myself. I feel more confident to be put in situations.

Rita's confidence developed in many ways; perhaps most significantly for her was that she became 'a lot less shy' in general, enabling her to 'become more a people person'. She captured something of the continuous flow of learning and the development of confidence:

> It wasn't necessarily a bad experience when I first arrived, it was just <u>new</u>, and I just learned from it and I, you know ... I tried every day, and I just got stronger and stronger from it, and in turn became more independent.

A contrasting 'vicious circle' might be identified in the way Joan's early home-sickness led her away from learning opportunities among cultural others because, 'it's difficult when I miss home to then spend time with people who I don't understand'.

Bringing it all back home – implications for campus communities

Highlighted above, then, are examples of learning processes brought to light in lived-experience:

- driven by participants being open, willing to engage and pushing themselves beyond their comfort zones
- socially situated, triggered in contact with 'others' and the dilemmas these posed
- flowing through and into their biographies as holistic virtuous circles of becoming, crossing learning dimensions in a process of self-actualisation.

This chapter presents global citizenship as self- and act-in-the-world dimensions to being-in-the-world, and argues the development of these is consistent with a model of learning as a holistic, three-dimensional change to the lifeworld, at times shifting self- and/or worldview meta-schemes. Such change is proposed to be significantly enacted through inter-subjective encounters, and triggered in the dilemmas encountered when established/unexamined lifeworld representations encounter un-ready-to-hand features and figures on lifeworld horizons. In such a model (echoing, perhaps, Martin Hague's account of the importance of the avant-garde community to Ghandi's transformative experience in Chapter 14 of this book), the importance of the community of practice, whether social, professional or academic, assumes great significance to the quality and the direction of learning. The lived-experiences of the UK undergraduate students have brought to light examples of learning triggers and virtuous circles through experiences of intercultural contact within communities of social practice established during international mobilities. In such encounters, the unexamined flow is interrupted and learning is personalised. Such experiences, I propose, are common also to international students experiencing lives as sojourners within many university campuses and community worlds, familiar to us but strange to them. It is, perhaps, strange how little these dimensions to their experience have been researched in comparison with their sojourning home student peers, a situation which in itself may speak to what constructs lie most ready-to-hand among those of us interested in the impacts of international education. In each case, however, while their experiences may appear particularly 'rich', the learning processes involved are, at root, exactly those which underpin all learning as represented in the experiential and constructivist models discussed earlier. In this light, I would suggest that we can look to our campuses and ask if we cannot offer similarly rich communities in which to enable global citizen becoming for all our students.

The participants in this study were 'alert' to their new milieu, mindful (Langer, 1989) of themselves in their interactions; they were perhaps anxious, but also *willing* to engage, ready to push beyond their comfort zones and open to learning. I would suggest that this is also a common affective state for (just about) all students, home or international, when they first enter the new milieu of their university. What we present as the expectations, rules and rituals of our campus community at that point *situates* their learning, quickly establishing norms and practices to move their university being into an unexamined flow. Extracted from that flow during their mobility experiences, participants in this research moved into emergent communities of social practice, in large part among cultural 'others'. We know that this does not appear to be the common experience of home or international students in the UK, the US, New Zealand or Australia, where our everyday observations, along with most research in the area (largely among international students) speaks of cultural/national silos rather than of an inclusive campus community (Trice, 2007; UNITE, 2006; Volet & Ang, 1998; Ward, 2001a,b). Social identity theories (Tajfel & Turner, 1986; Ting-Toomey, 2005) tell us the tendency to in-group and out-group communities is natural, giving shape to our unexamined identities, reinforcing our established and ethnocentric representations of the 'other' and her worlds, and providing securities which can sustain us in uncertain times or places. However, the business of the university is to enable us to grow beyond ourselves, not to constrain us within established self-views or worldviews.

In situating the exploration of the learning of students on mobility within learning and development theories rather than solely within theories of interculturality, it has been possible to see that their learning, while richly significant, is not differently realised to any other form of lifeworld change. This enables us to question the uniqueness of the international sojourn as a site for holistic, global learning. However, if we are to enable *all* our students to move to a sense of *self-in-the-world* as one at ease dwelling among alterity, then our campuses must present themselves at every encounter as genuine spaces of intercultural community, and our curriculum – in its content, delivery and assessment – must *require and enable* the capabilities to enact that sense of self. Otherwise, the significant learning available to the very few home students who participate in international mobility will be denied to the majority who stay at home. Our current practice, I suggest, is largely culpable in sustaining, even re-enforcing, the ethnocentrisms of an unexamined existence. As we have seen, students, given appropriate learning situations, are willing and capable of so much more.

References

Ashworth, P. (2003). The phenomenology of the lifeworld and social psychology. *Social Psychology Review*, 5(1), 18–34.

Bamber, P. (2008, December 2007). *The impact of student participation in international service-learning programs.* Paper presented at the Education for Sustainable Development: Graduates as Global Citizens, Bournemouth.

Bandura, A. (1997). *Self-efficacy: The exercise of control.* New York: Freeman.

Bennett, M. J. (1993). Towards ethnorelativism: A developmental model of intercultural sensitivity. In R. M. Paige (ed.), *Education for the intercultural experience.* Yarmouth, ME: Intercultural Press, pp. 21–71.

Bennett, M. J. (2008). On becoming a global soul. In V. Savicki (ed.), *Developing intercultural competence and transformation. A path to engagement during study abroad* Sterling, VA: Stylus, pp. 13–31.

Bourdieu, P. (1986). *Distinction: A social critique of the judgement of taste.* London: Routledge.

Bourdieu, P. (2006/1986). The forms of capital. In H. Lauder, P. Brown, J.-A. Dillabough & A. H. Halsey (eds.), *Education, globalization & social change* Oxford: Oxford University Press, pp. 105–118.

Brookfield, S. D. (1987). *Developing critical thinkers.* Milton Keynes: Open University Press.

Byram, M. & Feng, A. (eds.) (2006). *Living and studying abroad – Research and practice.* Clevedon, England: Multilingual Matters Ltd.

Charlesworth, S. J. (2000). *A phenomenology of working class experience.* Cambridge: Cambridge University Press.

Deardorff, D. K. (2008). Intercultural competence. A definition, model, and implications for education abroad. In V. Savicki (ed.), *Developing intercultural competence and transformation* Sterling, VA: Stylus, pp. 32–52.

Deardorff, D. K. & Hunter, W. (2006). Educating global-ready graduates. *International Educator, May/June,* 72–83.

Dewey, J. (1916/1966). *Democracy and education.* Toronto, Canada: Collier-Macmillan.

Gmelch, G. (1997). Crossing cultures: Student travel and personal development. *International Journal of Intercultural Relations, 21*(4), 475–490.

Goleman, D. (1995). *Emotional intelligence.* New York: Bantam Books.

Goleman, D. (1998). *Working with emotional intelligence.* London: Bloomsbury.

Heidegger, M. (1998/1962). *Being and time* (J. Macquarie & B. Blackwell, trans.). Oxford: Blackwell.

Hunter, B., White, G. P. & Godbey, G. C. (2006). What does it mean to be globally competent? *Journal of Studies in International Education, 10*(3), 267–285. doi: 10.1177/1028315306286930.

Husserl, E. (1936/1970). *The idea of phenomenology.* The Hague: Martinus Nijoff.

Jarvis, P. (2006). *Towards a comprehensive theory of human learning. Lifelong learning and the learning society.* Vol. 1. London: Routledge.

Killick, D. (Forthcoming). Seeing ourselves-in-the-world: Developing global citizenship through international mobility and campus community. *Journal of Studies in International Education.*

Krathwohl, D. R., Bloom, B. S., & Masia, B. B. (1964). *Taxonomy of educational objectives. The classification of educational goals. Handbook II: Affective domain.* London: Longman.

Langer, E. (1989). *Mindfulness.* Reading, MA: Addison-Wesley.

Lave, J. & Wenger, E. (1991). *Situated learning. Legitimate peripheral participation.* Cambridge: Cambridge University Press.

McLeod, M. & Wainwright, P. (2009). Researching the study abroad experience. *Journal of Studies in International Education, 13*(1), 66–71.

Mezirow, J. (1991). *Transformative dimensions of adult learning.* San Francisco, CA: Jossey-Bass.

Mezirow, J. (2000). Learning to think like an adult. Core concepts of transformational theory. In J. Mezirow & associates (eds.), *Learning as transformation* San Francisco, CA: Jossey-Bass, pp. 3–33.

Nussbaum, M. (1988). Nature, function, and capability: Aristotle on political distri-
bution. *Oxford Studies in Ancient Philosophy, supplementary volume.*
Oberg, K. (1960). Culture shock: Adjustment to new cultural environments. *Practical
Anthropology 7*, 177–182.
Piaget, J. (1972). *The psychology of the child.* New York: Basic Books.
Rogers, C. R. (1959). A theory of therapy, personality and interpersonal relationships
as developed in the client-centered framework. In S. Koch (ed.), *Psychology: A study
of a science. Vol. 3: Formulations of the person and the social context* New York:
McGraw-Hill, pp. 184–256.
Rogers, C. R. (1969). *Freedom to learn: A view of what education might become.*
Columbus, OH: Charles E. Merrill.
Savicki, V. (ed.) (2008). *Developing intercultural competence and transformation:
Theory, research and application in international education.* Sterling, VA: Stylus.
Skinner, B. F. (1953). *Science and human behavior.* New York: Macmillan.
Tajfel, H. & Turner, J. C. (1986). The social identity theory of intergroup
behavior. In S. Worchel & W. G. Austin (eds.), *Psychology of intergroup relations*
Chicago, IL: Nelson-Hall, pp. 33–47.
Ting-Toomey, S. (2005). Identity negotiation theory: Crossing cultural boundaries.
In W. Gudykunst (ed.), *Theorizing about intercultural communication*
Thousand Oaks, CA: Sage, pp. 211–234.
Trice, A. G. (2007). Faculty perspectives regarding graduate international students' iso-
lation from host national students. *International Education Journal, 8*(1), 108–117.
UNITE (2006). *The international student experience report.* Bristol: UNITE.
Volet, S. & Ang, G. (1998). Culturally mixed groups on international campuses: An
opportunity for inter-cultural learning. *Higher Education Research & Development,
17*(1), 5–23.
Vygotsky, L. S. (1962). *Thought & language.* Cambridge, MA: MIT Press.
Vygotsky, L. S. (1978). *Mind in society: The development of higher psychological
processes.* Cambridge, MA: Harvard University Press.
Ward, C. (1996). Acculturation. In D. Landis & R. Bhagat (eds.), *Handbook of
intercultural training*, 2nd edn. Thousand Oaks, CA: Sage, pp. 124–147.
Ward, C. (2001a). The A, B, Cs of acculturation. In D. Matsumoto (ed.), *The handbook of culture and psychology* Oxford: Oxford University Press, pp. 411–445.
Ward, C. (2001b). *The impact of international students on domestic students and host
institutions.* Wellington, NZ: Ministry of Education. Electronic version available
at: http://www.educationcounts.govt.nz/publications/international/the_impact_
of_international_students_on_domestic_students_and_host_institutions
Ward, C., Bochner, S. & Furnham, A. (2001). *The psychology of culture shock*, 2nd edn.
London: Routledge.
Ward, C. & Kennedy, A. (1993). Psychological and sociocultural adjustment during
cross-cultural transitions: A comparison of secondary students at home and abroad.
International Journal of Psychology, 28, 129–147.
Yershova, Y., DaJaeghere, J. & Mestenhauser, J. (2000). Thinking not as usual:
Adding the intercultural perspective. *Journal of Studies in International Education,
4*(1), 39–78.

Chapter 14

Towards the intercultural self
Mahatma Gandhi's international education in London

Martin Haigh

> *It is alarming and also nauseating to see Mr. Gandhi, a seditious Middle Temple lawyer of the type well known in the East, now posing as a fakir, striding half naked up the steps of the Vice regal palace to parley on equal terms with the representative of the King Emperor.*
>
> (Winston Churchill, 1931, *on Gandhi's meeting with the Viceroy of India*)

Introduction

A recent survey of international staff at Oxford Brookes University, UK, revealed that many manage their identities to mesh with the dominant culture (Clifford et al., 2010). Those in unfamiliar settings often create a 'dramaturgical self' or selves, multiple alternative identities and role-play strategies, to survive and thrive in their interactions with the world (Collinson, 2003; Goffman, 1959). For many, life is enacted as a cinematic spectacle, where they create their own characters and guide the development of the script (Starratt, 1993; Lumby & English, 2010). Dramaturgy is a key benefit of an intercultural education that helps learners consciously develop and manipulate personae that, otherwise, might be adopted subconsciously.

However, intercultural learning is much deeper than mere play acting, it is about reshaping the learner's way of being-in-the-world (Delors, 1996). Learning in multicultural contexts could be more effective if those who help new international staff settle in, and teachers who work with international sojourners, develop learning situations that explore new ways of being and constructing identity.

These ideas are explored through a case study of a special international student; it concerns the creation of the Mahatma Gandhi from the law student Gandhi who studied at the Inns of Court, London from 1888 to 1891. This chapter interprets the development of Gandhi's personae through analysis of his memoirs as an international learner (Gandhi, 1922) using theories that evaluate how acculturative stress, culture shock, is expressed in student behaviour (Pedersen, 1995). It explores some of Gandhi's explorations and personal awakenings and how they influenced his subsequent career. Gandhi's experiences as an international learner, partly triggered by his isolation in an alien culture, were an awakening to the spiritual strengths of his own culture. The end result remains iconic. However, more important was Gandhi's construction of himself as a person capable of transcending both his home cultural and other cultural personae: Gandhi's emergence as a true moral cosmopolitan (Hill, 2000).

Mahatma Gandhi's experience as an international student proved traumatic, transformative and ambiguous. It started him on the path that made him internationally famous; it perhaps created the Mahatma he became. However, its impacts were far from totally positive. He lost caste on his departure, struggled while overseas, his mother died while he was away, and he developed sentiments of isolation and distance that he never entirely shed (Hunt, 1993). In later life, he wrote:

> *I have never been an advocate of our students going abroad. My experience tells me that such, on return, find themselves to be square pegs in round holes.*
>
> (Gandhi, 1946, p. 308)

Like others, Gandhi's sojourn in another culture set him apart from those who immersed in their home culture. He became simultaneously more self-aware of the strengths and weaknesses of that culture and somewhat hybridised, in Hindu terms 'polluted', by his immersion within an Other way of life.

This chapter interprets Gandhi's own memoirs as the testimony of 'just another International Student' (Gandhi, 1922). It considers what light this sheds on Gandhi's experience, the emergence of his later intercultural self and his subsequent actions (Bhana & Vahed, 2005).

Theory

The experience of total immersion in an alien culture can be traumatic. Culture shock, acculturative stress, is what happens when someone moves from a familiar cultural environment to one that is not (McLeod, 2008). Chapdelaine and Alexitch (2004, p. 168) talk about: 'multiple demands for adjustment … at the cognitive, behavioural, emotional, social, and physiological levels' (p. 168) and the importance of social interaction with the hosts.

The shock for those arriving in London from the tropics arises from differences in climate, food, language, dress, social roles, rules of behaviour and social values and the cultural distance between their home and host society (Berry, 1992) and prejudice and preconception within the host culture. However, the most severe emerges from the realisation that their empathic emotional intelligence has been stripped away (Mayer & Salovey, 1993). The incomers are unable to control their impact on others because their normal cultural cues and codes no longer apply and they are unable to read the cues, body language and codes that frame others' actions. The experience can elicit extreme reactions that include high anxiety, blind panic and depression, before some form of accommodation is discovered. Oberg (1960) summarises:

> *Culture shock is precipitated by losing all of our familiar signs and symbols of social intercourse... the thousand and one ways that we orient ourselves to the situations of daily life...*

(p. 177)

Mandelbaum (1973) evaluates Gandhi's life history in terms of adaptation, dimension and turning points, noting that, in some respects, each subject is a performer of the 'pre-programmed'. However, the model that best describes the process of adaptation, including the 'psychological acculturative stress' called 'culture shock' is Pedersen's five-stage model (Pedersen, 1995, Figure 14.1). These stages are:

1   'Honeymoon', the excitement of everything being new.
2   'Disintegration', when the problems, embarrassments, frustrations and stress of dealing with unpredictable cultural encounters begin to create feelings of inadequacy, isolation and homesickness.
3   'Reintegration/Reversion', a 'These people...' phase that involves distancing and often rejection of the new culture.

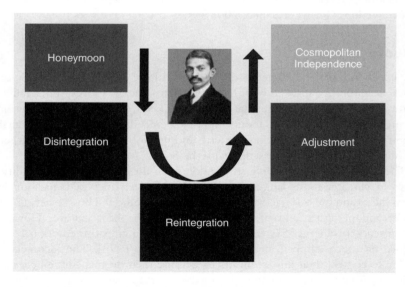

Figure 14.1 Stages of the international learner (adapted from Pedersen, 1995)

4   'Adjustment', when the sojourner begins to learn the ways, rules and 'performance skills' required by the new culture and so begins to feel comfortable enough to operate autonomously. During this phase, the sojourner begins to construct a new emotional intelligence that fits with their host culture.

5   'Cosmopolitan Independence', the final stage, arrives when the sojourner can cope with the possibilities and differences between the two cultures, make decisions based on this cross-cultural awareness, and even become enthusiastic about the new culture. Such people become 'cultural hybrids', cosmopolitans who may even place certain cultural traits of the new culture above those of their own (Hill, 2000) and learn how to enact their two cultures. They learn to perform in ways that are not merely acceptable but actively influential to audiences of one, other, or both cultures using the signs, symbols and forms that will affect the feelings of their audience in ways they intend.

Recognition of this process of adjustment is often modelled as a U-curve – or a double-U if the phases of 'reverse culture shock' are added for their return to their host culture (Figure 14.1).

This model has been criticised as an over-generalisation, and later researchers have used a larger matrix of social, cultural and individual personality parameters (Furnham & Bochner, 1986; Ward Bochner & Furnham, 2001). Pedersen (1995) also discounts rival 'disease' models, which conceive cultural shock as a malady that must be remedied by treatment. Foster (1962, p. 187) describes culture shock as 'A mental illness, and as true of much mental illness, the victim usually does not know he is afflicted'. Journey or 'pilgrimage' models have a distinctive Kuhnian flavour in their discussion of the resolution of cognitive differences and 'the migration from ethnocentrism to ethnorelativism' (Kuhn, 1970; McLeod, 2008, p. 31).

In fact, only some reach the bicultural cosmopolitan stage. Others, 'Rejectors', reject their new host culture and isolate themselves from it, while a minority, 'Adopters', fully merge into the host culture and allow their own cultural origins to fade into the background (Barnett, 1953). Berry describes four outcomes of psychological 'acculturative stress'. These vary depending on whether the sojourner regards their own cultural identity valuable enough to maintain and whether building relationships with members of the host society seems worthwhile. If the answer is yes to both, then 'integration'; if no to both, then 'marginalisation'; if yes to the first and no to the second, then 'separation'; and if no to the first but yes to the second, then 'assimilation' (Berry, 2001; Berry et al., 1989, 2002; Figure 14.2).

However, as the following analysis of Gandhi's student days in London shows, even short-term sojourners may shift quickly between these stages and stances. The U-curve does not really do justice to the complexity of cultural adaptation.

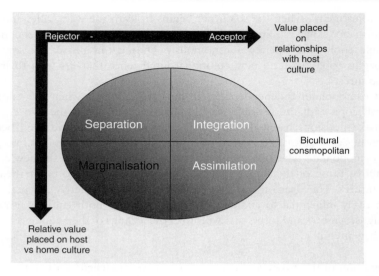

Figure 14.2 Outcomes of acculturative stress and sojourner stances (Barnett, 1953; Berry, 1992)

Analysis

Table 14.1 analyses Gandhi's testimony about his sojourn as a student at the Inns of Court in London and shows key text quotations, a description of the stance it implies, the outcome of the stress, and finally, the stage it represents on the culture shock U-curve.

Discussion

Gandhi's description of his time in London tells little of his 'Honeymoon' stage or its value. However, evidence for both of these high points can be found in his other writings. Perhaps pre-programmed by his English education at the Albert (Prince of Edinburgh) School in Rajkot, Gujarat, and the high ideals of social reform in his departing speech (in Gandhi, 1999, 1, p. 1), Gandhi set forth to seek his fortune: 'I thought to myself, if I go to England not only shall I become a barrister (of whom I used to think a great deal), but I shall be able to see England, the land of philosophers and poets, the very centre of civilization' (Gandhi, 1999, in Hay, 1989, p. 76). On arrival, he was hugely impressed by the size and modern conveniences of London, as well as the qualities of his first hotel room: 'I thought I could pass a lifetime in that room' (Gandhi, 1999, in Hay, 1989, p. 78). Later, in 1908, after his return, he commented that 'even now, next to India, I would rather live in London than in any other place in the world' (Doke, 1909, p. 51).

Table 14.1 Gandhi's experiences as a international student in London (Gandhi, 1922)

Text	Stance	Stress outcome	Stage
… we reached Southampton… On the boat I had worn a black suit, the white flannel one… having been kept especially for wearing when I landed…. Those were the last days of September, and I found I was the only person wearing such clothes…. The shame of being the only person in white clothes was already too much for me (p. 55)	Adopter – MG tries to fit in but fails	Aim is integration	A first step towards disintegration
I would continually think of my home and country. My mother's love always haunted me. At night the tears would stream down my cheeks, and home memories … made sleep out of the question…. Everything was strange – the people, their ways, …. I was a complete novice in the matter of English etiquette and continually had to be on my guard. …. England I could not bear, but to return to India was not to be thought of … (pp. 56–57)	Rejection	Marginalisation – rejection of both England and of returning to India	Disintegration – homesickness (hiraeth) – and collapse in the face of alien English society
Dr Mehta …said. 'We come to England not so much for the purpose of studies as for gaining experience of English life and customs. And for this you need to live with a family. … I gratefully accepted the suggestion and removed to the friend's rooms. …. He treated me as his own brother, initiated me into English ways and manners, and accustomed me to talking the language. My food, however, became a serious question (p. 57)	Towards bicultural cosmopolitan	Assisted assimilation	Towards adjustment
'Pray excuse me. … I admit it is necessary to eat meat. But I cannot break my vow. I cannot argue about it. … I am helpless. A vow is a vow. It cannot be broken. (p. 58)	Rejection	Separation in the matter of food	Reintegration – with original tradition
But I had found my feet … I had just begun reading newspapers… I launched out in search of a vegetarian restaurant (p. 59)	Acceptance	Towards integration	More adjustment
I once hit on a vegetarian restaurant … I noticed books for sale … among them Salt's *Plea for Vegetarianism*. This I… read … from cover to cover …. From the date of reading this book, I may claim to have become a vegetarian by choice (p. 59)	Bicultural cosmopolitan	More integration	Cosmopolitan

(Continued)

Table 14.1 (Continued)

Text	Stance	Stress outcome	Stage
I undertook the … task of becoming an English gentleman. The clothes … that I was wearing were… unsuitable … and I got new ones … While in India, the mirror had been a luxury …. Here I wasted 10 minutes every day before a huge mirror, watching myself arranging my tie and parting my hair (p. 61)	Acceptor	Full integration	Adjustment
I had not to spend a lifetime in England…. What then was the use of learning elocution?…. I was a student …I had discovered that I was pursuing a false idea. …. The punctiliousness in dress persisted for years. But henceforward I became a student (pp. 62–63)	Rejector	Separation	Reintegration
My life was certainly more truthful and my soul knew no bounds of joy. As I searched myself deeper, the necessity for changes both internal and external began to grow on me. …I now relished the boiled spinach … such experiments taught me that the real seat of taste was not the tongue but the mind (pp. 63–66)	Rejector	Marginalisation	Transformative reintegration
I decided to start a vegetarian club …. I myself became the Secretary (p. 69)	Bicultural cosmopolitan again	Integration	Cosmopolitan confidence
I was elected to the Executive Committee of the Vegetarian Society… but I always felt tongue-tied…. This shyness I retained throughout …. My last effort to make a public speech …was on the eve of my departure …. But …. I only succeeded in making myself ridiculous (p. 69)	Acceptor	Assimilation	Cosmopolitan – but without confidence
There were comparatively few Indian students in England …. It was a practice with them to affect the bachelor even though … married. …. in the event of the fact being known it would be impossible … to go about or flirt with the young girls. …I saw that our youths had …chosen a life of untruth …. I too caught the contagion. I did not hesitate to pass myself off as a bachelor though I was married and the father of a son (p. 73)	Acceptor	Integration	Reintegration

Towards the end of my second year in England I came across two Theosophists …. They talked to me about the Gita. … I felt ashamed, as I had read the divine poem neither in Sanskrit nor in Gujarati. I was constrained to tell them … that I would gladly read it with them. The book struck me as one of priceless worth…. I regard it today as the book par excellence for the knowledge of Truth (pp. 76–77)	Bicultural	Integration in the area of religion	Cosmopolitan – but extending back into own culture
But the New Testament produced a different impression, especially the Sermon on the Mount which went straight to my heart. … My young mind tried to unify the teaching of the Gita, The Light of Asia and the Sermon on the Mount. That renunciation was the highest form of religion and appealed to me greatly (pp. 77–78)	Bicultural	Integration in the area of religion	Home cultural rediscovery
Narayan Hemchandra… did not know English. His dress was ….. a clumsy pair of trousers, a wrinkled, dirty, brown coat after the Parsi fashion. …. Such a … person was bound to be singled out in fashionable society'. I have heard a good deal about you. … I should be very pleased if you were kind enough to come to my place.' Hemchandra … replied?' 'Yes…. I want to learn English. Will you teach me?' … Soon we were close friends (p. 81)	Bicultural interpreter	Integration in the role of social life	Building cosmopolitan skills
… we both called on the Cardinal. I put on the usual visiting suit. Narayan Hemchandra was the same as ever, …. I tried to make fun of this, but he laughed …. and said: *'You civilized fellows are all cowards. Great men never look at a person's exterior. They think of his heart'.* (p. 83)	Bicultural	Experiencing separation from the outside	Experiencing the cosmopolitan as outsider
Dining at the Inns of Court: …every one ate and drank the good commons and choice wines… To us in India it is a matter for surprise… that the cost of drink should exceed the cost of food. …. Later I came to understand (pp. 86–87)	Rejection	Marginalisation in the area of social networking	Experiencing the hidden curriculum
I passed my examinations, was called to the bar … and enrolled in the High Court on the 11th. On the 12th, I sailed for home. …But … there was no end to my helplessness and fear. I did not feel myself qualified to practise law…. I had learnt nothing at all of Indian law … with just a little leaven of hope mixed with my despair, I landed at Bombay (pp. 88–90)	Rejection		Towards the second U-curve of disintegration and reintegration

The other stages are more apparent, although their sequence is not 'clean' and the processes seem to divide according to different areas of life. Gandhi was enthusiastic about dress and appearance but solidly rejected the British meat-eating diet. Both these facts are important. His rejection of Western culture was important to constructing his adjustment and eventual bicultural cosmopolitanism.

Why did Mahatma Gandhi adopt a traditional Indian form of dress and make this his 'trademark'? Gandhi clearly understood the performative aspects of cultural adaptation, the need to look the part, which in his student days manifested as his 'dandy' phase in dress suit and top hat. This echoes his later appearance as Churchill's 'half-naked fakir' and Churchill was not alone at being unimpressed by this affectation. As in London, Gandhi was dressed for effect, in clothes calculated to resonate with his audience, in India and overseas. Hence, ironically, much of Gandhi's subsequent Indian-ness of performance was suggested by his experience as an international student in London.

However, it was Gandhi's defence of his vegetarian diet that led him furthest into cultural assimilation by bringing him into contact with the vanguard of social change. His first experience of campaigning came through the Vegetarian Society. Similarly, it was reading its theory that translated obedience to a mother's wish into belief in a moral cause. In London, vegetarianism was Gandhi's main campaign: 'A convert's enthusiasm for his new religion is greater than that of a person who is born in it' (Gandhi, 1922, p. 69).

His conversion bought him into contact with 'some of London's most eccentric idealists' (Hay, 1989, p. 81):

> *Through personal contacts with the Londoners he met, lectures he listened to, and books, pamphlets, magazines, and newspapers he read in 1888–91, he came not only to a deeper understanding of his family's beliefs and traditions but also absorbed convictions compatible with them that were to strengthen and guide him for the rest of his life.... Gandhi had "brought from England" his belief in democracy and the equality of women, along with his habits of cleanliness, self-discipline, and hard work.*
>
> (p. 77)

Hay speculates that Gandhi's creed of non-violence was influenced by the Humanitarian League in London. Gandhi thrived in 'the free atmosphere of the great Metropolis' (Gandhi, 1999, 3, p. 375). He 'learned English and English ways and conceptions, he absorbed the Englishman's passion for political freedom' (Shirer, 1979, p. 21). These skills were important in his subsequent negotiation of freedom for India from the Imperial yoke.

Gandhi also learnt about Hinduism in London. He found himself having to explain his tradition to outsiders. 'Surrounded as he was by Christians, Gandhi found that personal contact with several of London's Theosophists, brimming with enthusiasm for Hindu and Buddhist beliefs, helped him resolve some of his doubts about his ancestral faith' (Hay, 1989, p. 84). He began to read the Hindu scriptures, but also the Christian New Testament (Gandhi, 1960). Gandhi's subsequent stance on religion and his ability to accept the scriptures of other traditions began from his experience with the proto-New Age Theosophists, which may also be seen as part of an ascending phase in his acculturation U-curve.

The final message from Gandhi's autobiography shows that while he absorbed a great deal in London and this changed him forever, there was much that he never did understand, such as the social networking of the Dining at the Inns of Court. This 'hidden curriculum' of the Inner Temple passed Gandhi by – perhaps because of his dietary obsessions or shyness from his lack of confidence in English society. This shyness is also a key to the later Gandhi as social awkwardness can be masked through performance. Such a masque can change from persona to person and a new pattern of being, much as those who teach eventually become the identity – 'teacher'.

Adjustment experience of international staff at Oxford Brookes University

Was Gandhi's experience as exceptional as his place in history? Exploration of the Mahatma's experiences in London was triggered by a study of Oxford Brookes University's international academics. This survey explored the effect of teaching and education overseas upon their teaching in the UK (Clifford et al., 2010). This involved three focus groups of about 30, followed by 15 individual interviews. Clifford's work in Australia had shown that little of their wealth of international experience was shared or valued (Clifford & Joseph, 2005). The Oxford Brookes focus group discussions and interviews, however, highlighted how these staff use their experiences at other institutions inside and outside the UK, to make sense of their experience at Brookes. Many saw the UK university culture as offering students more independence and as more student-centred but with lower levels of attainment (Clifford et al., 2010). However, the most surprising outcome was how they position themselves not as 'international staff' but as 'local staff with international experience'. The shifting identities move along a continuum from 'foreign' (with negative connotations) to 'international transitioning to local' (among recently arrived) to 'local (formerly international) with international experience' to 'local with international experience'. This continuum seems to mirror the 'culture shock' U-curve (see Figure 14.1).

These outcomes generated thinking about the university's induction processes for international staff and students alike. The present study of Gandhi's documented experience was sparked by the observation that these Brookes academics had all progressed, already, to the U-curve's rising limb (see Figure 14.1). Their distinguishing feature was that they were willing to talk about their experience and confident enough to offer their hosts advice.

Their reflections demonstrate that Gandhi's experiences were not exceptional and that the driving motivation was the need to fit in. One noted: 'I upset people

an awful lot in those early months' and described how s/he achieved more positive response from new colleagues, 'Your language starts to shift... anyway I'm
now, I think, fully English' (Clifford et al., 2010, pp. 10–11). Some respondents
sought to reassure that they were 'local'. 'I am [ ] by nationality... a local member
of staff ... I've only worked really full-time in Britain'. Another commented:
'At some point I realised that I was here for a significant period....That's when
I began to see myself as local' (Clifford et al., 2010, p. 11). Hill proposes that
'the right to forget where we came from' is fundamental for all cosmopolitans
(2000, p. 6) but this can be difficult to assert. As one participant said, 'You've
got this other identity label, which for some people... will be the only thing
they think about you... one thing that an international staff member definitely
wants is ... to be treated as normal' (Clifford et al., 2010, p. 11).

Another who had been at the university for more than a decade, commented:
'I still don't see myself as being local, I'm still not of here' (Clifford et al., 2010,
p. 11), to which they might have added, as Gandhi finally agreed, 'nor anywhere else'. Clifford notes (personal communication): 'The experience is great
for personal development – but, actually, you never can completely go home
again – you have been "transformed"...you don't quite fit in... but there again,
you would no longer really want to... although you can role-play nicely'. As a
cosmopolitan, you are transformed and no longer fit in even at home, which is
why Pedersen's five stages repeat themselves for those who do return (Pedersen,
1995).

"Cosmopolitans are individuals who, against their origins, choose a transnational identity situated at the crossings of boundaries" [and] "Moral cosmopolitanism... is concerned with the not-yet self, the self that ought to exist" (Hill,
2000, p. 7 and p. 8). This emergent not-yet self is clearly visible in Gandhi's history. The scriptures that Gandhi first accessed in London (and that helped him
rediscover his Vaisnava heritage) stress self-development, duty, sacrifice and self-
realisation. These texts agree with Hill that: 'we remake our world by individually
remaking the images of our own selves' (p. 6) and that ultimately, we may become
the image that we create and perform. Hence, the man-made Gandhi, reviled by
Churchill, is the same person who is the heroic 'great soul' revered across the
world.

So, the question becomes how can international staff and students remake
themselves as such moral cosmopolitans? Goffman (1959) stresses that the key
element – if this learning experience is to be transformative – is self-belief. Self-
development is not play-acting; it is negotiating a socially acceptable pattern
of being forged through experience, and constructed through experiential
learning.

'Experiential education is the process through which a learner constructs
knowledge, skill, and value from direct experiences' (Luckmann, 1996, p. 7). As
Delors (1996) and others hint, the key to successful experiential learning is
mutual participation in social experiences that involve shared, conceptual challenges where the emotions and interactions engaged are pretty much real.

The way to encourage transformative self-development may be to create learning invitations that foster social participation in cross-cultural experiential situations (Haigh, 2011). In staff development situations, this might involve mutual learning in team-teaching situations or in cross-cultural communities of practice. In the multicultural classroom, this might involve developing teaching exercises from an 'Other' cultural base (e.g. Haigh, 2009). The foundations of such exercises involve 'Learning to Be' more than the more performative 'Learning to Live Together' (Delors, 1996). How Gandhi would react is unknowable. However, his memoirs make clear that his learning owed little to his formal study and everything to the challenges and opportunities of being in London. In Chapter 13 of this volume, Killick emphasises the need of learning for global citizenship to be open, socially engaged, to push learners outside their 'comfort zones' into dealing with 'Otherness' and for these experiences to trigger 'virtuous circles of becoming'. The challenge is to build such social learning processes into staff and student induction and use them constructively within the curriculum.

Conclusion

This chapter applies theory from international education and the cross-cultural psychology of culture shock and acculturation to Gandhi's testimony of his time as an international learner in London (Gandhi, 1922; cf. Hunt, 1993). The study was triggered by the findings of a survey of international staff and staff with international experience at Oxford Brookes University, which highlighted their efforts to fit in with the local ethos, often downplaying their 'Otherness' and developing a 'local' persona deemed more acceptable. This chapter explores the processes of acculturation expressed in Gandhi's memoirs that illustrate how this influential international migrant managed to self-develop, explore various personae and, ultimately, transform his own way of being. This analysis suggests that much of the iconic Gandhi of later years emerged from his struggle to adapt to the alien culture of London and his search, less for 'Truth, which came later, but for a workable persona for Gandhi himself.

The first conclusion from this is one perhaps hidden from those without intercultural experience. It concerns the development of a capability for intercultural performance rather than 'intercultural understanding'. Goffman's ideas of dramaturgy provide a valuable insight into the processes at work (Goffman, 1959). However, the greater problem for immigrants, at least to the point where they feel confident within their new cultural context, is less to comprehend than to avoid offence and to fit in (cf. Clifford et al., 2010). This was Gandhi's first lesson in London and his performance as a 'London Dandy' may be the archetype of his later life of material simplicity.

However, the life of the later Gandhi shows a reality much deeper than the theatre metaphor implies (Lumby & English, 2010). What began as a search for a socially acceptable mask expanded into a re-evaluation of the self.

Finally, Gandhi's life became his message (Desai, 2009). Towards this goal, Gandhi's education in London was truly transformative. Its final product was a whole new way of being, forged by the fires of experience that both transcended and included its prototypes.

Perversely, it was Gandhi's rejection of the English diet in favour of vegetarianism that gifted Gandhi a cause, which taught him the skills of organisation, and contacts with London's avant-garde thinkers. Through them, Gandhi learnt about English ideals and religion, the religions of others, but most importantly the strengths and scriptures of his own. Robert Burns (1786) has written; 'O wad some Power the giftie gie us, To see oursels as ithers see us! It wad frae mony a blunder free us'. This power, to see one's own tradition from the outside, to have to justify its ways both to oneself as to others, and to learn to appreciate both its strengths and weaknesses, is something uniquely gifted to international sojourners, whether they arrive as students, academics or immigrants (Hill, 2000). The experience permanently changes those who go through it (cf. Hay, 1989; Pedersen, 1995). Moral cosmopolitanism, possibly the major outcome of an international education, remains a breeding ground for revolutionaries because it grants a perspective on what needs to be changed. In Gandhi's case, it also provided him with some of the tools he would need. The rest is history.

Gandhi's story indicates what is needed to drive effective internationalisation in a university is more than the creation of social learning situations through simulation, role-playing and games. Gandhi's learning was constructed in response to the learning invitations provided by direct experiential involvement with the Vegetarian Society and the Theosophists (Haigh, 2011). His formal education at the Inns of Court achieved almost nothing. So, Gandhi's educational message is clear and echoes that of Delors' UNESCO Commission (1996). An effective pedagogy for internationalisation, both of staff and students, needs experiential learning constructed around learning invitations that draw the learner into negotiated social experiences through involvement in meaningful projects of cross-cultural scope.

References

Barnett, H. G. (1953). *Innovation: The basis for cultural change.* New York: McGraw-Hill.

Berry, J. W. (1992). Acculturation and adaptation in a new society. *International Migration, 30,* 69–86.

Berry, J. W. (2001). Psychology of immigration. *Journal of Social Issues, 57*(3), 615–631.

Berry, J. W., Kim, U., Power, S., Young, M. & Bujaki, M. (1989). Acculturation attitudes in plural societies. *Applied Psychology, 38,* 185–206.

Berry, J. W., Poortinga, Y. H., Segall, M. H. & Dasen, P. R. (2002). *Cross–cultural psychology: Research and applications,* 2nd edn. Cambridge: Cambridge University Press.

Bhana, S. & Vahed, G. (2005). *The making of a political reformer: Gandhi in South Africa, 1893–1914.* New Delhi: Manohar, p. 44.

Burns, R. (1786). *To a louse: On seeing one on a lady's bonnet at church.* Available at: http://www.robertburns.org/works/97.shtml (accessed December 2008).

Chapdelaine, R. F. & Alexitch, L. R. (2004). Social skills difficulty: Model of culture shock for international graduate students. *Journal of College Student Development,* 45(2), 167–184.

Churchill, W. (1931). *Comment on Gandhi's meeting with the Viceroy of India.* Available at: http://refspace.com/quotes/d:1/Winston_Churchill/gandhi (accessed March 2011).

Clifford, V. & Joseph, C. (2005). *Internationalisation of the Curriculum Project Report.* Melbourne, Australia: Monash University Higher Education Development Unit.

Clifford, V., Adetunji, H., Haigh, M., et al. (2010). *Fostering interculturality and global perspectives at Brookes through dialogue with staff.* A BSLE Project Report. Oxford: Oxford Centre for Staff and Learning Development.

Collinson, D. L. (2003). Identities and insecurities: selves at work. *Organization,* 10(3), 527–547.

Delors, J. (1996). *Learning: The treasure within.* Paris: UNESCO.

Desai, N. (2009). *My life is my message: Sadhana (1869–1915).* New Delhi: Orient Black Swan.

Doke, J. J. (1909). *M. K. Gandhi: An Indian patriot in South Africa.* Varanasi: Akhil Bharat Sarva Seva Sangh (1956 reprint).

Foster, G. M. (1962). *Traditional cultures and the impact of technological change.* New York: Harper & Brothers.

Furnham, A. & Bochner, S. (1986). *Culture shock: Psychological reactions to unfamiliar environments.* London: Methuen.

Gandhi, M. K. (1922). *An autobiography: The story of my experiments with truth.* Harmondsworth: Penguin Classics (2001 reprint).

Gandhi, M. K. (1946). University education. *Harijan,* 8(9), 308.

Gandhi, M. K. (1960). *Discourses on the Gita.* Ahmedabad: Navajivan Trust.

Gandhi, M. K. (1999). *The collected works of Mahatma Gandhi* (98 vols). New Delhi: Publications Division Government of India. Available at: http://www.gandhiserve.org/cwmg/cwmg.html (accessed March 2011).

Goffman, E. (1959). *The presentation of self in everyday life.* New York: Doubleday.

Haigh, M. (2009). Fostering cross-cultural empathy with non-Western curricular structures. *Journal of Studies in International Education,* 13(2), 271–284.

Haigh, M. (2011). Invitational education: theory, research and practice. *Journal of Geography in Higher Education,* 35(2), 299–309.

Hay, S. (1989). The making of a late-Victorian Hindu: M. K. Gandhi in London, 1888–1891. *Victorian Studies,* 33(1), 75–98.

Hill, J. D. (2000). *Becoming a cosmopolitan: What it means to be a human being in the new millennium.* Lanham, MD: Rowman and Littlefield.

Hunt, J. D. (1993). *Gandhi in London,* 2nd edn. New Delhi: Promilla.

Kuhn, T. S. (1970) *The structure of scientific revolutions. International encyclopedia of unified science,* 2nd edn, vols 1 & 2. Chicago, IL: University of Chicago.

Luckmann, C. (1996). Defining experiential education. *Journal of Experiential Education,* 19(1), 6–7.

Lumby, J. & English, F. G. (2010). *Leadership as lunacy and other metaphors of educational leadership.* Thousand Oaks, CA: Corwin (Sage).

McLeod, K. D. (2008). *A qualitative examination of culture shock and the influential factors affecting newly-arrived Korean students at Texas A&M University*. PhD dissertation. College Station, TX: Texas A&M University.

Mandelbaum, D. G. (1973). The study of life history: Gandhi. *Current Anthropology*, *14*(3), 177–206.

Mayer, J. D. & Salovey, P. (1993). The intelligence of emotional intelligence. *Intelligence*, *17*, 433–442.

Oberg, K. (1960). Cultural shock: Adjustment to new cultural environments. *Practical Anthropology*, *7*, 177–182.

Pedersen, P. (1995). *The five stages of culture shock: Critical incidents around the world*. Westport, CT: Greenwood.

Shirer, W. L. (1979). *Gandhi: A memoir*. New York: Simon & Schuster.

Starratt, R. J. (1993). *The drama of leadership*. London: Falmer.

Ward, C. A., Bochner, S. & Furnham, A. (2001). *The psychology of culture shock*. Hove: Routledge.

Chapter 15

A mismatch of expectations? An exploration of international students' perceptions of employability skills and work-related learning

Sabine McKinnon

Introduction

Employability has been the subject of considerable debate in the British higher education sector for some time now. It is a controversial concept that is difficult to define (Harvey, 2001; Lees, 2002; Yorke, 2006). Employers, academics, students and government have struggled to agree on a definition. In Scotland, the new 'Graduates for the 21st Century' QAA Enhancement Theme has re-ignited the debate (QAA, 2009). Knight and Yorke's (2003) understanding of the term is still the most commonly cited; they define employability as 'a set of achievements, understandings and personal attributes that make individuals more likely to gain employment and be successful in their chosen occupations' (Knight & Yorke, 2003, p. 5). More recently, the Confederation of British Industry (CBI) presented their definition of employability in their 'Future Fit' report on how graduates can be prepared for the workplace. It puts the emphasis on the needs of a 'modern competitive economy', which requires employable workers who can adapt their 'skills, knowledge and attitudes' continually to 'prosper in a changing world' (CBI, 2009, p. 8).

How universities can improve their students' employability skills is far from clear. Ever since the Dearing report in the UK (Dearing, 1997), the debate about the best way of doing so has shown no signs of abating. Bolt-on or embedded? Subject specific or generic? A job for the careers service or the academic departments? There seems to be no one-size-fits-all solution, neither within the UK (Connor & MacFarlane, 2007; QAA, 2006) nor internationally (Harvey & Bowers-Brown, 2006; Little, 2003). In her study of different national approaches to enhancing graduate employability, Little points out that 'there is little evidence of systematic thinking about how best to do it, let alone any model that can be badged as "best practice" and adopted wholesale' (Little, 2003, p.4).

The arrival of an ever-increasing number of international students on the UK campuses has given the employability debate a new focus. What employability skills are important for them and their future careers? Which employment markets and which communities are they preparing for and how can staff at British universities support them in their efforts?

Given increasing graduate mobility in the global employment market, universities need to base their academic provision on an understanding of international employers' graduate recruitment criteria. While there is some evidence that there are similarities in the expectations employers have of graduates (Andrews & Higson, 2008), there are also indications that employer demands vary from country to country. In the UK, the CBI regularly asks their 240,000 members for their views on the importance of different graduate skills. The results from their latest survey on education and skills (CBI, 2010) show that businesses expect their new recruits to possess a wide range of transferable, 'soft' skills such as self-management, communication and teamworking. Other UK studies reveal that employers from all industries agree on the importance of these generic skills but that they are dissatisfied with the skills levels they see in their graduate applicants (Archer & Davison, 2008; Levy & Hopkins, 2010).

At European level, large-scale European Union (EU) surveys show that employers from different countries are looking for similar skills, but they disagree in rating their importance (Eurobarometer, 2010). Whereas 91 per cent of the Maltese and 76 per cent of the British respondents considered communication skills very important, only 40 per cent of the Danish and 26 per cent of the French participants felt the same. The views from graduates in the EU reflect this diversity. Large-scale European studies (Allan & Van der Velden, 2007; Schomburg & Teichler, 2006) reveal that they perceive the relevance of graduate employability skills differently. Brennan and Little (2009) point to the importance of 'local and cultural traditions and histories' which define 'meanings and practices associated with graduate employment' (p. 3).

Evidence from countries outside Europe and the English-speaking world about desirable employment skills is more scarce. Brennan et al. (2001) compared the perceptions of European graduates with those of their Japanese counterparts and found some interesting differences. When asked what they considered to be the top 10 competencies from a list of 36 that they possessed at time of graduation, the Japanese respondents placed 'loyalty and integrity' at the top of their list and put 'working in a team' last. European graduates put 'loyalty and integrity' in fifth place, whereas the UK participants did not include them at all.

Given such a variety of views, it is likely that international students who study at the UK universities arrive with an understanding of employability that differs from that of their British teachers, employers and fellow students. What they consider to be important in preparing for employment might clash with the ideas that shape the academic curriculum and careers advice in the UK host institution. Results from international student surveys[1] point to a potential conflict. In the case of Glasgow Caledonian University, the data from the surveys show that international students were very positive about the learning experience overall but they were the least satisfied with the employability-related aspects of their studies.[2] This picture is repeated across the British higher education sector. International students complain most often about a lack of careers support when questioned about their experience at the UK universities (Connor & Brown, 2009).

What might be the reasons for their dissatisfaction? What do they expect when they arrive? The study presented here aimed to answer that question. More specifically, it sought to identify international students' understanding of employability skills and their views on the UK learning and teaching styles designed to improve them.

The strategic context at Glasgow Caledonian University: Embedding employability through work-related learning

At Glasgow Caledonian University, employability is at the heart of its Learning, Teaching and Assessment Strategy (GCU, LTAS, 2008–2015). It requires all schools to build students' competencies in the skills demanded by employers through embedding work-related learning activities in the taught curriculum. The slogan 'Learning for the Real World' has become its main marketing tool (GCU, 2010). A new university-wide strategic change initiative named the Real WoRLD Project (**Real**ising **Wor**k-**R**elated Learning **D**iffusion) was launched in 2008 to advise academic staff on different ways of engaging students in work-related learning (Real WoRLD, 2008). To provide a clear definition of the term, the project team developed five 'Principles of Work-Related Learning' (McKinnon & Margaryan, 2009) which identify work-related learning as activities that:

- provide students with learning opportunities to integrate theory and practice
- achieve learning outcomes that state what the students will be able to do in the workplace
- encourage and support students' interest in a wide variety of careers
- require students to take on an active rather than a passive role in the learning process
- accommodate cultural diversity.

Examples of work-related learning activities are work placements and internships, industry mentoring and work shadowing schemes, case studies, simulation exercises and student-led projects which are based on an employer brief. One of the Real WoRLD Project's aims was to identify what students' perceptions of employability skills are. A first round of focus groups with the UK students was conducted in the summer of 2008. A second series with international students took place a year later. The findings of the focus groups with international students are presented in this chapter.

The study

Students were recruited for this study through an invitation in the university newsletter for international students and e-mail invitations sent out by programme leaders whose courses were most popular with international students in the academic year of 2008–09. A total of 27 students from three academic schools (Business, Computing and Engineering and Law and Social Sciences) and 10 countries participated in the five focus groups: 16 students were post-graduates on one-year taught programmes; 11 were undergraduates from all years of study. Forty-four per cent of the sample was Nigerians, who represent the largest group of international students at the university. Table 15.1 shows the participants' countries of origin.

It must be acknowledged that such a high percentage of students from one country (Nigeria) can lead to somewhat skewed results because of a national bias in the data set. The results of this study should therefore be viewed with a certain degree of caution. Nevertheless, cross-cultural research has established that Nigeria is representative of the 'collectivist' cultures[3] most of the UK's international students come from (Hofstede, 1986; UKCISA, n.d.). Hofstede's work shows that Nigerian students share certain values and assumptions with their contemporaries from other collectivist societies such as Pakistan, India or Malaysia. Given the limitations of this small-scale study, it does not claim to present a complete picture of *all* international students' perceptions.

The focus group discussions were based on a framework of questions designed to explore how these students prepare for future employment. In the first section, they were asked to reflect upon their criteria for choosing a subject, a programme and a UK university. The second section investigated their perceptions of employ-ability skills and their learning experience at Glasgow Caledonian. Students were asked to compare learning and teaching methods in their home countries with those they had experienced in Scotland. They were also encouraged to reflect on potential differences in employers' recruitment criteria at home and in the UK. A final set of questions focused on their future career plans. Each session

Table 15.1 Focus groups participants' countries of origin

Country of origin	Number of participants	Percentage of sample
Nigeria	12	44
India	3	11
Poland	3	11
Russia	2	7
Ghana	2	7
Pakistan	1	4
Uganda	1	4
France	1	4
Spain	1	4
Portugal	1	4
Total	27	100

lasted between 60 and 90 minutes, depending on the number of students and the strength of the discussion. The data were recorded and transcribed and analysed inductively by clustering the responses around the key themes from the question framework.

Findings

Given the large amount of data created, only a small percentage can be presented here. This chapter focuses on participants' views of essential employability skills and their response to the learning and teaching styles they had experienced in British higher education.

Perceptions of employability skills: Adaptability and cultural awareness

The students in this sample were very aware of the national variations involved in the definition of employability skills. During their short time in the UK (from four to nine months at the time of the study), they had already realised that recruitment practices in Britain differ from those in their home countries and that they needed to adapt the local context in their search for employment.

When asked what they considered to be the most important graduate recruitment criteria, the non-European students felt that evidence of a highly regarded qualification, technical knowledge and practical work experience rather than 'soft' skills mattered most in their countries. The degree certificate as physical proof of knowledge was considered to be the most important element of the job application process in India, Pakistan, Ghana and Nigeria.

> *I think it's really different when you compare the UK and Nigeria. In Nigeria what is most relevant is your qualification, first qualifications.... The document is really, really, really very important, more than in other countries.*
>
> (Nigerian student)

He continued to explain that employers in his country are forced to look for documented evidence of academic achievement because the Nigerian education system is '*not trusted by the people*'. In his view, they have more confidence in a British degree than a Nigerian one: '*The system in Nigeria has broken down... papers can be bought*'. Although the 12 Nigerian students in this study were by no means representative of their country's student population they seem to reflect a widely held view that the quality of their higher education system is poor and insufficiently related to labour demand requirements (Saint, Hartnett & Strassner, 2003).

Another Nigerian student explained that he felt ill-prepared for the UK labour market because he lacked the 'soft', interpersonal skills employers are looking for. He had applied unsuccessfully for a job with a British energy company and when he asked the recruitment officer what graduate qualities they were looking for she explained:

> *...we want to see your interpersonal skills, we want to see how you can interact, how you are able to work with others because we are going to train you. He added: ...because they don't want a situation whereby the student is ... only concerned about his education. They don't want to work with that kind of person.*

He realised that his Nigerian understanding of the most essential employability attribute – that is, the ability to achieve high grades on a prestigious degree programme – differed from the UK definition which focuses on generic, 'soft' skills.

Other cultural differences in defining employability became obvious in the focus group discussions. Highly developed technical skills and subject knowledge were perceived as more important in India and Pakistan and in the African countries represented here (Nigeria, Ghana and Uganda) than they are in Britain.

> *I felt that to quite some extent that in the UK interpersonal skills are more important compared to Pakistan. In Pakistan they ask for more technical skills... employers need specific technical skills and they ask you the technical questions [in the interview].*

He added that employers in Pakistan may also test the candidates' general knowledge in an interview to make sure they are as educated as they claim to be. They do not always trust the quality of the degree certificate. Evidence of highly developed 'soft' skills such as team working was not required.

Practical work experience was considered the most important recruitment criterion by all participants. They felt that employers in the UK as well as in their home countries value graduates who have some understanding of real-life working practices.

> *The degree gets me into the interview room but it's the experience that will get me the right job.*

(Nigerian student)

They were very aware that there are different ways of providing students with an insight into the workplace. Placements were considered the most valuable, but they also recognised the importance of other work-related learning activities such as employer talks, industry visits, job shadowing opportunities and case studies. When asked whether they were satisfied with the provision of work-related learning opportunities on their programmes, all but one gave a negative answer. The students felt that the university could do more to help students gain practical experience. The lack of placements and industry-based projects concerned them the most.

The debate about practical work experience revealed interesting cultural differences.[4] The African participants felt very strongly that academics should use their contacts in industry to give their students an advantage in the job application process. They expected to be given a special recommendation, an invaluable introduction to their lecturers' industry networks. One Ghanaian participant expressed his disappointment that the university had given him a standardised form to confirm his status as a student rather than a personal letter of recommendation for a summer placement.

> *I don't think the university are doing enough in that field... they gave me a letter and it was just the basic 'to whom it may concern', he is a student of this school, I hope that suits your purpose and that was it. No, I expected something more.... Interviewer: 'A recommendation?' Yeah.*

The Nigerian students agreed. They pointed out that personal contacts matter a great deal in the employment market in their own country:

> *Nigeria is all about, let me use this phrase, man knows man, that's it. It's everywhere. If I know him, you know, you can just say, please help me...*

The African students' dissatisfaction with the 'service' provided by the academic staff in Scotland reveals their cultural values and understanding of the relationship between student and teacher, which has been widely recognised as culture specific (Carroll & Ryan, 2008; Hofstede, 1986; Palfreyman & McBride, 2007; Timm, 2008). They come from cultures that Hofstede terms 'collectivist'; that is, societies where the individual expects an 'in-group', be it the extended family, clan or organisation, to protect the interests of its members (Hofstede, 1986). In return, loyalty to the collective is expected of them. The participants in this study expected a 'favour' from the academic community they felt they had joined and they claimed that it would be common practice in their home countries. When they did not receive it in Scotland, they were disappointed. The European students in the focus groups did not seem to expect such an 'entry ticket' to the employment market. They did not raise it as an issue of concern.

Other employability skills cited by the students included team working, communication skills and cultural awareness. All participants felt that the ability to work in a team is essential for any graduate job in any country.

> *The group work is better because in any situation, especially now that we're going global, we are going to have to work with people of different cultures, of different behaviours and most times you're going to work with people you don't like personally.*
>
> (Nigerian student)

Cultural awareness as an important employability skill was raised by the two Russian participants who had found it difficult to understand British culture when they first arrived. They had chosen to study in the UK to improve their knowledge of different cultures and looked to their course at university to give them an insight into all aspects of British society, including business etiquette and networking skills.

> I think one of the great skills to have is building good relationships, working relationships. See, in Russia, people are... much more friendly. So they use different persona of yourself to build these relationships. Here you need different things... if you are trying to implement the same ways as you did in your own country it doesn't work here and it chokes you.

The Nigerian participant in the same focus group also felt that British people are more reserved than his fellow nationals and that he needed to adapt to their communication styles to be successful in the UK workplace.

> In my country we are very effusive, we are very boisterous, show the emotion, shake hands... (here) you have to learn to value their privacy, they don't like it... it's not that they are not friendly but they want not to be too open.

He suggested that the university offer international students an introductory course in British business etiquette and networking skills to help students understand such cultural differences.

Views on learning and teaching styles: An abdication of responsibility?

The feedback on the learning and teaching styles the students had experienced in Scotland was generally positive. The student-centred approach adopted there compared very favourably with the more distant student–staff relationship they had experienced at home. All of the participants reported that academic status and authority matter more in their countries. Staff in their own countries were perceived to be less interested in answering questions from individual students and insist on more formality in communicating with them. By contrast, academics in the UK were seen as helpful and supportive:

> You can ask as many questions as you want.... I don't think I have ever been turned down...the relationship between the teacher and the student here is amazing because I call my teacher George, I don't call him 'Sir'... In Poland they [the students] are probably seeing some of them [the staff] as God.

(Polish student)

Same in my country. They are so big-headed.

(Nigerian student)

Students were also aware of the different learning styles in different countries. Almost all of them felt that the rote-learning method in their home countries was inferior to the practice-based approach in the UK. They agreed that they were learning more from lecturers who illustrate theory with practical, real-life examples rather than just presenting the theory in a formal lecture. They praised the use of case studies and course work instead of traditional end-of-year exams because it helps them develop useful employability skills:

I think it (the teaching) is really great because we do mostly case studies. I have never done so many case studies in my life...it really opened my knowledge... you put yourself in the situation of a manager, what would you do if you were there and stuff like that...

(French student)

...about the coursework. I think it is more tailored to the industrial system of doing things...coursework is more fashioned to the work that's expected in the industry where people will be made to go out and find out something and present a report, maybe present it before a board.

(Nigerian student)

While most of the feedback on the learning and teaching methods they had experienced in the UK was positive, there was also some criticism. The full-fee-paying students who make considerable financial sacrifices for studying abroad complained about the low number of contact hours. They want to see value for money, which they perceive to manifest itself in high input from staff:

I have been told that the university prepares you ...to work by yourself and study by yourself. But then, I think, don't call it full-time, call it self-teach or distance learning. This is not full-time.

(Russian student)

These complaints about low contact hours point to a similar conflict between two value systems. The Russian students clearly felt that their Scottish teachers did not care sufficiently about their students' progress when they did not teach them every day, did not check up on their attendance in class and expected them to learn on their own. Their idea of a good-quality education seemed to clash with the UK perception. They wanted to see much more input from academic staff and the university as a whole because they were used to it in their own country. One of the students explained that the attitude of academic staff in Russia reflected employers' more paternalistic approach to managing their staff:

> ...*post-Soviet bosses, they are looking after you because it's in their habit to look after their employees...*
>
> (Russian student)

In a similar vein, the participants struggled to understand the benefits of independent student learning, which is generally at the heart of the UK university experience (Biggs, 2003). While they appreciated the British staff's best intentions to support their students, they were also critical of what they perceived to be an abdication of responsibility and a lack of interest in students' academic progress:

> *[In Russia]... teachers are very interested in teaching you... at times they are bugging you, why don't you come to lectures, why don't you do this and that? Here it is... more self- teaching, so you should do it yourself... but you pay money. So you are paying to get some knowledge from someone.*
>
> (Russian student)

These Russian students perceived the British approach to university teaching as *laissez-faire* at best and irresponsible at worst. They appeared unconvinced that they could learn as much here as they could in their own country. The participants from Africa and Poland agreed with them.

Evaluating these views from an intercultural perspective points to a potential culture clash based on conflicting values. Values can be defined as 'desirable, transsituational goals, varying in importance that serve as a guiding principle in people's lives' (Schwartz & Bardi, 2001). The values that shape students' perceptions of the purpose of a university education, the role of a teacher and the responsibilities of a student are not universal. There is sufficient evidence that they differ from culture to culture (Carroll & Ryan, 2008; Hofstede, 1986; Teekens, 2003). Teekens (2003, p. 114) refers to a country's education system as an 'expression of a national cultural code' which is learnt in childhood and 'very hard to unlearn'. Like most of the full-fee-paying international students at the UK universities, the students in this study came from 'collectivist cultures' with a 'high power distance'. Hofstede defines power distance as 'the extent to which the less powerful persons in a society accept inequality in power and consider it as normal' (Hofstede, 1980). In high power distance cultures, students respect and admire teachers for their 'wisdom' and their subject knowledge (Hofstede, 1986). They expect them to provide a great deal more guidance and advice than British academics, who come from an 'individualist culture' with a 'low power distance', are prepared to give. Whereas the UK staff expect their students to be independent learners who take responsibility for their own academic progress (Knight, 1996), students from collectivist cultures such as India, Pakistan and Nigeria often feel that it is the teachers' duty to do that for them (Hofstede, 1986). As a result, British academics or careers advisers who are not aware of such cultural differences might perceive international students as too demanding or dependent.

Conclusion

This study provided a glimpse of the complex interactions between cultural value systems and perceptions of quality in learning and teaching. Reflecting on employability acted as a catalyst for a debate about the value of studying at a Scottish university. The respondents in these focus groups challenged the validity of pedagogic concepts such as independent learning that often form the basis of curriculum planning in the UK and other Western countries. They also raised the question whether British academics are aware of the cultural implications of their teaching styles and the different employer recruitment criteria in their students' home countries. What and how students need to learn to be successful in finding a graduate job in different national employment markets will continue to be the subject of the educational debate at global level. Teekens emphasises the importance of understanding the 'system' that has produced the foreign student (Teekens, 2003, p. 117). If programme teams who teach a class of almost exclusively international students on their postgraduate programmes are not aware of the hidden values and assumptions students bring to their classroom, the likelihood of misunderstandings and conflict is high.

It would, therefore, be helpful for busy academics if the university could provide cultural awareness training for academics and careers advisers which focuses on the role of values in learning and teaching rather than the detail of specific national customs. Reflecting on one's own culture and how it might be perceived by foreign nationals would be the best starting point for an enlightened debate (Carroll & Ryan, 2008). Colleagues who have lived and worked in different countries could share their first-hand experience of the difficulties involved in adjusting to a new culture to inform those who have not. Current and former international students could be invited to speak about their experiences when they first arrived in the UK. Academic induction programmes that explain the rationale for and value of an independent learning approach to new student cohorts would further assist in avoiding potential confusion, disappointment and disaffection.

An improved level of cultural awareness could potentially ease the culture shock which so often obstructs successful communication at university and in the workplace (Marx, 1999; Oberg, 1960). *All* students, including those from the UK, would benefit from courses on national differences in business etiquette and the job application process. Glasgow Caledonian University ran a successful series of workshops on improving international students' networking skills where students took part in highly interactive interview simulations and networking role-plays which were acted out by professional actors. The workshops were followed by a networking lunch with a selection of local employers, which gave the students the opportunity to put their newly acquired skills into practice.

Given international students' often reported difficulties in gaining access to placement and internship opportunities because they lack employer contacts and networks in the UK (Connor & Brown, 2009), it would be beneficial to embed campus-based, alternative work-related learning activities in the taught curriculum. Employers can contribute to the teaching by providing real-life project briefs which students work on. That way international students gain a first-hand insight into the UK employers' needs and expectations. In some subjects employers are also called upon to assess and provide feedback on students' reports and presentations. Glasgow Caledonian offers simulated assessment centres to prepare international students for real-life interviews. An alumni mentoring scheme which matches employers with current (international and the UK) students to provide them with information and advice on the graduate recruitment process has been particularly popular with international students.

British universities are tasked with providing a well-educated workforce for the global employment market (UKCES, 2010). In the current funding climate they rely very heavily on the financial contribution from international students to achieve that. High priority should therefore be given to understanding the cultural differences which shape international students' attitudes and expectations.

Notes

1 See International Graduate Insights group (i-graduate) Student Barometer.
2 The ISB questionnaire defines employability as 'learning that will help me get a good job'.
3 For a more detailed definition of collectivist cultures, see later in this chapter.
4 This chapter bases its understanding of 'culture' on the most commonly cited definition by Hofstede (1980), who defines culture as 'collective programming of the mind that distinguishes the members of one group or category of people from another'. More recently, the GLOBE research programme (House et al. 1999) interprets the term as 'shared motives, values, beliefs, identities, and interpretations or meanings of significant events that result from common experiences of members of collectives and are transmitted across age generations'.

References

Allan, J. & Van der Velden, R. (eds.) (2007). *The flexible professional in the knowledge society: General results of the REFLEX project.* Maastricht University, the Netherlands: Research Centre for Education and the Labour Market.

Andrews, J. & Higson, H. E. (2008). Graduate employability: 'Soft skills' versus 'hard' business knowledge: A European study, *Higher Education in Europe*, *33*(4), 411–422.

Archer, W. & Davison, J. (2008). *Graduate employability: What do employers think and want?* London: The Council for Industry and Higher Education.

Biggs, J. (2003). *Teaching for quality learning at university.* Buckingham: SHRE/ Open University Press.

Brennan, J. & Little, B. (2009). Graduate competences and relationships with the labour market: The UK case. In *Development of Competencies in the World of Work and Education, Conference Proceedings 2009*. Ljubljana, Slovenia: DECOWE.

Brennan, J., Johnston, B., Little, B., Shah, T. & Woodley, A. (2001). *The employment of UK graduates: Comparisons with Europe and Japan*. Bristol: HEFCE.

Carroll, J. & Ryan, J. (eds.) (2008). *Teaching international students: Improving learning for all*, 4th edn. Abingdon, Oxon: Routledge.

Confederation of British Industry (CBI) (2010). *Ready to grow: Business priorities for education and skills. Education and skills survey*. London: CBI.

Confederation of British Industry (CBI) and Universities UK (2009). *Future fit: Preparing graduates for the world of work*. London: CBI.

Connor, H. & Brown, R. (2009). *Global horizons: Recruiting international students and graduates from UK universities*. London: Council for Industry and Higher Education.

Connor, H. & MacFarlane, K. (2007). *Work related learning (WRL) in HE – a scoping study*. Centre for Research in Lifelong Learning, Glasgow Caledonian University: The Higher Education Academy. Available at: http://hlst.ltsn.ac.uk/assets/York/documents/ourwork/employability/work_related_learning_in_HE.pdf (accessed 10 January 2011).

Dearing, R. (1997). *Higher education in the learning society*. Norwich: HMSO.

Eurobarometer (2010). *Employers' perception of graduate employability*. Flash EB Series #304. EU Directorate-General for Education and Culture.

Glasgow Caledonian University (GCU) (2008–2015). Learning, Teaching and Assessment Strategy (LTAS). Available at: http://www.gcu.ac.uk/quality/strategy/ltas.html (accessed 16 December 2010).

Harvey, L. (2001). Defining and measuring employability. *Quality in Higher Education*, 7(2), 97–109.

Harvey, L. & Bowers-Brown, T. (2006). *Employability: Cross-country comparisons, graduate market trends, Winter 2004–05*. Prospects Net. Available at: http://ww2.prospects.ac.uk/cms/ShowPage/Home_page/Members___Log_in/Labour_market_information/Graduate_Market_Trends/Employability_cross_country_comparisons__Winter_04_05_/p!epmjlid (accessed 17 December 2010).

Hofstede, G. (1980). *Culture's consequences: International differences in work related values*. Beverly Hills, CA: Sage.

Hofstede, G. (1986). Cultural differences in teaching and learning. *International Journal of Intercultural Relations, 10*, 301–320.

House, R.J., Hanges, P. J., Ruiz-Quintanilla, S. A., et al. (1999). Cultural influences in leadership and organizations: Project GLOBE. In W. H. Mobley et al. (eds.), *Advances in Global Leadership*. Vol. 1. Stamford, CT: JAI Press.

Knight, P. (1996). Independent study, independent studies and 'core skills' in higher education. In J. Tait & P. Knight (eds.), *The management of independent learning*. London: Kogan Page in association with SEDA.

Knight, P. & Yorke, M. (2003). *Assessment, learning and employability*. Maidenhead, UK: Open University Press.

Lees, D. (2002). *Graduate employability: Literature review*. LTSN Generic Centre. Available at: http://www.palatine.ac.uk/files/emp/1233.pdf (accessed 5 January 2011).

Levy, C. & Hopkins, L. (2010). *Shaping up for innovation: Are we delivering the right skills for the 2020 knowledge economy? A Knowledge Economy programme report.* London: The Work Foundation.

Little, B. (2003). *International perspectives on employability, a briefing paper.* York: The Higher Education Academy. Available at: http://www.heacademy.ac.uk/resources/detail/employability/employability524 (accessed 6 January 2011).

McKinnon, S. & Margaryan, A. (2009). *Principles of work-related learning.* Available at: http://www.academy.gcal.ac.uk/realworld/documents/Principlesofwrl180909.pdf (accessed 17 November 2010).

Marx, E. (1999). *Breaking through culture shock.* London: Nicholas Brealey.

Oberg, K. (1960). Culture shock: Adjustment to neo-cultural environment. *Practical Anthropology, 17,* 177–182.

Palfreyman, D. & McBride, D. L. (eds.) (2007). *Learning and teaching across cultures in higher education.* Houndsmills, Basingstoke: Palgrave Macmillan.

Quality Assurance Agency (QAA) (2006). *Graduate enhancement themes outcomes: Employability.* Available at: http://www.enhancementthemes.ac.uk/publications/default.asp#Employability (accessed 17 November 2010).

Quality Assurance Agency (QAA) (2009). Graduates for the 21st century enhancement theme. Available at: http://www.enhancementthemes.ac.uk/themes/21stC Graduates (accessed 25 November 2010).

Real WorLD Project at Glasgow Caledonian University (2008). Available at: http://www.academy.gcal.ac.uk/realworld (accessed 5 January 2011).

Saint, W., Hartnett, T. A. & Strassner, E. (2003). Higher education in Nigeria: A status report. *Higher Education Policy, 16,* 259–281.

Schomburg, H. & Teichler, U. (2006). Higher education dynamics 15: Higher education and graduate employment in Europe: Results of graduate surveys from 12 countries. Dordrecht, the Netherlands: Springer.

Schwartz, S. H. & Bardi, A. (2001). Value hierarchies across cultures. *Journal of Cross-cultural Psychology, 32,* 268–290.

Teekens, H. (2003). The requirement to develop specific skills for teaching in an intercultural setting. *Journal of Studies in International Education, 7*(1), 108–119.

Timm, A. (2008). *Final report on educational practices in India: Student diversity and academic writing project.* Available at: http://www.sdaw.info/lecturers/SDAW%20India_Final%20report%202008.pdf (accessed 16 December 2010).

UKCISA (UK Council for International Students Affairs) (n.d.). *International students in UK higher education: Key statistics.* Retrieved 7 January 2011 from http://www.ukcisa.org.uk/about/statistics_he.php#table1 (accessed 7 January 2011).

UK Commission for Employment and Skills (UKCES) (2010). Skills for jobs: Today and tomorrow. *Volume two: The evidence report.* London: UKCES.

Yorke, M. (2006). *No. 1 of the ESECT Learning and Employability Series: Employability in higher education: What it is – What it is not.* York: The Higher Education Academy.

Part 4

New ways of listening

Pathologies of silence? Reflecting on international learner identities amidst the classroom chatter

Yvonne Turner

Introduction: Learning and talking in the Anglo-Western tradition

In the Anglophone education literature, active learner constructions have tended to identify talking in the classroom as an indicator of student engagement (Shaw, Carey & Mair, 2008). Student-centred learning approaches advocate classroom methods, including group work, presentations and in-class questioning which are dependent on oral communication as a key mechanism for student-to-student and student-to-lecturer contact (Buswell & Becket, 2009). Consistent with the notion of Socratic argumentative/dialogic learning, the pedagogical foundations of such constructions of learning are culturally rooted and may not reflect social learning traditions which take a different perspective on silence and talking (Ollin, 2008). At the same time, contemporary notions of reflective learning identify a concern with quiet thinking, silence and critical contemplation in the intrapersonal learning process (Moon, 2004). Within this paradoxical context an interesting strand in the discourse emerges focused on the degree to which silence is a public or private phenomenon and how far it is intrinsic to the collective learning process in the classroom.

Practically, the contribution of silence to learning is sometimes drowned out in the clamour of the student-centred classroom. A co-identification of noisy students with effective learners asks particular questions about the dynamics of participation in internationally diverse learning spaces. A range of factors may militate against the talkative engagement of all students, bringing a consequent risk of marginalisation or the potential for negative characterisations of those who prefer quiet reflection to noisy participation (Ryan & Viete, 2009). Some research has indicated the challenges posed for silence in the international classroom (Zhou, Knoke & Sakamoto, 2005). Studies have documented student struggles to engage orally in classroom activities because of language challenges, confidence or cultural preferences for communication styles (Bartram, 2008). Others have identified a range of contextual factors, both cultural and pedagogical, which influence participation (Turner & Robson, 2008). These include cultural and academic literacy, cultural stereotyping, a lack of cross-cultural competence among teachers and student skills gaps in turn-taking and participative dynamics. Practitioner research has characterised student participation as primarily a student skills gap to be overcome in order to enable more effective engagement in the talkative classroom environment (Cathcart, Dixon-Dawson & Hall, 2006; Mainkar, 2008). Relatively little literature has explored the notion of silence from the perspective of cultural pedagogy and considered issues of power and knowledge legitimacy in the classroom context. This chapter briefly explores 'active' and 'reflective' learning in the context of the international classroom, drawing on the emerging results from small-scale qualitative research conducted in business school classrooms in a UK higher education institution.

Participative dynamics in the Anglo-Western higher education classroom

The contemporary Anglophone higher education environment is dominated by suggestions that correlate noisy, talkative students with critical thinking and learning:

> *One of the purported aims of Anglo-western higher education is to encourage students to think critically; and their courses require them to construct knowledge through agonistic forms of arguments and to express themselves directly and assertively. Students are invited to join their lecturer in challenging received wisdom, and their efforts are approved so long as they follow conventional approaches...students who are reluctant to participate in challenging received wisdom – who value reticence and the appearance of consensus – are less likely to engage the interest and respect of lecturers in this system.*
>
> (Chanock, 2010, p. 544)

In this context, silence may become implicitly associated with a lack of engagement either with the social community of learners or with the objects of learning, marginalising a student's right to reticence in the classroom (Chanock, 2010).

To some degree cultural norms co-identifying talkative involvement with engagement have underpinned incipient cultural dynamics of participation. Such preferences can encourage a unidimensional perspective on silence among teachers because they have tended simultaneously to identify quietness with social isolation or social loafing. This is particularly evident in less formal, more student-centred teaching settings such as those which feature group work (Pieterse & Thompson, 2010). Yet silence is culturally plastic and loaded with many meanings across social and learning settings (Marlina, 2009; Ramburuth & Tani, 2009; Wilkinson & Olliver-Gray, 2006). Zhou, Knoke & Sakamoto (2005), in their study of Chinese students in Canadian higher education, explore the contribution of silence in the legitimation of cultures of knowing and suggest that: 'Classroom power dynamics are not only about gender, race and so on, but also about *linguistic and cultural disparities in knowledge production, dissemination and vali-dation'* (Zhou et al., 2005, p. 304, authors' italics).

Zhou et al.'s study emphasises cultural dichotomies in modes of participation, such as formal versus informal, serious versus relaxed, knowledge-based versus spontaneous and personal versus impersonal, and identifies the need to create a 'safe' (Zhou et al., 2005, p. 295) and inclusive learning space in which indigenous ways of knowing are provided sufficient space for articulation and are listened to in order to engage students more fully in learning.

Other work suggests that the silent student risks characterisation as 'less able' more than those who represent their knowledge orally. Turner's (2009) small-scale study of student peer-group work identified a 'pathologising' of silence by cultural insiders and an evolving punitive dynamic in the classroom setting which enforced noisier participation. Particularly in the context of student-centred and less formal learning environments, therefore, interplay between vocalisation and silence becomes more important as a socio-cultural marker of the classroom space. Shaw et al. (2008) characterise the tutorial classroom as a socio-cultural space in which 'active', talking participation is foregrounded:

> *participation is not just about attending classes, it is also about actively taking part in them. Making contributions in a tutorial…requires skills on the part of the contributor…even in settings which are designed to maximise opportunities to participate, those with less experience can feel marginalized or excluded…this is often more a reflection on the way in which higher education is socially and culturally organised, than a reflection on the 'inherent' intellectual capabilities of individual students.*
>
> (Shaw et al., 2008, pp. 704–705)

In this context, additional pressures of cultural adaptation on international learners are clear. Bartram (2008) identifies socio-cultural support as a primary requirement for international students – above the need for academic support. In the context of semi-formal and participative classrooms, emphasis on social learning within a cultural context poses particular stresses on international students. This research prompts further reflection on attitudes towards 'silent' students as a means of exploring underlying assumptions within higher education pedagogy.

Public versus private orientations in cross-cultural literature

In the wider context of cross-cultural communication, communication preferences are identified with a cluster of cultural factors which position style as a key cultural indicator (Samovar, Porter & McDaniel, 2007). In particular, links between notions of public versus private space and collective versus individual orientations to society coalesce to reflect patterns of influence in the classroom (Holmes, 2005; Kim, 2006). In this environment, an inevitable conjunction between notions of 'active' learning and participation and language throws into focus the challenges of silence in the classroom. Accepting Vygotsky's notion of learning as dialogic, and the Freirian model of learning as conversation, one of the markers of active learning is an oral articulation in classroom settings (Freire, 1970; Wertsch, 1983). Indeed, active use of verbal language is identified as a medium through which teachers adjudge students' intellectual skills and capabilities. Additionally, the coalescence of speech and inclusion foregrounds interesting dimensions in classroom power dynamics. Who speaks and how they approach the act of speaking represent an enactment of personal power in the Anglophone context (Ryan & Viete, 2009). By association, silence is often associated with a lack of personal power, social marginalisation or even a lack of intellectual ability.

To some extent this view of talking and silence relates to embedded cultural notions of communication. Hall's (1988) – for whom communication and culture were synonymous – low context/high context characterisation of national cultures addresses the degree to which cultures give explicit verbal expression to thoughts and feelings or prefer implicit, less direct modes of expression. Equally, the literature on cross-cultural communication identifies that in low context cultures silence is regarded as a negative, an *absence* of or *withdrawal* from communication, whereas the high context environment identifies a strong role for silence to play as a positive part of the communication process (Schneider & Barsoux, 2003). Consequently, for low context cultures, silence is regarded as uncomfortable or potentially antisocial, whereas high context cultures tend to regard silence with psychological equanimity. Broadly, cultures vary in their perspective about the usefulness of verbal language to convey important messages – high context cultures tend to regard verbal language as less helpful in relating significance of meaning. Additionally, more obvious matters of cultural etiquette and politeness vary, with widely different interpretations given to turn-taking, interrupting and taking the lead as legitimate communication strategies. These factors contribute to differences in attribution of the status of classrooms as either private or public spaces and co-learner groups as composed of insiders – with whom talk and its consequences would be more easily shared – or outsiders – with whom social norms of politeness are more formally in place.

Reflection: Individual or shared?

Flowing from this context, questions arise that explore silence as an individual, private or collective, public learning activity. This links into considerations of the nature of reflective learning in the higher education classroom. Numerous characterisations of Asian classrooms identify relatively high levels of classroom silence. At the same time, descriptions of Anglophone classrooms tend to be noisier. The nature of reflective learning is given to a quiet thoughtful pondering of questions, issues and style (Hedberg, 2009; Peltier, Hay & Drago, 2005). Yet within the Anglo context it is highly suggestive that such reflection takes place privately, individually outside the classroom. The classroom context, it seems, is more about the shared declaration of the *outcomes* of the individual reflective process rather than providing a site for quiet collective reflection (Gray, 2007). The individualistic focus in the Anglo learning literature tends not to make explicit the potential of shared quietness to enhance individual silent reflection.

Ideas about reflective learning have evolved from a range of intellectual roots from systematic reflections about professional development to psychological constructions of complex learning processes. Increasingly, notions of reflection have become more 'invasive' and engage concepts of 'confession and self-surveillance' (Ross, 2011, p. 115), suggestive of more collaborative elements in the reflective process. In expanding ideas about the outcomes of reflection in shared learning spaces, greater focus on classrooms as venues for oral communication becomes clear, particularly in the broader context of the participative classroom. Nonetheless, mainstream thinking about reflective learning tends to emphasise intrapersonal reflection through reflective writing, whereas reflective practices and skills development are scaffolded by teachers (Moon, 2004). To some extent, therefore, constructions of reflective learning appear to offer a partial counterpoint to the talkative classroom. Equally, reflective learning constructs tend to construct reflective processes in an individualised cognitive context which underlines an atomistic intimation of silence as a properly individual activity external to the classroom learning space.

Talking and silence: What can they tell us about learning that happens in the classroom?

While it is important not to overstress sharpness in the dichotomy between silence and talking in classroom spaces, the relative lack of research provides insufficient insights from which to generalise. Nonetheless, suggestions that Anglo-Western classrooms are constructed more as noisy, talking spaces inhabited by individual minds rather than contemplative collective spaces which harness the benefits of shared quiet reflection is interesting when explored from an intercultural perspective. Suggestions that teachers' judgements about classroom behaviours which privilege particular modes of talking engagement also question the degree to which classrooms are inclusive or are characterised by cultural norms which may not recognise or undervalue certain participatory styles.

Project and method

Drawing on these strands in the discourse, this chapter reports the emerging findings of a small-scale project which explored student perspectives on their own classroom participation from a standpoint of talking or quietness. The project evolved from earlier research, which explored intercultural dimensions of student engagement in classroom-based peer groups (Turner, 2009). The study site was within the business school of a UK higher education institution.

Over the past 20 years, the UK business schools have been characterised by growing levels of participation by non-UK nationals and have experienced high levels of international diversity in the classroom. A large number of studies have explored issues specific to the diverse business and management classroom but relatively little research has been undertaken to explore the dynamics of talking, silence and learning within them. As a vocational discipline, Anglo-Western business and management pedagogy has developed practice norms focused on development of students' oral skills and related particularly to notions of employability (Desiraju & Gopinath, 2001; Mainkar, 2008). Such approaches have adopted extensive use of student-centred peer-group working and oral presentations, particularly those using case study methods. The business and management discipline therefore provides a fruitful site from which to explore the relationship between oral communication, learning and assessment.

The study commenced during 2010–11 using a conventional research design focused on a short online survey sent to a cross-section of 200 international and the UK students in the School across postgraduate and undergraduate levels (100 postgraduates and undergraduates, respectively). The undergraduate sample drew from stage 1 and stage 4 students, focusing on direct entrants as a means of mirroring the postgraduate sample composition. An initial pilot survey was undertaken in autumn 2010. This survey identified useful revisions in the design of individual items, the data from which, for the purposes of this chapter, are disregarded. The main data collection period took place in spring 2011.

Responding to the functional limitations mentioned above, online survey methods provided an accessible approach to obtaining a reasonably wide surface sample of students across the school and to generating data which would suggest themes for subsequent exploration in interviews. The questionnaire design was simple – 10 choice-based, tick-box questions – to incentivise participation. Students were emailed a standard message introducing the study with a request to participate. The sample constitution was broadly an opportunity sample, drawing from student cohorts that the researcher had taught over the current academic year. Given that the focus of the work was aimed at exploring the perceptions of international students in particular, the sample was constructed from 150 international and 50 UK students to provide a limited initial comparison. For the purposes of the project, European Union (EU) students were included within the international learner group since the focus of the data collection was towards perceptions of those who were non-UK learners rather than on the basis of fee-paying status. Response rates were low but within a reasonable range of expectations for such surveys – a total of 80 people participated (40 per cent), 63 international and 17 UK students. Additional tranches of data collection will take place in autumn 2011 to provide a more substantive interpretive base from the survey data.

The design of individual items, question summaries and results are shown in Table 16.1. The survey drew specifically on student perceptions and preferences

Table 16.1 Preliminary survey results

Question	International respondents (N = 63; figures indicate positive responses to question)	UK respondents (N = 17; per cent of those who responded to question)
Thinking about how you take part in a class, how talkative do you tend to be in tutorials, seminars or workshops?		
I tend to be one of the most talkative people in class	5 (8%)	2 (12%)
I talk more than most people	19 (31%)	7 (41%)
I talk but tend to be quieter than most	31 (50%)	7 (41%)
I tend to be quiet in class	7 (11%)	1 (6%)
Do you talk more in tutorials, seminars or workshops if you have spent more time preparing in advance?		
No, I always participate in the same way	8 (14%)	5 (29%)
I talk a little more if I am better prepared	18 (29%)	3 (18%)
Yes, I talk more when I'm prepared	34 (54%)	9 (53%)
I talk more when I have not prepared as much	2 (3%)	0
How satisfied are you with the way in which you participate in tutorials, seminars or workshops?		
I am very satisfied with my participation	24 (39%)	6 (35%)
I am mostly satisfied but would like to change my participation a little	26 (42%)	9 (53%)
I am not very satisfied with my participation	12 (19%)	2 (12%)
Of the following list of factors, what is the main factor that influences how much you talk in tutorials, seminars and workshops?		
How much I have prepared in advance	10 (16%)	4 (24%)
The style of the class	13 (21%)	4 (24%)
Feedback from the lecturer	12 (19%)	4 (24%)
The behaviour of other students	5 (8%)	1 (6%)
How confident I feel with my language skills	8 (13%)	0
My learning preferences – I am a talkative learner	6 (10%)	1 (6%)
My learning preferences – I am a quiet learner	8 (13%)	3 (18%)
I am a shy person and do not like to talk in groups of people	0	0

continued

Table 16.1 (Continued)

Question	International respondents (N = 63; per cent of those who responded to question)	UK respondents (N = 17; per cent of those who responded to question)
Of the following factors, what is the main factor that would help you to change your style of participation in tutorials, seminars or workshops?		
Marks for class participation as part of the module	13 (21%)	7 (41%)
Punishment for those who do not speak a lot	2 (3%)	0
Clearer instructions on what to do and how to take part in classes	10 (16%)	3 (18%)
Clearer feedback and support from the lecturer during classes	31 (49%)	5 (30%)
Nothing, I cannot change my approach to learning	7 (11%)	2 (12%)
What kind of classroom style do you find most supportive to your learning?		
A classroom in which the students do more talking than the teacher	3 (5%)	1 (6%)
A classroom in which the teacher guides the students in their participation but in which all students talk	39 (60%)	9 (53%)
A classroom in which the teacher asks students to participate at particular times	18 (29%)	6 (35%)
A classroom in which the teacher does most of the talking and students listen to what they have to say	4 (7%)	1 (6%)
What kind of classroom style do you prefer?		
A classroom in which the students do more talking than the teacher	2 (3%)	2 (12%)
A classroom in which the teacher guides the students in their participation but in which all students talk	39 (62%)	7 (41%)
A classroom in which the teacher asks students to participate at particular times	15 (24%)	6 (35%)
A classroom in which the teacher does most of the talking and students listen to what they have to say	7 (11%)	2 (12%)
What kind of classroom style do you like the least?		
A classroom in which the students do more talking than the teacher	24 (39%)	6 (35%)

Table 16.1 (Continued)

Question	International respondents (N = 63; per cent of those who responded to question)	UK respondents (N = 17; per cent of those who responded to question)
A classroom in which the teacher guides the students in their participation but in which all students talk	9 (15%)	1 (6%)
A classroom in which the teacher asks students to participate at particular times	8 (13%)	1 (6%)
A classroom in which the teacher does most of the talking and students listen to what they have to say	20 (33%)	9 (53%)
How much does talking with other students in tutorials, seminars and workshops contribute to your learning?		
Discussion with other students in class is the most important part of my learning	9 (14%)	1 (6%)
Discussion with other students in class is quite important, among other activities	42 (67%)	13 (77%)
Discussion with other students in class does not contribute very much to my learning	10 (16%)	3 (18%)
Discussion with other students in class does not contribute at all to my learning	1 (2%)	0
Discussion with other students in class obstructs my learning	1 (2%)	0

in terms of oral engagement and classroom participation. The survey isolated responses to tutorial, seminar and workshop classrooms in the business school in order to focus on learning spaces in which oral communication occurred most frequently. Individual items explored respondents' perspectives on the link between advance preparation for classes and their engagement as well as the contribution of oral interaction with peers. Basic analysis using simple descriptive statistics was undertaken to classify categories, themes and trends within the results.

Reflecting on the emerging outcomes

Though such a small data set provides only a limited insight into student perceptions, the data ARE suggestive of some potentially interesting themes for further exploration. Across certain areas, broad similarities in preference existed between the UK and international students in terms of classroom style, for example. The distribution of results across the range of categories explored highlighted some variation in orientation and preference between the two groups, particularly in terms of preferences for highly student- or teacher-centred approaches.

In terms of basic self-perceptions about participation in the classroom, more international students identified themselves as less talkative than their UK peers and suggested a stronger link between advance preparation and talking behaviours in the classroom. This resonates with previous research suggesting that many non-UK students identify knowledge-based criteria as a basis for participation in the classroom, preferring to remain quiet when feeling that they lack sufficient expertise to participate in discussion and debate. Interestingly, a similar percentage of international and the UK students expressed satisfaction/dissatisfaction with their current style of participation, with approximately two-thirds of both groups seeking to make some change. These outcomes perhaps suggest opportunities for structured skills development work in the area of interpersonal communication and collaborative working to enhance students' understandings of interpersonal etiquettes and communication styles. In terms of the direction of developmental change, the underlying assumption for all groups of students appeared to be towards increasing levels of talking participation rather than reducing it. The survey questions attempted to balance out descriptors of both talking and quiet participation, making the incipient suggestion of changes to become more talkative on the part of respondents an interesting one for further exploration. Do these responses reflect perceptions about underlying classroom norms, for example, or more universal preferences for communicative participation that would modify the socio-cultural expectations encouraged in previous research?

In considering factors that would influence a change in behaviour, both groups identified a range of factors across the available categories. Perhaps, unsurprisingly, international students identified language confidence within the range that was absent from the UK responses, possibly highlighting a definitional differentiation in the groups between a focus on technical language skills and broader issues of communicative competence. Although the same three factors emerged for both groups in terms of influence over their classroom behaviour – advance preparation, class style, lecturer feedback – to some degree international students ranked preferences for communicative scaffolding in-class from teachers more highly, a theme which emerged more strongly in later questions. Collectively, responses foregrounded the importance of infrastructural and design factors, such as class style and teacher involvement, as the most important influences on participation strategies. These responses suggested that active teacher engagement in the detailed design and creation of learning spaces is an important underpinning factor in student participation and communication styles.

Linking to the question about factors influencing talking participation in classes, the next survey question – exploring factors to encourage students to change their behaviour – showed similar general emphasis on assessment for class participation and lecturer feedback but within different proportions. Half of international student respondents focused on feedback from lecturers as a key factor, with 40 per cent of the UK students suggesting that assessment of student participation would most clearly support participative change. Little support from either group was expressed for punitive measures to change behaviours. Interestingly, little emphasis was placed on improving or making explicit instructions about how to engage in the classroom, which may suggest a divergence between understanding and preference or other factors in shaping student participation. These responses tend to underline a facilitative/supportive rather than an instructive/directive contribution for lecturers, with an emphasis on active communicative feedback and encouragement for particular behaviours. The contrast in this category of responses between international and the UK students is interesting, suggestive that the UK students are more encouraged by formal incentives, whereas international learners are more encouraged by lecturer support. Nonetheless, these two key areas emerged very strongly in combination as key opportunities to support and encourage students' talking participation where it is desired.

The following three survey questions focused on student preferences in terms of classroom style. Across the questions, a clear preference for a participative classroom style emerged in terms of approaches which respondents felt best supported their learning and met their basic preferences. This is interesting because it is suggestive that all groups of students identified a positive contribution from social-dialogic learning in classroom settings, a perspective reinforced strongly in the final question. At the same time, however, international students show a stronger preference for higher levels of teacher-centred methods and structured teacher facilitation for student peer-to-peer engagement, whereas the UK students showed a much lower tolerance for formal teacher-centred approaches, which may suggest the potential for teaching practitioners to reflect on their interactive styles in the classroom. In particular, international student responses seemed to show a lower preference for highly student-centred classrooms, seeking active in-class engagement with teachers as part of the learning process.

Talking, learning, being quiet: Any insights?

Within the context of the limitations of the survey data, some potentially useful themes and issues emerged from the preliminary stages of the research exercise. Descriptively, international students did seem to make a stronger account of themselves as less talkative in classroom settings, although with varying levels of satisfaction with that set of behaviours, whereas more UK students identify themselves as talkative compared with their international peers. This certainly resonates with the suggestions from both the international education and intercultural communication literature which would tend to strand preferred communication strategies for Anglo-Western peoples as among the most orally centred.

Equally, the international respondents in the survey identified that lecturers had a central role in actively facilitating student engagement, although this seemed to be echoed across both groups to a large extent. Certainly more international respondents expressed an unfavourable view of highly student-centred approaches, which poses some interesting questions in terms of the design of inclusive learning spaces. The majority of respondents associated importance to student-to-student discussion in the UK classroom within a context of active teacher facilitation and support. To some degree the survey data hinted at variances in preference about the stylistic norms underlying engagement between the UK and international respondents which linked into earlier discussions about participative dynamics from a cultural standpoint. These areas may only be further illuminated through more qualitative work to probe underlying beliefs and values about the status of the classroom and perspectives on the nature and value of peer-based social learning.

In general, the survey data took a very small and tentative step into the area of culture, talking and learning in the Anglophone higher education classroom, highlighting areas of similarity as well as some potential differences between the UK and international learners in their preferences for participation. An assumptive focus on high levels of talking participation within a framework of active teacher support and facilitation as a positive element of semi-formal classroom settings is perhaps the most striking theme to emerge from the initial survey data. Furthermore, more qualitative data collection will attempt to explore the cultural situatedness of this set of apparent preferences and will attempt to deconstruct the degree to which the particularities of Anglo-Western classroom norms have influenced student responses. To a large extent the outcomes of this initial stage of the research is both tantalising and muddling. Some elements of the data support the notion that perspectives on classroom engagement are universalised rather than subject to cultural norms; other elements show differentiation between the UK and international learners. One as-yet implicit dimension in this is the degree to which student recent experiences in the UK university classroom have shaped participants' notion of assumptive norms and therefore influenced style of response to the questions. This aspect of the data collection will contextualise further research, reflecting the multidimensional character of both intercultural communication and learning, which is composed of both behavioural and affective aspects. In doing so, it will explore in more depth participants' perspectives and preferences for silence as more than a mere absence of talking.

References

Bartram, B. (2008). Supporting international students in higher education: Constructions, cultures and clashes. *Teaching in Higher Education*, *13*(6), 657–668.

Buswell, J. & Becket, N. (2009). *Enhancing student-centred learning in business and management, hospitality, leisure, sport and tourism*. Newbury: Threshold Press.

Cathcart, A., Dixon-Dawson, J. & Hall, R. (2006). Reluctant hosts and disappointed guests? Examining expectations of cross cultural group work on postgraduate business programmes. *International Journal of Management Education*, 5(2), 13–22.

Chanock, K. (2010). The right to reticence. *Teaching in Higher Education*, 15(4), 543–552.

Desiraju, R. & Gopinath, C. (2001). Encouraging participation in case discussion: A comparison of the MICA and the Harvard case methods. *Journal of Management Education*, 25, 394–408.

Freire, P. (1970). *Pedagogy of the oppressed*. New York: Herder and Herder.

Gray, D. E. (2007). Facilitating management learning: Developing critical reflection through reflective tools. *Management Learning*, 38, 495–517.

Hall, E. T. (1988). *Silent language*. New York: Bantam Doubleday Dell Publishing Group.

Hedberg, P. R. (2009). Learning through reflective classroom practice: Applications to educate the reflective manager. *Journal of Management Education*, 33, 10–36.

Holmes, P. (2005). Ethnic Chinese students' communication with cultural others in a New Zealand university. *Communication Education*, 54(4), 289–231.

Kim, S. (2006). Academic oral communication needs of East Asian international graduate students in non-science and non-engineering fields. *English for Specific Purposes*, 25(4), 479–489.

Mainkar, A. V. (2008). A student-empowered system for measuring and weighing participation in class discussion. *Journal of Management Education*, 32, 23–36.

Marlina, R. (2009). 'I don't talk or I decide not to talk? Is it my culture?' International students' experiences of tutorial participation. *International Journal of Educational Research*, 48(4), 235–244.

Moon, J. (2004). *A handbook of reflective learning*. London: RoutledgeFalmer.

Ollin, R. (2008). Silent pedagogy and rethinking classroom practice: Structuring teaching through silence rather than talk. *Cambridge Journal of Education*, 38(2), 265–280.

Peltier, J. W., Hay, A. & Drago, W. (2005). The reflective learning continuum: Reflecting on reflection. *Journal of Marketing Education*, 27, 250–263.

Pieterse, V. & Thompson, L. (2010). Academic alignment to reduce the presence of 'social loafers' and 'diligent isolates' in student teams. *Teaching in Higher Education*, 15(4), 355–367.

Ramburuth, P. & Tani, M. (2009). The impact of culture on learning: Exploring student perceptions. *Multicultural Education and Technology*, 3(3), 182–195.

Ross, J. (2011). Traces of self: Online reflective practices and performances in higher education. *Teaching in Higher Education*, 16(1), 113–126.

Ryan, J. & Viete, R. (2009). Respectful interactions: Learning with international students in the English-speaking academy. *Teaching in Higher Education*, 14(3), 303–314.

Samovar, L. A., Porter, R. E. & McDaniel, E. R. (2007). *Communication between cultures*. Belmont, CA: Thomson Wadsworth.

Schneider, S. C. & Barsoux, J. (2003). *Managing across cultures*. Harlow: Pearson Education.

Shaw, L., Carey, P. & Mair, M. (2008). Studying interaction in undergraduate tutorials: Results from a small-scale evaluation. *Teaching in Higher Education*, 13(6), 703–714.

Turner, Y. (2009). 'Knowing me, knowing you', is there nothing we can do? Pedagogic challenges in positioning the HE classroom as an international learning space. *Journal of Studies in International Education, 13*(2), 240–255.

Turner, Y. & Robson, S. (2008). *Internationalizing the university: An introduction for university teachers and managers.* London: Continuum Press.

Wertsch, J. W. (1983). *Vygotsky and the social formation of mind.* Cambridge, MA: Harvard University Press.

Wilkinson, L. & Olliver-Gray, Y. (2006). The significance of silence: Differences in meaning, learning styles and teaching strategies in cross-cultural settings. *Psychologia, 49*(2), 74–88.

Zhou, Y. R., Knoke, D. & Sakamoto, I. (2005). Rethinking silence in the classroom: Chinese students' experience of sharing indigenous knowledge. *International Journal of Inclusive Education, 9*(3), 287–311.

Chapter 17

Raising students' awareness of the construction of communicative (in)competence in international classrooms

Rachel Wicaksono

As a teacher of the UK and international undergraduate and postgraduate students who use English as their medium of communication, I am reminded daily of how the spread of English around the world presents both opportunities and threats for all of its speakers. This chapter explores the construction of (in)competence in classroom talk where English is used as a lingua franca between the UK and international students. I begin with a review of two misguided but, frequently occurring, ways of thinking about English as a language, followed by a look at how this thinking may be playing out in three examples from recordings of my students' classroom talk. Finally, I attempt to consider how new ways of listening and acting/talking may benefit British students who are using English in international situations.

English is the medium, or lingua franca, of my mixed nationality and mixed language classrooms and this situation can result in, sometimes unforeseen, opportunities and threats for both the UK and bi- or multi-lingual international students who are using English as an additional language. For the UK students, misguided ideas about their ownership of English can mean that the responsibility for intelligibility is rested wholly on the shoulders of the international students: if I can't understand you, you need to learn more of my language. Such attitudes may go some way to explain, for example, minimal take up by the UK students of international communication opportunities, as well as being associated with a less successful experience in mixed language group work for all group members. For international students, ideas about the UK students' ownership of English can mean that their well-developed (international) communication skills are not widely recognised. More seriously, the 'the English own English' idea means that well-established, but non-UK, varieties of English are judged, including by the international students themselves, to be 'incorrect' and in need of improvement (Widdowson, 1994).

Of course, my students are by no means alone in their beliefs about English; indeed, they are in powerful company. In January 2008, the then UK Prime Minister Gordon Brown, on a visit to India, made the generous offer of a 'new gift' to the Indian people – the English language. He suggested that benefits for the recipients would include increased business and access to global knowledge, as well as improved progress, and respect for other nations and cultures. Conveniently, Brown chose to gloss over the disrespect, lack of technological progress, economic and political troubles that exists within, not to mention between, English-speaking countries. Furthermore, the fact that English has been part of multilingual India for generations (Gargesh, 2006), and is a well-established lingua franca both within India and with her international trading partners, was not explored by Brown. Instead, his 'gift' was predicated on the belief that English is something Britain owns and that giving English is a way for Britain to help, 'anyone – however impoverished and however far away' (Brown, 2008). What linguists have to say about these beliefs is the subject of the next section. Suffice to say for now that sociolinguists and critical discourse analysts have long argued that the spread of English was, and continues to be, linked to the agendas of both the multinational business community, and the economic and political interests of the UK and US governments. In his 1992 critique of the English language teaching industry, Robert Phillipson claims:

> That there are now several centers of power that compete in promoting several native models of English and market distinct [English language teaching] methodologies cannot be denied. The motivation is clearly the exploitation of the economic power of English, as is obvious from the following quote: 'As the director of a dynamic worldwide chain of English language schools puts it, "Once we used to send gunboats and diplomats abroad; now we are sending English teachers"'.

(p. 8)

Aside from the cynically self-serving beliefs about *English* exemplified by Brown and highlighted by Phillipson, beliefs that both grant and deny power to the speakers of the world's most widespread lingua franca, there are more fundamental beliefs about *language* which underpin the UK/international student practices and which I will very briefly mention here. Linguists have documented how all speakers of all languages use different styles of speaking, writing and signing, including vocabulary, pronunciation, grammar and ways of getting their meaning across, depending on the communities they belong to (age, residence, job, hobby, religion, ethnicity, clubs, etc.). Linguists have also noted how any one speaker can belong to multiple communities, shifting their speaking, writing or signing style to fit who s/he is talking to and what s/he is trying to achieve (Clark, 1997). The linguistic reality is that languages do not have a core, a default version, a monolithic lexicon, but that there are alternative modes of expression, between which speakers of the language switch, depending on the context in which they find themselves. But because this style shifting largely goes on without our conscious awareness, we are, encouraged by self-styled 'authorities' (from national governments to BBC Radio 4 pundits), unlikely to realise that:

> *The assumption of a default, "accent-free", version of each language is one of our most powerful linguistic beliefs... the judgements involved are not linguistic at all, but social.*
>
> (Hall, 2005, p. 252)

Languages, including English, are not the same thing as the idealised systems that exist in grammar books and dictionaries:

> *Rather, they are sociocognitive systems, mediating between isolated individuals and named groups living within regional or national borders. Because of this, their own borders, in both the minds of individuals and communities of speakers, are very fluid indeed. Believing that governments and academies can ring-fence a language from outside influence is as naive as believing that everyone outside the Italian border can be prevented from eating pizza, or that everyone outside the Chinese border can be forced to celebrate the new year without fireworks.*
>
> (Hall, Smith & Wicaksono, 2011, p. 12)

So, how do speakers of English, who may be using varieties that are geographically disparate, communicate? Canagarajah (2007) suggests that recent studies of lingua franca English reveal:

> *what multilingual communities have known all along: language learning and language use succeed through performance strategies, situational resources, and social negotiations in fluid communicative contexts. Proficiency is therefore practice-based, adaptive and emergent.*
>
> (p. 923)

This is not a stripped down, simplified variety of English but a theory of language in which understanding is created between willing subjects, in real time and in specific contexts. Describing lingua franca English, Canagarajah (2007) says:

> *The speakers are able to monitor each other's language proficiency to determine mutually the appropriate grammar, lexical range and pragmatic conventions that would ensure intelligibility.*
>
> (p. 925)

Approximately 80 per cent of users of English around the world are bi- or multilingual and using English as an *additional* language; a greater number in fact than those who are monolingual speakers of English (Brutt-Griffler, 2002).

Furthermore, the varieties of English evolving around the world, wherever it is used as a lingua franca, may increasingly have little to do with English as it is used in the UK. According to David Graddol (2006), in a report on English for international communication:

> *Research is also beginning to show how bad some native speakers are at using English for international communication. It may be that elements of an [English as a lingua franca] syllabus could usefully be taught within a mother tongue curriculum.*

(p. 87)

In mixed language situations in the UK university classroom talk, how do these beliefs about ownership of English and language as a monolithic system play out? Data I have collected from mixed language groups of students show a number of ways in which the UK students treat the achievement of mutual understanding as potentially threatened by the English language 'incompetence' of their international interlocutors. Evidence includes the multiple proactive repetition/rephrasing of questions and the substitution of 'easier' lexical items for those diagnosed as troublesome. While these and other strategies can provide a resource for maintaining the flow of talk, they also, in some cases, result in further misunderstanding and a reinforced perception of the international student as an incompetent user of English. An example of how this occurs can be seen in the following extract from a discussion between Ollie, a UK student, and Stavros, an international student (for a glossary of transcription symbols, see the end of this chapter).

Transcript I

```
01   O:   What- what parts of ummm like your lessons (.) have you
02        enjoyed (.) doing (.) with Rachel.
03   S:   (2.0) Hmm?
04   O:   What parts of your ermmm ((LS)) (1.0) foundation
05        programme have you enjoyed doing with Rachel.
06   S:   (.) We- I don't have Rachel.
07   O:   Oh you DO:N't? oh right. So what- (1.0) what lessons d-
08        what lessons are you doin'?
```

Ollie's question is punctuated by three micropauses, the second and third of which precede additional information, 'doing' and 'with Rachel'. Stavros responds to Ollie's question with a long pause and a complaint noise, 'Hmm?'. This is taken up by Ollie as evidence of some kind of trouble; specifically, as a request for some clarification of his previous utterance. In line 04 of the transcript, Ollie repeats his question using some of the same words as in his previous turn, 'What parts of', but instead of saying 'lessons', he substitutes 'foundation programme'.

Ollie's substitution comes after a number of features which delay its delivery; 'ermmm', a lip smack and a one-second pause. 'Foundation programme' is the institutionally sanctioned name for Stavros's current academic course of study, in contrast to the more generic word 'lessons'. The question that was relaunched in line 04 is then completed with the same words as were used in the first attempt, 'have you enjoyed doing with Rachel'. In line 06, Stavros, after a micropause and a false start 'We- I' supplies what might be the explanation for his initial hesitation: Rachel is not his teacher. Ollie has made an incorrect assumption which Stavros wishes to correct, before, or instead of, answering the question. Ollie accepts the correction in line 07 and, without pausing, asks another question. In his third question, after a short pause of one second to relaunch the question, Ollie changes the focus of from asking about *enjoyable* parts of lessons with Rachel to asking a more general question about the type of lessons Stavros is currently having. The third question, as well as including a one second pause mid-question, starts and then restarts twice: 'So *what*- (1.0) *what* lessons d- *what* lessons are you doin'?'.

In the extract above, Ollie seems to treat the problem signalled by Stavros in line 03 as a possible issue of lexical (non-) competence; Stavros does not appear to understand his question, perhaps the blocking word is 'lessons'. Ollie attempts to solve the problem by trying again with an alternative phrase which he will have frequently heard used to describe Stavros's current programme of study, like using a familiar brand name such as 'Hoover', instead of a more generic and perhaps less familiar term like 'vacuum cleaner'. It turns out, of course, that the problem here is not Stavros's English language competence but his desire to correct Ollie's mistaken idea that I was his teacher. Stavros orients to the assumptions behind Ollie's question rather than to the reason it is being asked, which is to find out what he has been studying. Stavros resists the linguistic incompetence interpretation and makes it clear that Ollie is the one who is mistaken.

Ollie's multiple rephrasing of his question, both prior and subsequent to what appears to be a misunderstanding, though in this case it is his, rather than Stavros's, is a very common feature of my mixed language group data. Other examples include Claire (UK) and Markus (international) in transcript 2, and Byrn (UK) and Giorgios (international) in transcript 3, below.

Transcript 2

01 C: (.h)err(1.9)which do you feel is most important when you
02   learn English th- the writing and understanding of the language
03   or the speaking and pronunciation which do you find (.h) you
04   should(.) you: should err (.) err work more active? err (.) to
05   be emm (1.2) so to grammatically understand the language or
06   err (.) just so you can speak and get by the pronunciation which
07   do you think is most important?
08 M: en it depends on situation I think=

Transcript 3

01 B: So whilst you've been learning English what kinds of things
02   have you done already (.) what kind of areas have you covered whilst
03   you've been here.
04 G: (.) What do you mean?
05 B: (.) (.h) Well, have you looked at (.) um (.) travelling and directions
06   ° have you looked at °°° how to you know like how to °°° actual
07   words. like in the supermarket ° like buying and selling [food?]
08 G: [yeah]

Such 'preventative' actions involving repetition and rephrasing by the person considered to be a 'native speaker' of the lingua franca have been found in other mixed language situations (English – Gardner, 2004; German – Hinnenkamp, 1987). In all these cases, the 'native speakers' demonstrate their willingness to support mutual understanding by modifying their talk. Their preventative modifications are based on judgements about their interactants' 'competence' in English and demonstrate how categories of 'membership' are created, a process with subsequent interactional consequences. When repetition or rephrasing occurs after a challenge to mutual understanding has been recognised, or indeed prior to and in order to prevent a challenge, it has the perhaps unintended consequence of ascribing an interlocutor to the category of 'non-understanding at this time' (see also Park, 2007). This ascription can create, as Hinnenkamp (1987) argues, a category which, in the speaker's mind may imply a *general* incompetence in English, or even, as Gumperz (1982) in his work on 'minoriza-tion' shows, incompetence in general. In other words, repetition and rephrasing, particularly where it is preventative,

> *as identifier of membership category may... be labelled* 'parasitic', *in that its application draws upon negative stereotyping at the expense of the stereo-typed, and to the benefit of the stereotyper, who has thus successfully legitimated his or her claim of being naturally endowed with more rights than her or his interlocutor.*
>
> (Hinnenkamp, 1987, p. 173, emphasis in the original)

The use of repeated and rephrased talk to create a particular kind of relationship and accomplish what one or more of the interactants perceive to be a 'normal' situation does not necessarily result in negative consequences, however. Repeating and rephrasing can also allow recognised roles to come into being in a way that creates the context necessary for a particular kind of institutional relationship. ten Have's (1991) work, for example, on doctor–patient interaction, shows that the asymmetrical relationship created by the use of doctor–patient categories acts not only as a constraint on interaction but also as a resource. In positioning each other as 'doctor' and 'patient', the interactants create a framework that provides structure and strategies for successful interaction. Similarly, interactants can use ways of talking conventionally associated with 'being a UK student' and 'being an international student' as a way of achieving their mutual aim of having a conversation (Park, 2007). One benefit of doing this repetition and rephrasing is that a handy and effective framework is provided by which the conversation may proceed. Though, as Hinnenkamp (1987) and Gumperz (1982) remind us, all the benefits are not always equally shared between all the participants. Although the students fulfil their mutually agreed aim of 'having a conversation', it may be at the expense of international students who, having been cast in the role of 'potentially incompetent', are then exposed to the UK students' multiple rephrasings and repetitions through which the potential for misunderstanding is actually created. A cycle is created: in orienting to misguided ideas, prevalent in our political and institutional discourse, about the UK as the legitimate owner and best user of English, and about English as a monolithic entity around which any variation is a sign of incompetence, the UK students create communicative conditions in which misunderstanding is more likely. When misunderstanding occurs, the misguided ideas which led to it in the first place are assumed to provide an explanation, and the cycle of designing talk for incompetent interactants continues. Resistance by the international students does occur, as in the case of Stavros, who points out that it is Ollie who has misunderstood. Markus appears to understand, despite Claire's repetition and rephrasing, and Giorgios makes it clear that he has not understood, without pointing out the barriers to understanding that Bryn has created.

If it is indeed the case, as the quote from Graddol (2006) above suggests, that monolingual speakers of English may lack proficiency in the use of English in international situations, what are we to do? According to Canagarajah (2007), also quoted above, proficiency in lingua franca English is a practice-based, adaptive and emergent phenomenon. Lingua franca communication succeeds where the speakers are willing, and able, to monitor each other's talk and determine mutually the appropriate grammar, lexical range and pragmatic conventions that are most likely to ensure intelligibility. So, successful international communication is mainly to do with having a positive attitude towards variety, the willingness and ability to monitor one's own talk and the talk of an interlocutor, and the opportunity to practise negotiating meaning in international situations. In an attempt to sensitise my students to these factors, a mixed language group of students worked with me to design an online learning activity which was subsequently published under a Creative Commons licence (Wicaksono, 2009). We submitted the activity, which we decided to refer to as an 'online tutorial', to Jorum, the JISC-managed national digital repository and we were awarded an Intrallect-sponsored prize at the 2009 Association of Learning Technologies conference. The link in the list of references below points to an online version of the tutorial; an editable MS Word file marked up in Wimba Create and an HTML version ready to be imported into a virtual learning environment.

Our online tutorial aims to raise awareness of English as a lingua franca and explore alternative models for the description of (mis)understanding and (in)competence in international situations. The awareness-raising approach we take runs counter to much of the overgeneralised 'communication skills' advice available for students, and staff, working in international situations, such as 'be direct', 'be clear'. Instead, we encourage students to take a 'bottom-up' approach to the effect of their talk on their classroom roles, task outcomes, identities and assessments of their interlocutors' (in)competence. Specifically, the tutorial introduces students to the idea of English as a lingua franca and to the benefits of recording and transcribing their classroom talk. There are instructions for how to do this, including interactive flashcards to help them memorise some of the most common transcription symbols and a short video of one of the international students, Ilias, talking about his first experience of transcription. The tutorial includes several examples of classroom talk recorded by the students and of their transcriptions of this talk. There are some focus questions to guide the discussion of the transcriptions, and a videoed discussion of Ollie and Stavros discussing the 'with Rachel' data included as transcript 1 of this chapter.

I have enjoyed working on our awareness-raising tutorial and hope that it encourages my UK students to monitor their talk and perhaps avoid always falling back on their usual strategies of repetition and rephrasing. By showing them how to pay attention to the small details of their talk, I have been able to focus them on how successful communication arises *between* people in interaction, and is the responsibility of *both* the speaker and the hearer. Rather than participating in the perpetuation of misguided ideas about English and about language in general, I have encouraged the students to *notice* what is happening in their talk, and, in this way, to become more aware of the powerful role language plays in the creation and resistance of their assessments of each other's competence and, ultimately, their (UK/international) identities. Feedback, especially from students without a background in language learning or linguistics, has indicated the need for more examples of ways in which their talk is dependent on, and perpetuating of, stereotypes about communicative competence. Based on this feedback, I am currently working on version two of the tutorial, which I aim to publish later this year. The Creative Commons licence means that others are also welcome to use or adapt the materials within the tutorial to suit the needs of their own students, and I would be very interested to share experiences with anyone who decides to do so.

Challenging widely held and, potentially beneficial, at least in the short term, ideas about English is a sensitive business and it is tempting to look for the usual 'top tips' such as 'be direct' and 'be clear'. But successful communication is person-, task- and situation-specific, and the only good tip is to put on hold assumptions about what English is and how it really should be used. Of course, this runs counter to the activities of national governments and anyone else who stands to benefit from a monolithic version of what English is. The UK universities with an international agenda are in a tricky position here: Are we promoting an opportunity to come and be taught where English is 'at its best', an attitude which only hampers successful international communication? Or, are we open to noticing how English is already successfully used around the world in multifarious ways, and to sending a strong signal of our willingness to learn?

References

Brown, G. (2008). *English – The world's language. 2008 speeches.* Available at: http://www.youtube.com/watch?v=6gxaN-hagTY&noredirect=1 (accessed 3 November 2011).

Brutt-Griffler, J. (2002). *World English: A study of its development.* Clevedon, England: Multilingual Matters Ltd.

Canagarajah, S. (2007). Lingua franca English, multilingual communities, and language acquisition. *Modern Language Journal, 91,* 923–939.

Clark, H. H. (1997). Dogmas of understanding. *Discourse Processes, 23,* 567–598.

Gardner, R. (2004). On delaying the answer: Question sequences extended after the question. In R. Gardner & J. Wagner (eds.), *Second language conversations.* London: Continuum Press.

Gargesh, R. (2006). South Asian Englishes. In B. B. Kachru, Y. Kachru & C. L. Nelson (eds.), *The handbook of world Englishes.* Blackwell Handbooks in Linguistics. Oxford: Blackwell.

Graddol, D. (2006). *English next.* British Council Learning. Available at : http://www.britishcouncil.org/learning-research-english-next.pdf (accessed 4 April 2011).

Gumperz, J. J. (1982). *Discourse strategies.* Cambridge: Cambridge University Press.

Hall, C. J. (2005). *An introduction to language and linguistics: Breaking the language spell.* London: Continuum Press.

Hall C. J., Smith, P. S. & Wicaksono, R. (2011). *Mapping applied linguistics: A guide for students and practitioners.* London: Routledge.

Hinnenkamp, V. (1987). Foreigner talk, code switching and the concept of trouble. In K. Knapp, W. Enniger & A. Knapp-Potthoff (eds.), *Analyzing intercultural communication.* Berlin: Mouton de Gruyter.

Park, J. (2007). Co-construction of nonnative speaker identity in cross-cultural interaction. *Applied Linguistics, 28*(3), 339–360.

Phillipson, R. (1992). *Linguistic imperialism.* Oxford: Oxford University Press.

ten Have, P. (1991). Talk and institution: A reconsideration of the 'asymmetry' of doctor–patient interaction. In D. Boden & D. H. Zimmerman (eds.), *Talk and social structure: Studies in ethnomethodology and conversation analysis.* Cambridge: Polity Press.

Wicaksono, R. (2009). *English as a lingua franca: An online tutorial.* Available at: http://www2.yorksj.ac.uk/enquirycommons/elf/ (accessed 5 April 2011).

Widdowson, H. G. (1994). The ownership of English. *TESOL Quarterly, 28*(2), 377–389.

Glossary of transcription symbols

[]	Overlapping talk: denotes when more than one person is speaking
=	Latching: denotes an utterance that follows another without a gap
(.h)	Audible inbreath
(.)	Micropause: a just noticeable pause
(5.6)	Timed pause: the number in brackets represents the number of seconds
?	Gradual rising intonation: not necessarily a question
.	Gradual falling intonation: the pitch gradually falls to this point
° °	Quieter talk
°° °°	Much quieter talk
CAPITALS	Louder talk
Wha-	A sharp cut-off
Ye:s	Colons show that the speaker has stretched the preceding sound
((LS))	Lip smack

Chapter 18

Internationalising the curriculum for all students

The role of staff dialogue

Valerie Clifford, Juliet Henderson and Catherine Montgomery

Introduction

Bringing about curriculum and pedagogical change in higher education is difficult. Disciplines have been imbued with a strong belief about the nature of knowledge and how that knowledge is best taught (Becher, 1989; Neumann, Parry & Becher, 2002). However, in recent times the growth of interdisciplinarity (Becher & Trowler, 2001) and interest in indigenous knowledges (Teasdale & Ma Rhea, 2000) have presented a challenge to traditional ideas. Alongside this, universities now plot their strategic directions and decree the redesigning of curricula to meet specific agendas, for example, by introducing research into the undergraduate curricula, changing assessment practices, introducing sustainability and internationalisation.

Internationalisation of the curriculum (IoC) has brought a range of responses from staff, from delight and creative action to dismay and resistance (Clifford, 2009). What has become apparent is that staff need to begin with their own education in the area before they can begin to redesign curricula and practise new pedagogy (Sanderson, 2011; Teekens, 2000). Overseas international educational experience is often promulgated, for staff and students, as the way to internationalise ourselves, but, as with students, finances, domestic and work obligations often make this very difficult. We, therefore, need to explore alternative ways of 'internationalising' ourselves. We need to draw on the strengths of our existing practice to develop new knowledge, expand our pedagogical repertoire and flex our creative imagination (Gough, 1999; Rizvi, 2002). It is imperative that universities provide staff with the support to explore what these new ideas mean in their disciplines.

Innovations in curricula have often been introduced to higher education staff through workshops, and while these are a good means of disseminating new ideas, they may not have an impact on pedagogic practice. Accredited, sustained courses are more successful in moving change into practice (Brew & Barrie, 1999; Gibbs & Coffey, 2004) but these are very time consuming and pursued by a minority. Other ways have to be found to bring about change in curricula.

This chapter introduces a one-month, fully online course which was set up as a possible way of offering tertiary staff a safe space (Clegg et al., 2004) in which to explore new troublesome concepts (Meyer & Land, 2003), gather ideas on curriculum development and encourage experimentation with new practice. As the topic of the course was internationalisation of the curriculum, a virtual platform was also seen as a way of bringing voices together from a range of global locations to offer a variety of perspectives to the discussions.

It is now generally acknowledged that even for learners not included in the 'net generation' technology has become a useful learning tool (Sharpe, Beetham & De Freitas, 2010). It has been shown that well-designed and facilitated online discussion encourages collaborative work (Dearing, 1997; Laurillard, 2002), accommodates heterogeneity in learning styles, epistemologies and goals (Bates et al., 2007–2008; Britain & Liber, 1999) and contributes to the building of community (Skinner & Derounian, 2008). Transnational discussions can lead to transformative learning through fostering recognition of diverse views of the world, challenging normative discipline curricula and encouraging staff to 'act as social agents of change' (Morey, 2000, p. 29).

IoC presents as troublesome knowledge to many academics, as its definition is unclear (Clifford, 2009; Green & Mertova, 2011), lines of responsibility not evident (Green & Mertova, 2011) and resources negligible. It is a radical pedagogy in that it questions the current positioning of higher education in different global contexts (Readings, 1996) and the interpretation of 'internationalisation' as the marketing of the university to attract international students. In the course, IoC is presented as needing to address the education students require to become global citizens in our globalised, multicultural, interdependent world. It moves beyond celebrating diversity through such artefacts as food and music, introducing 'international' case studies into courses and encouraging international and home students to work together, to students' active engagement with real-world issues such as sustainability, equality and justice, so moving into the realm of values and ethics (Haigh & Clifford, 2011). These are contentious areas, and staff often feel underprepared to deal with these in their course and their classrooms. This course was seen as offering a forum to introduce these issues and invite exploration in a safe space with others also curious and eager to learn.

The course

The data for this chapter derive from four iterations of a one-month fully online course on IoC. The course has been taken by 73 people, who were predominantly faculty academics (48) and academic developers (21). These have included people in leadership positions at university, faculty and department level charged with progressing IoC. Fifteen disciplines have been represented, the most populous being health with 14 participants and business with eight. There has been a steadily increasing demand for the course and an increase in the number of participants from 10 to 27. The course has mainly attracted participants from around the UK (25 UK, 3 Scottish, 2 Irish and 1 Welsh university) and Australia (five universities), the last iteration also including staff from Western Cape, South Africa. The participants themselves identified, in terms of their nationality, as from a range of European, African, Australasian and Asian countries.

The course was structured over four weeks to move the participants through, firstly, a range of theoretical perspectives on IoC designed to introduce them to a critical reading of IoC, then to an exploration of the positioning of their institutions on IoC, followed by an exploration of IoC in their own discipline. Alongside this, participants were contributing to a 'how to do it' list on Google docs to help bridge the gap between theory and practice. This list was used for tasks exploring different aspects of IoC (global perspectives, intercultural communication and global citizenship) (CICIN, n.d.) and to work with Kitano's (1997) framework of exclusive, inclusive and transformative approaches to IoC. In the final week, the participants drew up an action plan for how they would take IoC forward in their institution. This structure allowed flexibility for participants to work with the ideas presented from the standpoint of their position in their institution, while exposing them to a range of institutional approaches and interactions with people in a variety of different roles.

Each week, readings and tasks, which included contributing to online discussions, were assigned. Most of the discussion forums were open to all participants, but as good practice indicates that some people prefer a more private space to contribute (Sharpe et al., 2010) in weeks 2 and 3 participants were put in either pairs or triads to pursue their online tasks. The first two iterations of the course had two tutors monitoring and contributing to the discussions, while, with the increase in numbers in the last two iterations, three tutors were assigned. The tutors' role was to contribute to the online discussions and monitor postings. If a participant's posting had not received a response from the group by the end of 24 hours, then the tutor would respond so that the participant did not get discouraged. Tutors also took it in turns to lead and summarise discussions.

The three tutors worked collaboratively on a thematic analysis of the texts from the online discussions of the four iterations of the course. They compared the focus and depth of the discussions in terms of the rapidly changing higher education context.

In this chapter, we show the participants using the discussions in three different ways. First, the participants use the forums to explore the meaning of internationalising the curriculum as transformative education, an interpretation new to most of them. Second, the participants develop an acute awareness of their own need to develop themselves as 'internationalised' and 'intercultural' persons, many starting the course with a focus on the needs of international students and finishing the course deep in debate about the possibilities of developing global citizens and universal value systems, discourses that some found uncomfortable. Third, participants, although highly personally committed to the internationalisation agenda, begin to see beyond a personal crusade to the crucial role of support in terms of developing communities of colleagues to share the journey and the workload, and the importance of leadership and the need to gain senior management support to embed the agenda in the institution.

The higher education context of IoC

In the first year of the course (2008), the focus of internationalisation for most universities still lay with marketing for, and support of, international students. Few of the participants' universities had developed internationalisation strategies, although several were in the process of writing them.

At the time the participants' universities did have international offices and management structures in place with senior management responsibility for the area. However, international offices did not have a focus on the curriculum beyond support for international students. However, by the fourth iteration of the course (two years later) university-level internationalisation strategies were common and many paid lip service to curriculum development in the area. Two examples of such curriculum references from the course participants were:[1]

> *To increase the international dimension on campus for all students by supporting innovations in the curriculum, learning and teaching approaches and services.*
>
> *This strategy does not advocate the use of any particular interpretation, favouring an approach that is based on an understanding of the skills and competencies that students should have gained once they had studied a curriculum that has been internationalised.*

However, an exception was one university (who had sent four members of staff on each iteration of the course) and had been through a two-year process of moving from a focus on international students, to applying internationalisation to both home as well as international students, through to framing internationalisation as 'responsibility, global citizenship and sustainability' in their strategy and institutional plans.

By the fourth iteration most of the participants' universities had a senior manager responsible for IoC, and a number of the course participants carried responsibility for IoC in their faculty or department, a few having a university-wide brief (e.g. as an educational developer). Also, reference to curriculum was appearing in a number of strategy documents, but few elaborated on the meaning of this or allocated resources to curriculum development. Who carried responsibility for curriculum development was often fuzzy and a number of people taking the course were exploring what their role might mean in their institutions. This ambivalence was often seen to stem from the ambiguity of the meaning of IoC and a reluctance by management and academics to step back and reappraise their curriculum in relation to internationalisation, often hoping that adding some international case studies, or encouraging students from different cultural groups to interact, was sufficient.

Development of IoC literacy

When the course began in 2008, the majority of the participants 'read' IoC as their institutions framed it, as about teaching international students, along with a focus on differences between Western and Asian learners. Some also saw celebrating cultural difference, adding international case studies to the curriculum and running specific international focused modules/units (an additive approach, Banks, 1993) as the extent of IoC. The participants were focused on their own acceptance of diversity and difference and on how they move away from their own ethnocentrism.

The pre-reading sent for the course was chosen to question these ideas right from the beginning. The participants expressed their surprise in different ways, one saying that 'I have only thought of internationalisation as a liberal term before, not as a radical one'. At first the participants were quite protective of their disciplines and their traditionally associated pedagogy, but then started to consider ways that they might overcome their own limited cultural frame of reference. Such questioning brought both the discomfort that exploring new ideas brings and identification of the key role of staff development in ensuring cross-disciplinary initiatives in IoC take place. Some participants expressed concern that by engaging in discussions of internationalisation they might be viewed as racist or colonialist by their colleagues. There was also an emergent discourse of 'internationalisation at home'. Early on, few participants had thought of IoC as an overall philosophy and pedagogy.

By the third iteration, with the higher education environment changing, many of the participants came to the course with a broader outlook and were already critically reflecting on different cultural viewpoints to form a better understanding of their own and other cultures. They were also seeing IoC as a debate on educational theory and pedagogies and were aware of their own historical and geographical situatedness and how this framed their own assumptions: for example, that democracy is a universal good. In parallel to this perspective, staff were more prepared to discuss the concept of global citizenship, in terms, not just of being knowledgeable and concerned about global issues such as sustainability, poverty, famine and injustice but also the need to take action about these issues, and to consider global citizenship as the goal of higher education for students. They also recognised that this moved many academics (sometimes themselves) outside their 'comfort zone'. Concerns over practical issues were also raised, such as how to avoid tokenism, the influence of professional associations over the curriculum, the limits of relativism and the place of indigenisation (the local within the global).

By the fourth iteration, the participants were more articulately expressing IoC as involving a wholesale transformation that challenges hegemonic ideas and practices, and as being cyclical and ongoing and requiring involvement and action. People generally saw these ideas as in line with their personal codes of ethics. Also, for the first time, this iteration involved South African participants, who introduced the idea of 'Africanisation': that is, the increasing strength of counter-hegemonic and postcolonial voices in Africa that challenge the Western concept of 'knowledge' and work to reformulate this from the perspective of local, previously subjugated knowledges (Prinsloo, 2003). Critical pedagogy and IoC were discussed as a Western discourse and questions were asked about how we can formulate a counter-narrative from within that discourse.

> *The dilemma is how to formulate a counter-narrative from within. How legitimate would it be? What alternatives are there? We need to formulate transformative agendas but be cognisant of our own locations and how they have shaped and are still shaping us.*

Participants struggled with ideas of possible global values, finding ideas of ethnorelativism difficult. Some became overwhelmed by the sense of their responsibilities to their students and wondered where they would find the time for all this change and how they would encourage their colleagues to become involved. They felt that the complexity at the pragmatic level may interfere with colleagues understanding the issue and that counter-hegemonic practices might alienate some of their colleagues.

Increase in awareness of internationalised-intercultural self

In the first iteration of the course, participants shared personal stories of becoming open to cultural difference and committed to internationalisation within their own curricula, this often being sparked by periods living and/or working abroad. For some, living abroad had led to enhancement of their personal approaches to communicating with others and an openness to difference:

> *My strategies are to observe first, know the details of local culture, and to understand the sign culture of the locals and then respond to the activities. I also follow the same pattern while I communicate with international students. There are a lot more cultures we don't know on the earth.*

While some participants felt that they had international experience that they could draw on and was appropriate, the new envisioning of IoC also led to expressions of nervousness about 'how to' internationalise the curriculum:

> *nagging thoughts of how might I do this better ... if we are to be inclusive of 'others' or incorporating of difference then we need to show how we could do this in a practical sense.*

Some of these doubts were also linked to questions about the difficulty of introducing a transformative model of education, given increasing workload, student numbers and current norms around student assessment:

> *How do we negotiate differences and develop respect and understanding when we also work with limited contact time and large classes?*
> *I often find the transformed model of IoC most difficult to practice, especially in some of the undergraduate modules and end up using exclusive and inclusive methods. This might be because of the type of assessment we have within the modules – essay and examination system.*

For one of the participants on the second course the need to bring about change also caused worry:

> *I feel a certain anxiety at the implications of internationalisation and the change required.*

This worry linked to internal struggles with the contested nature of an international approach:

> *I am always struggling with how to balance a truly international approach without any whiff of a colonial influence ... if not sensitively handled, the very raising of internationalisation could create a learning environment which appears racist and/or patronising.*

Despite more general critical awareness of their historical and geographical situatedness, participants in the third course also experienced anxiety at moving outside 'comfort zone' assumptions. This was seen by one participant as a challenge particularly linked to academic identity as a teacher:

> *Wonder whether some of the obstacles to IoC are less to do with a refusal to consider particular canons of knowledge and more to do with a nervousness in academic identity within a new model of learning and teaching.*

Another participant described the opportunities for creativity and co-generation of knowledge associated with their 'internationalising' academic identity in motivational terms:

> *For me the carrot is about not just elaborating on the same old bullet points (stick) but looking forward to explore issues I deeply care about with a different set of people every time I teach a class (ideally).*

In the last run of the course to date, a growing awareness of the ethical and professional self as a central locus of IoC was widespread amongst participants:

> *We have a tendency to talk about Internationalisation as something that is out there rather than within ourselves.*
>
> *It's a new idea that rather than internationalising others, e.g. students, we need to start with internationalising ourselves.*

On the most recent run of the course, it was generally seen as a given that transformative education and bringing questions of ethics and justice into the curriculum was 'the goal'. Instead of expressing anxiety at the unknown, participants spoke the language of experienced, radical campaigners who at times saw the potential of IoC as redemptive:

> *In striving for it [transformative education] there will be setbacks and there will be uneven development.*
>
> *It is our challenge as educators to create awareness and willingness for students to make choices and not just be chosen by fate.*
>
> *I live in the constant defiant hope that courses and colleagues like this will help us to grow a more compassionate and just society.*

Whereas some participants declared a wholehearted personal engagement with the ethical dimensions of IoC, one academic commented on the complexities of making teaching and learning sites of ethical practice and the fact that the premises of IoC are based on Western values of teaching and learning:

> *Should we be assessing values per se. On the face of it, doesn't this infer that if you (student) don't accept the values I (teacher) promulgate, you'll fail. What we should be assessing is the extent to which students have the critical facility to challenge values including their own ... which is itself a value of western education. Conundrum.*

Finally, one participant summarised the process of internationalising the self as follows:

> *Read, discuss, do. Read, discuss, do ...*

Development of awareness of need for support

The participants' growth in awareness during the course of the broad agenda of IoC, and the implications in terms of their own development and their own values and beliefs, also led to a realisation that the implications for curriculum and pedagogical change were greater than originally envisioned. This opened up a renewed consideration of what support their institution had to offer them and where else they could look for support. While they saw their departments as the pertinent work unit, and their heads of departments as the link for translating university strategies at the local level and to assist with resourcing, the participants saw the need to work collaboratively and develop communities of practice beyond their own work units and institutions.

> *The reading has brought home to me that IoC is a journey rather than necessarily a destination and that I will need to work with colleagues over a period of time to develop their ideas on how to bring about change to the curriculum.*

For two other participants, who championed IoC in their institutions, a first step towards building communities of practice was open discussion about staff and student perspectives on IoC:

> *a useful effort for me after this course, will be to set up some informal staff/ student sessions where we can reflect upon what we're doing at the moment and start to air some thoughts about new ideas and developments.*

The sense that participants saw themselves as pioneers of new transdisciplinary approaches to teaching and learning, that necessarily required cross-campus communities of practice and support from strong leadership, came through in several comments:

> *As an academic within the disciplines of Marketing, Strategy and Negotiations, I am aware that simply sowing seeds for the possibility of new ideas, as well as giving time and space for these ideas to be socialised, may promote authentic change to occur. Hence, I am actively considering how I may go about facilitating change within my own sphere, which may become contagious to those around.*

Related to the notion of 'sowing seeds' was the recognition by one participant that the 'insights of colleagues' were the driver of IoC and these needed to 'be harnessed'. A similar idea was expressed in terms of the key to IoC being 'to get staff to take ownership of the issue and propose the solution'. 'Buy-in' of colleagues was identified by an educational developer as the only way to ensure IoC 'was embedded into the whole curriculum'. However, as one participant highlighted, the real challenge was building communities of practice with 'shared commitment and vision'.

> *There is something about the role of caring and being part of a community – creating communities of practice within disciplines that can be models for communities in the wider world.*

Communities of practice were seen to provide a vital opportunity to 'share further resources and ideas'. A discussion of disciplinary differences in IoC saw some disciplines such as Geography are 'instinctively international', and that perhaps an understanding about 'how this has emerged over time' could inform the process of IoC in other fields.

Having established that communities of practice were the way forward for embedding IoC, participants were also positive about the potential of such approaches to overcome 'tokenistic' and 'static or tick-box exercise' renderings of internationalisation. Yet again, as mentioned above, finding the time to do the 'hard work' associated with discussing the challenges of IoC with colleagues meant participants sometimes chose to leave discussion at the 'integrative' level and not to try and extend it to the 'transformative' level.

One university deliberately used the course to build a community of practice at their university, enrolling four staff members from around the university on each iteration of the course. These participants formed a study group each time to work together on the course and for one course an educational developer partnered an academic, who could not attend, and worked through the tasks each week with him, applying the tasks to his discipline. Also, on two occasions, people from the same university met online and joined forces, submitting joint action plans for taking the IoC agenda forward at their institutions.

Discussion

What is striking amongst these insights into staff perspectives on IoC is the impression that participants see themselves as pioneers opening up new areas of higher education curricular practice. It is through the online dialogue that the anxieties and challenges of the 'pioneer work' of internationalisation are engaged with by staff and linked to broader social concerns in all the runs of the course. However, what was particularly noticeable for the tutors was the sense that each cohort articulated the pioneer work differently. Certainly for the first two iterations of the course it was an unexpected debate, but one entered into willingly. Whereas the greater awareness of participants of the broader debate in the third and fourth iterations of the course might be attributed to the inclusion of more participants from a broader range of global locations, it may also reflect the increased engagement with the debate around IoC in the higher education sector in the UK and worldwide (de Wit, 2011), and the concomitant growth of policy directives and positions of responsibility in the area.

The course allowed the participants to pause, to critically reflect on their curriculum for a few brief weeks and to engage in debates about the purpose of higher education and the meaning of IoC in terms of the future of our graduates, such time being a luxury in academia nowadays. Whereas the participants embraced the opportunity to explore a wider vision of IoC and to explore the implications for themselves and their teaching, the communal nature of this exploration allowed them to see the advantages of strengthening their individual quests through increased institutional support and collaboration with a variety of communities of practice. This broader vision fitted with the increasing institutional strategic developments and structures.

The course itself became a site of increasing IoC literacy; participants became more familiar with ideas of global citizenship and expressed their tensions associated with having to deal with different value systems. It was a discourse of multiplicity and fragmentation, moving back and forth from views of the global to the importance of local interpretations of IoC rather than Western-centred hegemonies, 'the local is now reshaped globally . . . idea of global is meaningless without its local reference' (Rizvi, 2002, no page numbers). Such conversations are described by Pinar (2005) as 'a bridge, a passage from here to there and elsewhere, in the spaces in between, a generative space of possibilities', a space for a global imagination (Rizvi, 2006). The conversation of IoC may be particularly well suited to the advantages of global connection that an online course has to offer.

There were people who did not fully engage with the course. Despite advanced publicity and a welcoming letter emphasising the need to timetable six hours online per week, a number of participants realised in the first week that they were not going to make the commitment and just monitored the course. Some had periods of sickness during the course and found it hard to catch-up on return and made use of the course being left open for one month after its official ending to continue to read the debates they had missed. One or two indicated a shyness to expose themselves online. For many it was their first experience of an online course and, although initially nervous, they became active participants.

Conclusion

This study has demonstrated the developmental needs of higher education staff to be able to engage with university strategic initiatives to 'internationalise the curriculum' and offers an effective way that this might be addressed.

The online participants used the course to address the fuzziness of the term of IoC and came to appreciate the scope of the idea, the need to engage in their own professional development of the idea, and that such initiatives were a matter of whole programme curricula reform and not just a matter of making a few changes to their own teaching.

Engaging busy academics in in-depth discussions of the fundamental purposes of higher education is a luxury rarely participated in nowadays. For that discussion to include an analysis of their institutional policies and structures, their role vis-à-vis those policies and structures, an exploration of the disciplinary consequences in terms of curriculum and pedagogy, through to drawing up a personal action plan, is unusual in professional development. The fact that this happens in a highly contentious, murkily defined field, and enticed participants to explore ideas of transformative curriculum, is even more exciting.

The use of an Internet site to achieve these outcomes for professional development with a group of staff who are not of the net generation is very encouraging.

Participants seemed able to express their hesitancy at the use of the medium at the beginning, but then established enough rapport with the others on the course to explore dissenting views and express their apprehensions about the practicalities of the theory and the way forward.

Much has been written about communities of practice, but being able to find an accessible critical mass of people with a deep interest in a specific topic can be very difficult. The online course gave people access to such a group and they were able to talk and think through their own positioning, access new resources and plan future action to take back into their local workspace. Online courses offer a way of developing international communities of practice between people not only positioned at a distance geographically but also in posts at different levels in their organisation, enhancing the understanding of all of the processes that institutions need to engage in to move curricula reform from a strategy to a reality.

Notes

1 All quotes are taken from the online discussion forums.

References

Banks, J. A. (1993). Approaches to multicultural reform. In J. A. Banks & C. A. M. Banks (eds.), *Multicultural education: Issues and perspectives*. Boston, MA: Allyn and Bacon.

Bates, S., Hardy, J., Hill, J. & McKain, D. (2007–2008). How design of online learning materials can accommodate the heterogeneity in student abilities, aptitudes and aspirations. *Learning and Teaching in Higher Education, 2*, 3–25.

Becher, T. (1989). *Academic tribes and territories: Intellectual enquiry and the cultures of the disciplines*. Milton Keynes: Open University Press.

Becher, T. & Trowler, P. R. (2001). *Academic tribes and territories: Intellectual enquiry and the cultures of the disciplines*, 2nd edn. Buckingham: Open University Press.

Brew, A. & Barrie, S. (1999). Academic development through a negotiated curriculum. *International Journal of Academic Development, 4*(1), 34–51.

Britain, S. & Liber, O. (1999). *A framework for pedagogical evaluation of virtual learning environments. JTAP report 41*. JISC. Retrieved 26 April 2011 from http://www.jisc.ac.uk/media/documents/programmes/jtap/jtap-041.pdf

Clegg, S., Rowland, S., Mann, S., Davidson, M. & Clifford, V. A. (2004). Reconceptualising academic development: Reconciling pleasure and critique in safe spaces. In L. Elvidge (ed.), *Exploring academic development in higher education: Issues of engagement*. Cambridge: Jill Rogers Associates.

Clifford, V. A. (2009). Engaging the disciplines in internationalising the curriculum. *International Journal of Academic Development, 14*(2), 133–143.

CICIN. (n.d.) *Internationalising the curriculum resource kit*. CICIN, Oxford Brookes University. Retrieved 10 May 2011 from http://www.brookes.ac.uk/services/ocsld/ioc/resourcekit.html

de Wit, H. (2011). Naming nationalisation will not revive it. *University World News, 23 Oct*, Issue 194. Retrieved 8 December 2011 from http://www.university worldnews.com/article.php?story=20111021215849411

Dearing, R. (1997). *National Committee of Inquiry into Higher Education (UK) 1997: Higher education in the learning society*. Report of the National Committee into Higher Education. Leeds: NCIHE.

Gibbs, G. & Coffey, M. (2004). The impact of training of university teachers on their teaching skills, their approach to teaching and the approach to learning of their students. *Active Learning in Higher Education, 15*(1), 87–100.

Gough, N. (1999). Globalization and school curriculum change: Locating a transnational imaginary. *Journal of Education Policy, 14*(1), 73–84.

Green, W. & Mertova, P. (2011). Engaging the gatekeepers: Faculty perspectives on developing curriculum for globally responsible citizenship. In V. Clifford & C. Montgomery (eds.), *Moving towards internationalisation of the curriculum for global citizenship in higher education*. Oxford, UK: OCSLD, Oxford Brookes University.

Haigh, M. and Clifford, V. (2011). Integral vision: A multi-perspective approach to the recognition of graduate attributes. *Higher Education Research and Development, 30*(5), 573–584.

Kitano, M. K. (1997). A rational framework for course change. In A. I. Morey & M. K. Kitano (eds.), *Multicultural course transformation in higher education: A broader truth*. Needham Heights, MA: Allyn and Bacon.

Laurillard, D. (2002). *Rethinking university teaching: A conversational framework for the effective use of learning technologies*. London: RoutledgeFalmer.

Meyer, J. & Land, R. (2003). *Threshold concepts and troublesome knowledge: Linkages to ways of thinking and practising within the disciplines*. ETL project occasional report 4. Edinburgh: University of Edinburgh.

Morey, A. I. (2000). Changing higher education curricula for a global and multicultural world. *Higher Education in Europe, XXV*(1), 25–39.

Neumann, R., Parry, S. & Becher, T. (2002). Teaching and learning in their disciplinary contexts: A conceptual analysis. *Studies in Higher Education, 27*(4), 405–417.

Pinar, W. (2005). A bridge between Chinese and North American curriculum studies. *Transnational Curriculum Inquiry, 2*(1), 1–12.

Prinsloo, P. (2003). The quest for relevance: Preliminary thoughts on the issue of relevance in higher education in South Africa. *Progression* 25(1). Retrieved 26 November 2011 from http://www.unisa.ac.za/default.asp?Cmd=ViewContent &ContentID=14090.

Readings, B. (1996). *The university in ruins*. Cambridge, MA: Harvard University Press.

Rizvi, F. (2002). *Internationalisation of the curriculum*. Retrieved 19 September 2007 from http://mams.rmit.edu.au/ioc/sf012iqo4uzn.pdf (no longer available).

Rizvi, F. (2006). Imagination and the globalisation of educational policy research. *Globalisation, Societies and Education, 4*(2), 193–205.

Sanderson, G. (2011). Internationalisation and teaching in higher education. *Higher Education Research and Development, 30*(5) 661–676.

Sharpe, R., Beetham, H. & De Freitas, S. (eds.) (2010). *Rethinking learning for a digital age*. London: Routledge.

Skinner, E. & Derounian, J. (2008). Building community through online discussion. *Learning and Teaching in Higher Education*, 2, 56–70.

Teasdale, G. R. & Ma Rhea, Z. (2000). *Local knowledge and wisdom in higher education*. Oxford: Pergamon Press.

Teekens, H. (2000). A description of nine clusters of qualifications for lecturers. In H. Teekens (ed.), *The international classroom: Teaching and learning at home and abroad*. The Hague: Netherlands Organization for International Cooperation in Higher Education (NUFFIC).

Chapter 19

Developing the multicultural community of practice

Starting at induction

Tony Shannon-Little

Introduction

The increasingly multicultural mix of students in higher education in Britain and elsewhere is rightly regarded as a fruitful opportunity for engagement, which will lead to greater understanding of different cultures including one's own.

However, De Vita (2001), among others, observes that the mere presence of international students on campus does not automatically trigger cross-cultural learning. The amount of contact between home and international students can be rather limited as local students often have pre-existing friendship networks (Sovic, 2009; Volet & Ang, 1998) and negative stereotypes about international students' language mastery (Harrison & Peacock, 2010; Schweisfurth & Gu, 2009; Volet & Ang, 1998), while sojourners themselves are often anxious about their own language level (Andrade, 2006; Halic, Greenburg & Paulus, 2009; Ramsay, Barker & Jones, 1999) and prioritise study over socialising (Leder & Forgasz, 2004; Lewthwaite, 1996). Similarly, there is disappointment at the quality of contacts which do occur (Cathcart, Dixon-Dawson & Hall, 2006; Sovic, 2009), much of which is characterised by Leask (2005) as 'cultural tourism'. De Vita and Case (2003) argue that real cultural learning must go beyond superficial mingling to 'the discovery and transcendence of difference through authentic experiences of cross-cultural interaction that involve real tasks and involve emotional as well as intellectual participation' (p. 388).

The development of such emotionally deeper links between students from different cultures through a range of ongoing shared experiences which De Vita and Case (2003) call for builds a sense of group cohesion and echoes Lave and Wenger's (1991) theory of socially situated learning, termed *legitimate peripheral participation*. This is the gradual learning of appropriate behaviour sanctioned within a particular social group, termed a 'community of practice', resulting in a move towards 'core' membership of that group. Wenger (1998) identifies three reciprocally reinforcing features as the source of coherence of a community of practice: *mutual engagement*, participation in common activities which build and maintain bonds over a period of time, in a *joint enterprise*, entailing mutual accountability and therefore negotiation and adjustment of roles, which develops a *shared repertoire* of styles of participation and of communication. Thus, meaning is socially constructed, according to Wenger, through collaboration, and individuals' identities within that community are both shaped by, and, in return, influence practice.

Similarly, Fay (1996) observes:

> *The process of becoming a student is in part the process of learning a set of expectations of appropriate behaviour, a code of conduct which defines what a student is permitted to do and not to do.... This code will be internalised in the sense that the student will make it their own.... Behaviour, feelings and relations are shaped by certain socially recognised principles such that persons conceive of themselves as bearers of rights and responsibilities within a system of ongoing relationships.*

(pp. 40–41)

The forging of such awareness and interrelations takes time, as the norms of tertiary education are new to all, domestic and international students alike. Harvey and Drew (2006) estimate an adjustment period of at least six months for domestic students, while the transition for international students may be further hampered by anxieties about language and cultural differences, and the onus is commonly perceived to be on them to assimilate into the 'dominant' academic and social cultures.

For international students, effective membership of communities of practice beyond their co-cultural networks may be difficult to achieve if their stay only lasts one academic year or less. A study of the experiences of students resident for longer than one year, allowing greater opportunity for construction of these deeper and more extensive cross-cultural links, may increase our knowledge of obstacles and successful strategies, and thus cast light on ways host institutions can support or accelerate the formation of such communities of practice.

In the first part of this chapter, a study of the experiences of students at a university in the UK, resident for 18 months or longer, is described. In the second part, the influence their comments have had on the planning of introductory sessions for new arrivals in one department in that university is outlined.

Method

This chapter describes the observations of 14 (9 females and 5 males) students from overseas on their experience of studying for 18–30 months at the University of Wolverhampton in central England. Students of nine nationalities from Europe, Central Africa and East Asia agreed to take part. Volunteers were aged between 22 and 38 and studying a range of disciplines on the Wolverhampton City site, including Linguistics, Media, Law, Computing and Business. During a semi-structured interview of approximately one hour, each student was asked about their domestic, social and study networks and the nature of their cross-cultural contacts. They described, retrospectively, their adjustment over time to a multicultural campus and the strategic choices that they made, and offered suggestions to improve communication between home and international students. Responses were recorded, transcribed and analysed to draw out common themes.

Findings

Interviewees described a wide range of strategies that they had successfully employed to allow them to adjust to a multicultural campus, including ways of evaluating different cultural norms without ethnocentric assumptions about their own culture's superiority, ways of increasing the amount of cross-cultural contact, and approaches and roles that they adopted to increase the quality of interaction that they had. Significant differences were described by interviewees in terms of their approach to social and domestic contacts, as opposed to in-class or study-related interaction.

Social and domestic contacts

As previous studies highlight, on arrival the overwhelming majority of the students tended to share accommodation and domestic life with co-culturals, in spite of their recognition that this defeated their declared aim to mix with local students (Brown, 2009). Significantly, in successive years this remains unchanged, but is not viewed as a failure or regressive choice, rather as a protective strategy providing them with a cultural and emotional safe zone to recharge their batteries. As one Polish student replied, when asked if it had been a definite decision to continue sharing with Poles:

> *Yes because we started to be very good friends, so we didn't want to change for other people who we didn't know so good... and I think actually that living probably with English people it would be like, not problems, but to accommodate with different culture as well, so basically we just stayed like let's say with the Polish group... without taking any risks.*

While a Chinese student explains why he feels more emotionally secure amongst co-culturals:

> *Actually there is one of my friends who lives with me, he is also my friend in China, so I think that's much easier, you can take care of each other.... My friends and me always go shopping and go to the gym and go for some foods together. When somebody is not feeling well, just give him medicine and cooking for him. A friend in need is a friend indeed.*

It would seem then that, for most, what Bochner, McLeod and Lin (1977) describe as the 'primary mono-cultural network' of co-culturals, is a key factor in emotional stability. As another student explains, in spite of her openness to her many English contacts, she stayed in Halls of Residence near other Chinese students because:

> *[i]f something bad happens to you, you feel lost because you can't really talk to English people because you have got different culture and they won't understand it. ... English are more laid back. They don't really worry about things like Chinese people do.*

Similarly many interviewees (8 of the 14) described their utilisation of more experienced co-cultural mentors in early stages, as informants to make sense of the culture of learning (Cortazzi & Jin, 1997), as a Cypriot student explains:

> *Actually a girl from Cyprus that she used to live with us in Hall, she was helping us, me and my friend, because she was in the Law School, but a older student. She was third year and we was in first year. Obviously she helped us a lot, because if you go on your first year you don't know how to start writing a law essay, and this is important for somebody to sit down and explain you; [the structure, how to quote, how to reference] This simple stuff is very important for your beginning... she help us. And I helped a lot of people after this... I done the same.*

Variation was reported in levels of socialising with other international students, termed 'tertiary multicultural' networks by Bochner et al. (1977), often due to shyness and language anxiety, but this was regarded as a short-lived problem. From the perspective of 18 months or more on campus, the interviewees found that social and domestic networks, predominantly involving other sojourners, were relatively easy to establish. The area of greatest concern for interviewees, when looking back to their first year of study, was disappointingly limited 'secondary network' contacts with academics and fellow students: these interlocutors are valued as they can contribute to the accomplishment of study-related goals, but also to an increase in understanding of the host culture and a sense of membership of an additional group.

Strategic positioning within class and group work

The process of internationalisation in universities is according to Thom (2010) often viewed as merely a one-sided adjustment by international students to the dominant host culture. The interviewees in this study accept the need for adjustment on their part, but do not view it as a process of assimilation. Reference is made to three roles where they recognise that they are dependent on the help of others in their study community. However, as we shall see later, this is balanced by other roles involving greater initiative or contribution. The three dependent roles are: non-native speaker, cultural 'apprentice' and less skilled mature learner.

Many examples are cited of help with linguistic expression given by home students during group work, and one Malaysian student explains how that extends to the classroom where she receives guidance on her English from tutors and fellow students:

> *We are only two Asian girls in the class and they do help me, even the lecturers, helping us a lot because we are sitting in the front seats and when we don't know they will just keep asking us whether we can understand, so I think it can help us a lot. Even the essay, I need to write the outline first, and I send to my lecturer and if they say it is alright I only will write the full essay, and they double check again before the due date. They will help me where you can find the sources.*

This is echoed by a Chinese student, who emphasises that as a cultural outsider she feels more tolerated and supported in her requests for clarification than if she were studying in her own country:

> *I am Chinese and I am glad people don't mind I keep asking questions. I worry about everything, so if they give me a paper I don't understand, I will keep following the tutor and ask him until I understand it. In China, people might happy to answer you but you will worry what they going to think, but in England I don't think I got to worry about that because I just asking. I am Chinese! So people will expect me to ask rather than in China people think "You are Chinese. Understand it! Deal with it!"*

She feels that others accept that she must learn the rules and values of this new culture and will patiently explain concepts and processes in more detail to her while she continues to learn. The third role is that of mature student who may find study harder, or in the following case, who has not had the same access to technology as younger students. The interviewee reports that making such a request creates bonds and improves the class atmosphere.

> *Where I come from we did IT but didn't have a computer! Young people here have so much knowledge. I go to them and am jealous in a happy way and I ask them to teach me – it's like a challenge. "I am a mummy here you are 19 call me mummy I'll call you son, I need this and you know it, you are brilliant you answered in the class, so please help me". Their reaction is to see me like a mum and help me. There are always challenges working internationally but it is the way you react, and open yourself to the people. It is not about the people from wherever, it is about how you blend with others.*

By contrast, four counterbalancing contributions which the interviewees make in group work, either in or out of class, were identified. The first was as social catalyst/motivator; as the interviewee quoted below (the one who provided the previous quote) had astutely realised, nearly everyone is shy, but it only takes one person to break the ice and the atmosphere improves dramatically. Her advice was:

> do not sit there and wait, because the same as they are feeling we have just come we don't know anyone, it's the same that us here feel that we don't know these people and somebody has to break through. Just do as I did: introduce yourself and ask for advice. It is very important and I know it is very difficult.... I am blessed because I can talk to small groups or large groups of people and do my best to help them feel better.

The second role is as able organiser/project manager, which four students claimed among their skills, as in the following case:

> I mean for me I always speak, tell them how to do it (You want to be the director of the group?) Sometimes, because maybe the students they are afraid to have the big responsibility, so they just ask me to do that, not because I am too smart, it's just because I want my work to be perfect before I hand it out to the lecturer. So they think I can take up the responsibility but I still need their help because some of them are really really creative and they give me a lot of ideas so I just compose everything to become a perfect job.

Several students positioned themselves as highly able students, as a result of one of two advantages. One was due to a claim to wider experience of life:

> You don't know what's really going to happen, but by the time goes by you just feeling confident, and because you know what you'd studied and the material, people get close to you because you are giving them something back. So you start seeing people asking you "Explain to me", someone from another different background so you kind of gain contact with them.

The second was because of a greater drive and commitment to studies than domestic students displayed, often because of the sacrifices that family were continuing to make to finance their stay, but often because of more discipline and focus on goals, as a mature student explains:

> I know what I want, and you are learning with some people who maybe are thinking C grade is enough, or even a D grade if I don't need to work hard. So it's been difficult in trying to deal with that... I am a lot more driven now, and so far I have had all 'A's in my modules from first year up to now, and I think that has a lot to do with the drive that I have now. I really know where I want to be and I'm focused on it, and if I had studied earlier I probably wouldn't want it as much as I do now.

Great importance is placed on balancing dependent roles with contributory roles in the community of practice: international students accept *legitimate peripheral participation* in some aspects of their study, but efforts are made to couple this with a sense of valued contribution to group work. Of course this is not always the case and there is reference by one interviewee to a distancing from cross-cultural contacts, where the individual withdraws to the co-cultural network, thus exerting a sense of control or justifying a marginal position. Having commented that he had reduced the number of friends of other nationalities he now had, one interviewee in his third year said he preferred to stick to the friends he arrived with:

> *Of course I am more comfortable and I have a lot of old friends and I don't need to make new friends, at the end of the day. That's why I said I don't want more relationships. I only want my friends, my old friends that I know them, and they know me. They know my bad things and my good things and they accept me like I am, and I accept them like they are… obviously.*

However, such withdrawal is generally seen as a negative move by other interviewees, who are still keen to maximise their cross-cultural contacts, and emphasise their continuing desire to learn more about all cultures, not just English culture.

This can be linked to the sense of direction to their efforts, in terms of plans and motivations, that they express. A range of such life aims or *trajectories*, as Wenger (1998) terms them, emerged from interviewees' self-description. Some individuals aim to settle in the UK for family or political reasons, while others have discovered highly attractive aspects of the host culture which have transformed their world view and self-image to the extent that they wish to remain. Some individuals are exhilarated by contacts with this new culture and want to continue the adventure by going on to engage with other cultures, while some want to take the cultural mediator skills that they have learned in the UK to use in their own country. Other individuals might be disillusioned by the difficulty of making cross-cultural contacts, or have found aspects of the culture itself unappealing, and have settled for aiming to gain their degree with the minimum of cross-cultural interaction before their eventual return to a more comfortable cultural milieu. In all cases, excluding perhaps the last one, all of the interviewees regard themselves as active co-contributors to the process of cross-cultural learning, not as simply receptive beneficiaries.

Students accept their own share of responsibility for the reportedly slow and painful development of cohesion in the classroom, and thus its delayed exploitation as a site of intercultural learning, but several call for help from tutors in structuring groups and activities, as in the following example:

> *Because basically in lectures … we could choose groups on our own. So probably Polish people will go with Polish people, and maybe if lecturer would*

> *mix the groups, English with international, that would help I think… because*
> *we are getting to know each other. I remember when I was in first year and we*
> *were doing some group task we were talking in Polish because the group was*
> *Polish so we didn't practice language as well.*

A more directive approach when setting up work groups, to achieve balanced membership and avoid self-replicating cliques, is advocated by many authors (e.g. Cathcart et al., 2006; Kelly, 2008; Osmond & Roed, 2010) to speed up integration, starting as early as possible.

Discussion

Yorke and Longden (2008), when addressing the broader issue of retention in higher education, observe that 'ways need to be found to enhance the chances of students developing the supportive network of peers that will sustain them when difficulties arise' (p. 48). For most international students, co-cultural networks providing domestic support appear to arise spontaneously. The issue of effective learning, on the other hand, requires us to face the challenge of developing communities of practice where all students can feel supported, respected and valued, and where international students' participation is seen as beneficial to themselves and to home students alike. At the same time, this is an opportunity for a more sophisticated management of the internationalisation of the curriculum, in response to the difficulties identified by Caruana (2010), among others, in the relative lack of awareness of global citizenship issues demonstrated by home UK students, and a common assumption by staff that their responsibility does not extend beyond provision of geographically varied examples.

Cross-cultural learning is not just a one-way street, and the earlier that collective recognition and mutual respect are achieved, the greater progress that can be made towards acknowledgement of both interdependence and reciprocal learning; the give and take that is vital for all students' self-esteem.

Obliging groups to have multicultural membership in order to engineer contact is a necessary but not sufficient step in this, and tutor support must be more proactive. Osmond and Roed (2010, p. 123) list five key recommendations to institutions/academic staff for smoother interaction in group work between domestic and international students:

- provide language support classes
- emphasise to home and international students the benefits of cross-cultural interactions
- establish clear rules and expectations in advance of group work for all students
- build in enough time for groups to gel, supported by regular tutorials
- include intercultural content to allow all students to make some unique contribution.

In the actual implementation of these recommendations, we must recognise the need for structured intervention right from the start to provide staged phases, beginning with low-risk contact and familiarisation with fellow course members through informal formative team building, before the gradient of risk increases with assessed group work. The crucial stage for construction of this platform for effective collaboration is when students first arrive for induction, upon which activities early in the semester can build. Thus, classmates, both home and international students, can create links and establish co-membership of the collective before co-cultural social networks become too entrenched.

Wingate (2007) advocates the use of the induction period to energetically initiate the process of reformulation of two fundamental notions which students will require in the transition into tertiary-level education; the academic discipline's conception of knowledge construction and application, and the different learning requirements for higher education. Wingate proposes that students be set pre-induction homework tasks of reflection on discipline-specific case studies and self-profiling (learning skills audit) to initiate this adjustment. Their responses to these tasks would be discussed in greater depth on arrival at university in a combination of a classroom-based induction programme and personal tutor sessions, to which Year 2 students' advice relating to transition to higher education can be added. These are described in more detail in recommendations below.

This approach values learning as a self-managed knowledge construction, echoing, for example, Knight and Yorke's (2004) USEM model which sees the four components of successful learning as understanding of subject, application of skilful practices, development of efficacy beliefs (confidence and understanding of one's own pro-active intellectual development) and metacognition. However, Illeris (2007), championing the social constructivist paradigm to which Lave and Wenger (1991) subscribe, criticises such a model for overemphasising the two areas of the cognitive and the psychodynamic, at the expense of 'sociality' (social integration, communication and cooperation). As stated above, Wenger (1998) considers that for such social integration within a student cohort to lead to the development of a community of practice, three conditions are necessary: mutual engagement over time; a joint enterprise with co-responsibility and a shared repertoire of participation. We, as tutors, have a significant part to play in providing such a context.

Conclusion

The presence of international students on campus does not in itself guarantee engagement or educational impact either for them or for home students and staff.

Initiatives promoting early engagement and an understanding of reciprocal benefits to all students within a cohort should lead to swifter integration and quality of dialogue within an academic community of practice. This may be of even greater benefit to the home students, who have few other opportunities on campus for cross-cultural learning, than to international students, whose daily life involves negotiation of a multicultural terrain.

Recommendations

The proposals in Table 19.1 build on Wingate's (2007) model of induction, but utilise peer contacts as the main vehicle of learning. In addition, they aim to build greater awareness of internationalism (following the recommendations of Osmond & Roed, 2010), and of employability issues. The aim is the establishment of a vibrant community of practice with cross-cultural learning at its core.

Table 19.1 Phased development of awareness of community of practice

Phase 1	Pre-induction – prior to the face-to-face course induction
Aims	At the end of this phase, students to be eager and curious to attend Phase 2
Activities	Facebook for co-nationals and classmates Case studies and questions, for engagement with discipline to understand pertinent issues and methods of investigation Self-profiling, to identify own learning approach

Phase 2	Face-to-face course induction in Freshers' week
Aims	At the end of this phase, students will have got to know each other in some depth and to have solved a formative task creatively, relying on each other's contribution. They will break down barriers, reduce anxiety and create bonds
Activities	Informal formative – multicultural Induction groups open-ended tasks requiring collaboration and contribution from all members of the team, and liaison with Year 2 student mentor and personal tutor. Three types: generic; discipline-specific; and input from Year 2 peers
I: Generic	Chain of connections between group members, their Year 2 mentor and personal tutor Team quiz (produced by Year 2 students) Interactive maps (link group members to countries around the world) Book club (selected chapter)
II: Discipline specific (examples)	Business Studies– Dragon's Den Film Studies – poster for hypothetical film 'Freshers' week' TESOL – resource hunt, materials to use with overseas visitors Linguistics – obtain translations of a phrase into as many languages as possible, including the local dialect
III: Peer (Year 2) input	Judge Year 2 creative writing drafts – topic 'Freshers' week' Videopaper of Year 1 experience of Induction Comics/posters – 'If you remember one thing in the first month, ...'
Conclusion	Discussion of issues with personal tutor

Table 19.1 Cont'd

Phase 3	Group work input – first three weeks of the course
Aims	At the end of this phase, students will have learned about interdependence in team work, and recognised rights and responsibilities of working in a community of practice
Activities	Structured formative peer tutoring tasks in multicultural groups. The first class is crucial in setting the tone: happy, intellectually engaging, active learning experience for students (Radloff & de la Harpe, 1998) – preparing them for collaborative learning. Groups given different research topics to present to the class as posters in Week 2 or 3 (Carter & McNeill, 1998; Sambell, Gibson & Montgomery, 2007)
Topics	• Group work theory (Belbin group roles, Tuckman group stages) with the proviso that what makes a good group member is culturally determined, particularly around conflict resolution • Employer priorities: transferable skills • SWOT analysis contrasting current and previous cultures of learning
Conclusion	At the end of this phase, the tutor establishes clear rules for the community of practice, recognising the range of contributions that class members can make

Phase 4	Applying for group membership
Aim	Students will assess their contribution to their group, and what they can gain from others.
Activity	The groups receive a case study in week 3 or 4 with an international/multicultural dimension, and the first task of each member is to prepare a 3-minute presentation of their strengths, imagining that they are applying to join the work group
Conclusion	Students are now more sensitised to the rights and responsibilities of collaborative learning, and may perform with greater awareness of the learning opportunities available to them, in their next group task and in participation in a community of practice

Issues

Such a programme takes valuable time to set up. However, the programme aims to be time efficient by initiating the *process* of developing effective learning and good study habits, to lead to better-quality collaborative learning and peer tutoring which will enhance the *product,* of subject-related research. As the interviewees observe, an earlier start is to everyone's benefit.

Further potential problems include the level of English of some non-native English speakers, which may prevent them from participating fully so early in the course, and the anxiety of many academics at their lack of training (Otten, 2003) for dealing with the cultural diversity that students in their courses represent, and indeed for coaching students in group work skills (Gueldenzoph Snyder, 2009).

Although these are relevant concerns, the issue here, however, is not whether such an approach would be difficult, but whether it would be preferable to not intervening at all, and institutional programmes of continuing professional development for staff and integrated English language support for students could be expected to meet such developmental needs.

References

Andrade, M. S. (2006). International students in English-speaking universities: Adjustment factors. *Journal of Research in International Education, 5*(2), 131–154.

Bochner, S., McLeod, B. M. & Lin, A. (1977). Friendship patterns of overseas students: A functional model. *International Journal of Psychology, 12,* 277–297.

Brown, L. (2009). Ethnographic study of the friendship patterns of international students in England: An attempt to recreate home through conational interaction. *International Journal of Educational Research, 48*(1), 184–193.

Carter, K. & McNeill, J. (1998). Coping with the darkness of transition: Students as the leading lights of guidance at induction to higher education. *British Journal of Guidance & Counselling, 26*(3), 399–415.

Caruana, V. (2010). The relevance of the internationalised curriculum to graduate capability: The role of new lecturers' attitudes in shaping the 'student voice'. In E. Jones (ed.), *Internationalisation and the student voice: Higher education perspectives.* London: Routledge.

Cathcart, A., Dixon-Dawson, J. & Hall, R. (2006). Reluctant hosts and disappointed guests? Examining expectations and enhancing experiences of cross-cultural group work on post-graduate business programmes. *International Journal of Management Education, 5*(1), 13–22.

Cortazzi, M. & Jin, L. (1997). Communication for learning across cultures. In D. McNamara & R. Harris (eds.), *Overseas students in higher education: Issues in teaching and learning.* London: Routledge.

De Vita, G. (2001). The use of group work in large and diverse business management classes: Some critical issues. *International Journal of Management Education, 1*(1), 26–34.

De Vita, G. & Case, P. (2003). Rethinking the internationalisation agenda in UK higher education. *Journal of Further and Higher Education*, 27(4), 383–398.

Fay, B. (1996). *Contemporary philosophy of social science: A multicultural approach*. Oxford: Blackwell.

Gueldenzoph Snyder, L. (2009). Teaching teams about teamwork: Preparation, practice and performance review. *Business Communication Quarterly*, 72(1), 74–79.

Halic, O., Greenberg, K. & Paulus, T. (2009). Language and academic identity: A study of the experiences of non-native English speaking international students. *International Education*, 38(2), 73–93.

Harrison, N. & Peacock, N. (2010). Interactions in the international classroom: The UK perspective. In E. Jones (ed.), *Internationalisation and the student voice: Higher education perspectives*. London: Routledge.

Harvey, L. & Drew, S. (2006). *The first year experience: Briefing on induction*. York: The Higher Education Academy.

Illeris, K. (2007). *How we learn: Learning and non-learning in school and beyond*. London: Routledge.

Kelly, P. (2008). Achieving desirable group-work outcomes through the group allocation process. *Team Performance Management*, 14(1/2), 22–38.

Knight, P. & Yorke, M. (2004). *Learning, curriculum and employability in higher education*. London: Routledge.

Lave, J. & Wenger, E. (1991). *Situated learning. Legitimate peripheral participation*. Cambridge: Cambridge University Press.

Leask, B. (2005). Internationalisation of the curriculum: Teaching and learning. In J. Carroll & J. Ryan (eds.), *Teaching international students: Improving learning for all*. London: Routledge.

Leder, G. C. & Forgasz, H. J. (2004). Australian and international mature students: The daily challenges. *Higher Education Research and Development*, 23(2), 183–198.

Lewthwaite, M. (1996). A study of international students' perspectives on cross-cultural adaptation. *International Journal for the Advancement of Counselling*, 19(1), 167–185.

Osmond, J. & Roed, J. (2010). Sometimes it means more work.... Student perceptions of group work in a mixed cultural setting. In E. Jones (ed.), *Internationalisation and the student voice: Higher education perspectives*. London: Routledge.

Otten, M. (2003). Intercultural learning and diversity in Higher Education. *Journal of Studies in International Education*, 7(1), 12–26.

Radloff, A. & de la Harpe, B. (1998). "What did you do in your first class?" What lecturers do in the first meeting with first-year students and its importance for their learning. *South African Journal of Higher Education*, 12(3), 192–197.

Ramsay, S., Barker, M. & Jones, E. (1999). Academic adjustment and learning processes: A comparison of international and local students in first year of university. *Higher Education Research and Development*, 18(1), 129–144.

Sambell, K., Gibson, M. & Montgomery, C. (2007). *Red Guides, Paper 34: Rethinking feedback: An 'assessment for learning' perspective*. Newcastle: Northumbria University.

Schweisfurth, M. & Gu, Q. (2009). Exploring the experiences of international students in UK higher education: Possibilities and limits of interculturality in university life. *Intercultural Education, 20*(5), 463–473.

Sovic, S. (2009). Hi-bye friends and the herd instinct: International and home students in the creative arts. *Higher Education, 58*(6), 747–761.

Thom, V. (2010). Mutual cultures: Engaging with interculturalism in higher education. In E. Jones (ed.), *Internationalisation and the student voice: Higher education perspectives.* London: Routledge.

Volet, S. E. & Ang, G. (1998). Culturally mixed groups on international campuses: An opportunity for inter-cultural learning. *Higher Education Research & Development, 17*(1), 5–23.

Wenger, E. (1998). *Communities of practice: Learning, meaning, and identity.* Cambridge: Cambridge University Press.

Wingate, U. (2007). Supporting 'learning to learn' in higher education. *Higher Education Quarterly, 61*(3), 391–405.

Yorke, M. & Longden, B. (2008). *The first year experience of higher education in the UK.* York: The Higher Education Academy.

Chapter 20

Listening to 'other' intellectual traditions

Learning in transcultural spaces

Janette Ryan

Introduction

In this chapter, I interrogate the dichotomisation of 'international' and 'Western' students using the Chinese learner as a case study. I explore this further by drawing on research into how notions of scholarship and learning are understood and practised in these two major world intellectual traditions: in Western (here, Anglophone) countries such as the UK and Australia, and in China with its Confucian-heritage intellectual traditions. Rather than identifying supposed 'differences' in these cultures, I instead explore similarities and point to the possibilities for learning across cultures in internationalised, transcultural spaces. These learning spaces have been opened up by the unprecedented movement of people and ideas across the world through international education. I discuss how ignorance in Anglophone countries about other intellectual traditions such as China's, however, means that opportunities for transcultural learning are being lost due to narrow approaches to internationalisation of the curriculum. Teaching and learning approaches continue to position 'home' students in the centre and 'international' students, whose task is to adopt the behaviours and knowledge of the 'home' context, on the periphery.

This chapter attempts to fill the vacuum about knowledge of the world's intellectual traditions and bodies of knowledge by examining differences and commonalities of Western and Chinese higher education systems through the views and practices of senior academics within them. It also interrogates why and how Chinese students in Westerns classrooms are viewed as problematic due to this lack of understanding of other intellectual traditions and academic practices. This chapter also addresses criticism of the 'Westernisation' of internationalisation and the lack of work that moves beyond theory and proselytising, and concerns about process over content, through an exploration of alternative conceptions of internationalisation that position cultural academic systems not in hegemonic relations of power but as partners in mutual intellectual enterprise. Such conceptualisations can inform debate about other cultural academic paradigms that can enrich teaching and learning in all systems of educational practice.

Internationalisation? The big questions

'Internationalisation' is a contested term and, as Montgomery argues in Chapter 12, this lack of clarity may be impeding its progress. Edwards (2007) argues that academics are 'still having the same conversations we were all having in the 1970s' (p. 373) and lecturers report the same 'pedagogical uncertainties' with teaching international students reported over a decade ago (Singh, 2009).

Academics urged to internationalise their curriculum rightly ask how precisely this can be done within their own discipline and practice: that is, What does it look like and how can it be enacted in their pedagogy? The lack of answers may lead them to accuse internationalisation advocates of not practising what they preach: namely, they urge others to learn about other academic paradigms while knowing little of alternative paradigms and bodies of knowledge themselves. The lack of understanding of what internationalisation means in education systems outside Anglophone or Western ones or its potential impacts provides some justification for this charge if international education is viewed as a one-way endeavour. For academics beginning work on internationalisation of teaching and learning, rather than looking to nebulous mission statements, starting questions could be: What is internationalisation for? Is it possible? and, What does it look like in my discipline, at my university, and in my own practice at this point in time? that is, What is it, what is its purpose, and is it worth it?

Beyond Western paradigms and understandings

The commonly used definition of 'internationalisation' in Anglophone countries is by Jane Knight (2004, p.11), a leading scholar on internationalisation from the University of Toronto:

> *Internationalisation is the process of integrating an international, intercultural or global dimension into the purpose, functions or delivery of post-secondary education.*

This is a useful definition for those looking to internationalise processes within and across a university. Knight herself argues that people have very different conceptualisations of internationalisation but a focus on process is not helpful in determining the purpose and nature of internationalisation, nor its implementation. Looking at how internationalisation is conceptualised in other academic cultures provides a different viewpoint. A definition of internationalisation by a leading education scholar in China, Gu (2001, p. 105) from Beijing Normal University, states:

> *The internationalisation of education can be expressed in the exchange of culture and values, mutual understanding and a respect for difference.... The internationalisation of education does not simply mean the integration of*

different national cultures or the suppression of one national culture by another culture.

Gu's definition implies a reaction to internationalisation as a Western academic imperialist endeavour and reflects the 'one-way' nature of the traffic to date: from developing countries to developed ones. It echoes the concerns reported by Mertova in Chapter 5 of Czech academics about impacts on national identity and Australian academics about the loss of indigenous cultures. The conceptualisation of internationalisation in non-Anglophone countries often centres on offering courses in English (especially in European and Scandinavian countries, as outlined by Slethaug and Vinther in Chapter 6), and the dominance of English as a *lingua franca* has led to concerns about the 'tyranny of the Anglosphere' (Klitgård, 2011a). In these countries, internationalisation may be viewed as oppressive and homogenising rather than enriching. Gu's conceptualisation views internationalisation not *within* a single system, but rather as an endeavour *between* civilisations. It envisages internationalisation not as a loss of national academic cultures but as an expansion of academic cultures, or in transcultural theory terms (discussed later), as 'a new, composite culture' (Murray, 2010).

The lack of clarity of the term 'internationalisation' and assumptions of its 'universality' (Nguyen et al., 2009) point to a need for further debate as well as its uncoupling from a Western-centred positioning. As Singh (2009) argues, there is still much ignorance between Western and Chinese or 'Confucian-heritage culture' (CHC) intellectual paradigms and this is inhibiting two-way or transcultural learning. 'Western' and 'CHC' academic paradigms are generally described as dichotomies and debates on the 'Chinese learner' are inaccurate and unhelpful (Ryan & Louie, 2007). This 'ignorance' about supposed differences between academic cultures and individuals within them inhibits the mutual and respectful *exchange* of ideas (as Gu advocates) rather than the simple *integration* of knowledge from one culture into another.

Furthermore, the core–periphery model of international education (Jiang, 2005; Pan, 2011) is beginning to change. Internationalisation is being pursued not just in Anglophone countries such as the UK, Australia, the US and Canada but also in Europe, Asia, the Middle East and South Africa (IIE, 2011). Many countries in these regions are aggressively competing for international students and actively pursuing internationalisation agendas. The direction of travel of people and ideas is becoming more 'two-way' and the previous pattern of unidirectional mobility of students is moving towards 'dynamic, mutual exchange' (IIE, 2011, p. 7). Changing national political, fiscal and immigration policies in countries such as the UK and Australia have had major impacts on international education patterns. China is pursuing a two-pronged internationalisation policy, internationalising its higher education through internal means (reform and increased expenditure on higher education institutions to make them world-class) and external means (sending students and scholars overseas) (Ryan, 2011a). China now attracts more international students than it sends and aims to attract over 500,000 foreign students each year by 2020 (IIE, 2011).

'Internationalisation', therefore, needs to engage with other educational systems and ideas rather than be limited to a process-driven approach. It must involve more than inclusion of international examples in courses or an international 'dimension' into university operations (Knight, 2004) but genuine attempts to pluralise the epistemological knowledge base (Webb, 2005). This requires engagement with diverse intellectual traditions so that their knowledge and perspectives are available for debate and learning by both academics and (all) students. As Singh (2009) argues, however, ignorance still typifies attitudes in many Western contexts about Chinese or CHC intellectual paradigms. This 'ignorance' about differences between academic cultures and individuals leads to poor outcomes for individuals and lost opportunities for learning across cultures.

Binary views of Western and Chinese cultures of learning

Much of the literature on cultures of learning takes a binary view of Western (usually Anglophone) and Chinese cultures of learning. Although there are dangers in adopting simple stereotypes, certainly for individuals within them, it is also true to say that national educational cultures derive from different historical and cultural circumstances and teaching and learning traditions within them can place emphasis on different academic values. What is viewed as 'good' or 'ideal' academic practice in one system can appear to be in opposition to the other. Table 20.1 outlines different 'Chinese' and 'British' academic values and derives from my experience over several decades as a student and academic in Western systems (in Australia and the UK) and in China, as well as extensive review of the literature and my own studies within each system (see Ryan, 2010 for further discussion).

Not all learners (or teachers) of course within each system exclusively hold these attributes; these are 'ideals' to which students and scholars are expected to aspire. What is more important than trying to ascribe individuals to these

Table 20.1 Comparison of Chinese and British academic values

China	UK
• Level of knowledge	• Type of (critical) thinking
• Learn from the teacher	• Independent learning
• Respect teachers and texts	• Question teachers and texts
• Harmony of the group	• Student-centred learning
• Consensus /avoiding conflict	• Argumentation /assertiveness
• 'Reflective' learners	• 'Deep' learners seeking meaning
• Critique of the 'self'	• Critique of the 'other'

columns, is recognition that there are different academic ideals that each system valourises, and that each holds value. These values play out in various ways, including in the behaviours of individuals within classrooms and in the work that they produce, and an appreciation of this can help those working with students or scholars from the other culture.

To illustrate this, looking at the first row in Table 20.1, a PhD student at a *viva voce* panel in China will most likely be asked what they found from their research: for example, What is the contribution to knowledge? In the UK, a panel is more likely to ask about their methodology, about how that knowledge was generated that is, How do you know that? The more respectful positioning of teachers and texts in China (third row) can make a student more cautious in expressing criticism, and they may keep their thoughts to themselves or diplomatically ask for clarification. A Chinese student in a Western classroom may internalise their thinking rather than express their opinion confidently to the whole class. Outward verbalisation of the thinking processes and learning through reflection and internalisation are both recognised as effective forms of learning. Confucian educational ideals have had an enduring impact in Chinese societies for millennia (and are being re-emphasised through the contemporary revival of Confucianism) and the importance of self-reflection and self-cultivation continues to permeate Chinese cultures (last row). As Confucius was reported to have said two and a half thousand years ago, 'One must first understand the self in order to understand the other', a portent of current debates in countries like the UK about learning about the 'self' through contact with the 'other'. In the current reform of education in China (see Ryan, 2011a,b), there is a concern for continuity of intellectual traditions and excellence while also learning from the best examples internationally, an apt example of a transcultural approach.

Construction of the 'Chinese learner'

As the largest national group of international students, most Western literature on international students focuses on Chinese students and often misinterprets and 'pathologises' them (Chung & Ingleby, 2011). Although differences do occur between systems, these attributes are not necessarily found in all members of a culture, especially in such large and diverse cultures as 'Western' or 'Chinese' ones, and in the later case, a system undergoing profound change and reform (Ryan, 2011a,b). Labelling students (or academics) on the basis of whole systems of cultural practice ignores the considerable diversity *within* cultures as well as *between* them (Ryan & Louie, 2007). Nevertheless, these terms are commonly used, and the term 'Western' education generally continues to be used to refer in fact to the 'Anglo-American model' (Klitgård, 2011a).

'Deficit' views stem from the fact that Chinese students' behaviours seem to be the opposite of those eulogised in Western academe (see Table 20.1). Research by Western academics often focuses on when international students arrive and are struggling to adapt to or 'de-code' the expectations of their new environment. These may require them to behave in ways that are counter-intuitive, as they need to 'unlearn' previous behaviours and learn new ones.

Chinese students thus encounter attitudes that interpret their behaviours as 'dependent' or 'deficit'. Their as-yet not fully developed English language skills may be misinterpreted as lack of ability or criticality and their initial lack of sophisticated language as lack of complex thought. Rather than being seen as an active and independent approach to learning about the expectations and standards of their new environment, and in the absence of specific and explicit explanations or examples, their questions about assignments or the 'correct' answer may be seen as a lack of independent learning. Their silence in the classroom may be seen as lack of connection with ideas rather than a deeper, internal engagement with these ideas, a reluctance to display their as-yet under-developed language skills, or even shyness or modesty. Unintentional plagiarism may arise from underdeveloped skills of paraphrasing rather than deliberate cheating or may even be a symptom of the overwhelming stress involved in experiencing steep learning curves early in their study. Lecturers may view 'acts of textual borrowing' (Schmitt, 2005) as plagiarism rather than a necessary step in their learning development (Klitgård, 2011b). Lecturers may develop views about Chinese learners and Chinese cultures of learning based on these partial and early observations.

Faced with these unfamiliar behaviours, academics may be unaware that modes of expression of critical thinking in one system may be considered impolite or lacking in self-reflection in another. The more deferential attitudes and behaviours towards teachers and knowledge in China contrast with more assertive and aggressive Western styles. With China's 5,000-year history of academic excellence and traditions of centuries of often intense intellectual debates about Confucian and other schools of thought, Chinese people know how to think 'critically' but they may conduct these debates differently. However, the apparent passivity of Chinese students is interpreted as an unwillingness to participate or an indication of a lack of ability. This lack of understanding can have unfortunate consequences for individuals. To give one example, a reference a school in China provided for its best student for his application to a UK university described him in the highest possible terms as 'the most modest student the school has ever seen'. Needless to say, this carried little weight in the minds of the UK admissions officer and was interpreted as 'damning' praise.

Academics expect incoming international students to learn about the indigenous academic culture and adopt its 'critical' traditions, yet there is little critical examination of their own systems of academic practice or their fit for purpose for vastly changed student cohorts. The majority of postgraduate students in the UK are now international, particularly in taught Masters courses, yet these courses remain largely unchanged despite recognition that they can be piecemeal, lack cohesion and involve a steep learning curve for international students. Analysis of the course satisfaction rates of international students in the UK shows that they are significantly less satisfied than 'home' students (Ryan, 2011c) and, sadly, many international students regard themselves as 'cash cows' for a finance-strapped higher education system, especially when their expectations of quality are not met.

'Western' and 'Chinese' systems of academic cultural practice

I turn now to a comparison of systems of 'Western' and 'Chinese' academic practice. Rather than interpreting Chinese cultures through the behaviours of newly arrived Chinese students in Western classrooms, a more authentic and evidential approach is to examine how scholarship and learning are understood and practised within these systems. This section reports on a study of Anglophone and Chinese notions of scholarship and learning in two Western (UK and Australia) and two CHC contexts (China and Hong Kong) (see Ryan, 2011d for a detailed discussion of methodology and findings).

Twenty-six senior academics (with at least 10 years' experience and at Associate Professor or equivalent level or above) in a range of disciplines in universities were asked (in English or Chinese):

- How do you define characteristics of 'good' scholarship and 'effective' learning?
- What differences and commonalities do you believe exist between Western and CHC paradigms of scholarship and learning?
- Do you believe that these paradigms are changing or should change?

In answer to the first question, participants' definitions in each system were strikingly similar, as can been seen in Table 20.2. Words and phrases are participants' *verbatim* responses and are representative of overall responses.

Few Western participants could answer the second question, but most Chinese participants stressed commonalities rather than differences. A Chinese Professor of Humanities at a southern Chinese university who has worked in both systems commented:

> *There are commonalities that good scholarship and effective learning share in both paradigms. An oft-cited belief in China is that the Western paradigm emphasises critical thinking whereas the CHC paradigm emphasises rote learning, memorisation and breadth of knowledge. I believe that differences exist only amongst individual scholars whether they are Eastern or Western.*

In response to the third question, most participants reported that their systems were changing but some Western participants noted that while paradigms are changing in China, this is mainly one-way learning, from the West. An American

Table 20.2 Definitions of 'good' scholarship and 'effective' learning

	Western	Chinese
'Good' scholarship ("好的" 学术)	Original, original ideas	Original, innovative (创新)
	Imaginative	Uses imagination
	Creative	Creative (创新), passion for pursuing knowledge
	Adds value, makes a difference	Has some value (价值), beneficial (有意义)
	Advances knowledge, application to existing knowledge	Contribution to knowledge, application (运用) of knowledge
	Rigorous, questioning, systematic	Systematic inquiry
	Sound theories and methods, innovative methodologies	Includes theory, methodology and subject knowledge; innovative methodologies (研究方法上的创新)
'Effective' learning ("有效"学习)	Understanding and applying knowledge	Deep and broad knowledge framework (既有深入,又有广泛...知识), applying knowledge (知识应用)
	Think for yourself	Critical thinking (思考)
	Work independently	Independent learner (有独立学习能力)
	Challenge and interrogate authorities	Challenge authorities' views (不能迷信权威)
	Build on what's known, develop new schema	[Combines] old and new academic knowledge (温故而知新)

Professor of Literature in Hong Kong commented that while China is learning from the West, it is trying to also maintain the best of Confucian education traditions, that is, combining the best features of both systems:

> *I don't think that the West is radically changing their views on the educational process but I do think that China is Westernising. It is trying to understand different kinds of skill sets to give their students an opportunity to feel comfortable with Western styles of learning, with Western styles of knowledge and they're incorporating that within the classroom in their own way... they don't lose what is quintessentially Confucian or quintessentially Chinese.*

Overall, the interviews provide evidence that although there are differences between the two systems, there are sufficient similarities and common aspirations (as seen in Table 20.2) to enable engagement between them and sufficient interesting differences (as seen in Table 20.1) to provide for mutual learning. The data (although only a relatively small sample) also suggest that negative views about

'Chinese learners' are not based on contemporary expectations and practices of educators within China.

Transcultural theory: New 'composite' cultures

Rather than seeing international education as a one-way transaction, transcultural theory focuses on its potential for reciprocal learning. Transcultural knowledge develops from contact between cultures and results in 'a new, composite culture in which some existing cultural features are combined, while some are lost, and new features are generated' (Murray, 2010). Transculturalism recognises that modern societies are no longer monolithic and that 'we are in an era where inter-culturality, transculturalism and the eventual prospect of identifying a cosmo-politan citizenship can become a reality' (Cuccioletta, 2002, p. 2). A transcultural approach can better equip all students to live and work in globalised contexts and in ways that make labels such as 'home' or 'international' obsolete.

Transculturalism can provide the answer to 'internationalisation of what?' As several authors in this volume point out, internationalisation can be a nebulous concept. By giving a specific destination for learning – that is, learning about the cultures of the world and the exchange of ideas across academic systems – this provides a clear pathway and rationale. Such approaches discard notions of hegem-ony and cultural superiority of one system over another and relationships become respectful and reciprocal. Systems of intellectual practice become learning partners rather than rivals. The vehicle for such changes is transcultural pedagogy and a curriculum that moves beyond interactions *between* cultures, with one culture positioned as more powerful or 'legitimate', to a stance which *arises from* mutual dialogue and respect amongst academic cultures and knowledge traditions.

As can be seen from the analysis here, supposed differences between systems can be a source not of derision or tension but of learning. Lecturers can find it hard to move outside of their comfort zones (as they expect of their students) and tend to notice differences rather than recognise commonalities. If we view internation-alisation as the mutual and respectful *exchange* of ideas (as Gu advocates) rather than the simple *integration* of knowledge from one culture into another, then this can provide answers to the questions, What is internationalisation for? and What does it look like in my discipline, at my university, and in my own practice?

Transforming lives through transcultural education

In addressing the final question, Is it worth it? I draw on my own experience as an international student and teacher of international students. I have taught thousands of 'home' and 'international' students over the past two decades. During each class, I ask students to sit next to someone with whom they have never spoken before. By the end of the semester, they have met everyone in the class. One year, a Sinhalese and a Tamil student working together during the time of the atrocities in Sri Lanka said afterwards they realised how much their cultural identities had been constructed and manipulated. A Chinese student who befriended a Japanese student reported how she had previously hated Japanese people for what they had done to her country during the Second World War but now understood how Japanese people had felt threatened and were worried about their security at the time. And at the end of the course a 'home' student said, 'I hated it at first when you made us move every class, but I wouldn't have got to know so many people otherwise. Our class has been like a "mini United Nations"'. Such examples show for me the value of transcultural approaches and their impacts on individuals.

So what is the ultimate impact of international education for those most closely involved? We need to be mindful that international education is not just an instrument of foreign or fiscal policy but also has a moral and ethical dimension. International education has the power to transform lives; my experiences as an international student, not just in China but also in the UK, profoundly changed my life, my thinking and my view of the world. This transformation is also poignantly evident in the testimonies of previous international students, as Haigh has so powerfully demonstrated in Chapter 14 through his analysis of the memoirs of Gandhi, perhaps the most famous international student of all. Although I can scarcely compare myself with Gandhi, I also came to understand my own 'Australianess'. It gave me the 'surplus of seeing' (Bakhtin, 1986, p. 7) not only into another culture but also my own. For those engaged in internationalisation work, it may seem like hard work, especially when marking a pile of essays not always in perfect English. We may not see it at the time, but internationalisation work transforms lives for decades to come.

References

Bakhtin, M. (1986). *Speech genres and other late essays.* Edited by C. Emerson & M. Holquist, trans. Vern W. Gee. Austin, TX: University of Texas Press.

Chung, M. & Ingleby, R. (2011). Overcoming the cultural challenges in supervising Chinese research students in Australia. In J. Ryan (ed.), *China's higher education reform and internationalisation.* London: Routledge.

Cuccioletta, D. (2002). Multiculturalism or transculturalism: Towards a cosmopolitan citizenship. *London Journal of Canadian Studies, 17,* 1–11.

Edwards, J. (2007). Challenges and opportunities for the internationalisation of higher education in the coming decade: Planned and opportunistic initiatives in American institutions. *Journal of Studies in International Education, 11,* 373–381.

Gu, M. Y. (2001). *Education in China and abroad: Perspectives from a lifetime in comparative education.* Hong Kong: Comparative Research Education Centre, University of Hong Kong.

Institute of International Education (IIE) (2011). *Student mobility and the internationalization of higher education: National policies and strategies from six world regions.* New York: Institute of International Education.

Jiang, K. (2005). The centre–periphery model and cross-national educational transfer: The influence of the US on teaching reform in China's universities. *Asia Pacific Journal of Education, 25*(2), 227–239.

Klitgård, I. (2011a). *The internationalisation of academic English writing in higher education: Anglo-American doctrines or transcultural hybridity?* Between tradition and change: 'The future of English in the light of globalization, transculturalism, and Internationalization' Conference, University of Southern Denmark, Kolding, Denmark, 11–12 October 2011.

Klitgård, I. (2011b). Plagiarism in the international university: From kidnapping and theft to translation and hybridity. In B. Preisler, I. Klitgård & H. Fabricius (eds.), *Language and learning in the international university*. Bristol: Multilingual Matters.

Knight, J. (2004). Internationalization remodeled: Definition, approaches, and rationales. *Journal of International Studies*, *8*(5), 5–31.

Murray, D. (2010). *Female North African-French students in France: Narratives of educational experiences*. Doctoral thesis, University of Nevada. Available at: http://digitalcommons.library.unlv.edu/thesesdissertations/344 (accessed 20 June 2011).

Nguyen, P., Elliott, J., Terlouw, C. & Pilot, A. (2009). Neocolonialism in education: Cooperative learning in an Asian context. *Comparative Education*, *45*, 109–130.

Pan, S. Y. (2011). Education abroad, human capital development, and national competitiveness: China's Brain Gain strategies. *Frontiers of Education in China*, *6*(1), 106–138.

Ryan, J. (ed.) (2011a). *China's higher education reform and internationalisation*. London: Routledge.

Ryan, J. (ed.) (2011b). *Education reform in China: Changing concepts, contexts and practices*. London: Routledge.

Ryan, J. (2011c). Teaching and learning for international students: Towards a transcultural approach. *Teachers and Teaching: Theory and Practice*, *17*(6), 631–648.

Ryan, J. (2011d). Access and participation in higher education of students with disabilities: Access to what? *Australian Educational Researcher*, *38*(1), 73–93.

Ryan, J. (2010). 'The Chinese learner': Misconceptions and realities. In J. Ryan & G. Slethaug (eds.), *International education and the Chinese learner*. Hong Kong: Hong Kong University Press.

Ryan, J. & Louie, K. (2007). False dichotomy? 'Western' and 'Eastern' concepts of scholarship and learning. *Educational Philosophy and Theory*, *39*(4), 404–417.

Schmitt, D. (2005). Writing in the international classroom. In J. Carroll & J. Ryan (eds.), *Teaching international students: Improving learning for all*. London: Routledge.

Singh, M. (2009). Using Chinese knowledge in internationalising research education: Jacques Rancière, an ignorant supervisor and doctoral students from China. *Globalisation, Societies and Education*, *7*(2) 185–201.

Webb, G. (2005). Internationalisation of the curriculum: An institutional approach. In J. Carroll & J. Ryan (eds.), *Teaching international students: Improving learning for all*. London: Routledge.

Index